KT-486-782

Ancient Rome

Ancient Rome

Duncan Hill

Parragon
Bath · New York · Singapore · Hong Kong · Cologne · Delhi · Melbourne

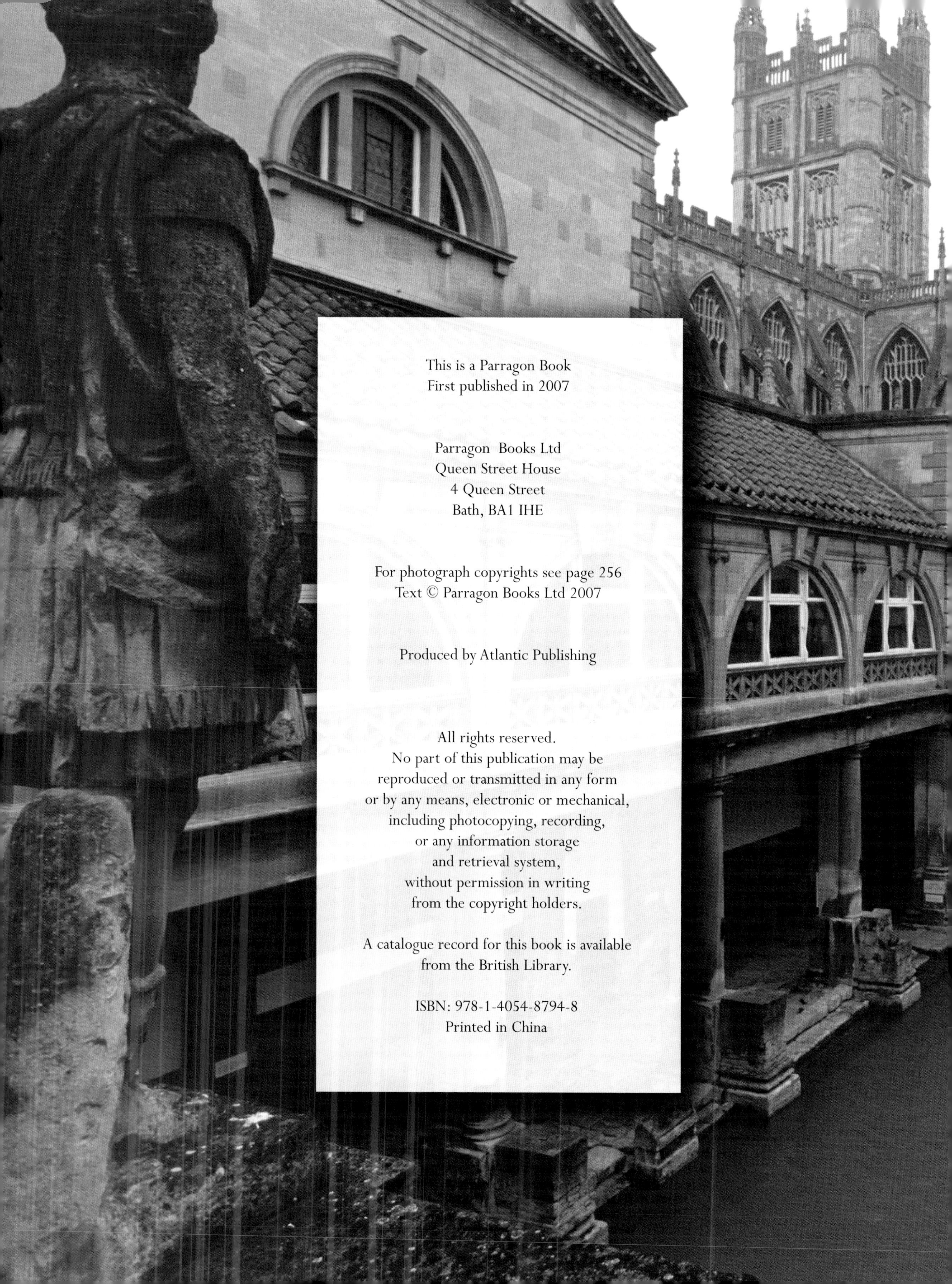

This is a Parragon Book
First published in 2007

Parragon Books Ltd
Queen Street House
4 Queen Street
Bath, BA1 IHE

For photograph copyrights see page 256

Produced by Atlantic Publishing

A catalogue record for this book is available
from the British Library.

ISBN: 978-1-4054-8794-8
Printed in China

Contents

Introduction

The rise of Rome from provincial settlement to imperial power is an epic story that reads like fiction rather than fact. Fable does indeed play a part: Romulus is said to have slain his twin brother Remus and founded the future city-state, both infants having survived abandonment on the banks of the Tiber thanks to the nurturing milk of a she-wolf.

When myth is stripped away, what remains is hardly less extraordinary. Despite possessing few strategic advantages, Rome mastered Italy, then looked outward. At its height the Empire encompassed territories from the Rhineland to Egypt, Britain to Armenia. Over two million square miles fell within Rome's orbit.

Conquest on such a scale required a formidable military machine, yet the Empire was not wholly underpinned by compulsion. The Romans were a largely civilizing force, urban and literate, a people who replaced tyrannical monarchy with citizenship, and who were proponents of selfless discipline, loyalty and order.

Rome is also associated with opulent decadence, particularly after power passed from the republican institutions into the hands of autocratic military commanders. During some reigns the Empire flourished; others were blighted by intrigue and blood-lust. Caligula, who appointed his favourite horse a consul, was just one emperor who fell victim to an assassin's hand.

Ancient Rome traces all facets of one of the world's great civilizations, from the legends surrounding Rome's foundation to the strife that precipitated the Empire's collapse. It describes a remarkable imperial power that left an indelible mark on the lands it occupied. The face of Europe today would be radically different were it not for the rich cultural, technological, linguistic and administrative legacy bequeathed it by the Romans.

The Roots of Rome

Origins

The vast Roman Empire, which at its peak stretched all the way from Britain in the west to Arabia in the east, had humble origins in the Latin-speaking settlements, collectively called Latium, surrounding the River Tiber.

Floor mosaic depicting the story of Romulus and Remus. The myth of the noble-born twins, saved from being killed at birth and raised by a she-wolf on the Palatine Hill, gave Rome, once one of the lesser Latium settlements, a grandeur to legitimize the city's domination of its neighbours.

Importance of the Tiber

The banks of the Tiber proved perfect for agricultural use and were well-defended by the nearby hills. The location further benefited from the river itself, which provided ready access to the sea for trade with seafaring merchants, but was sufficiently distant to protect the settlements from seafaring enemies. In their ideal location, the Latin settlements were able to develop during the early centuries of the first millennium BC.

Rome was among the younger of these Latin settlements, its foundation was dated by Roman historians to approximately 750 BC, but without sufficient archaeological evidence, this has proved impossible for modern historians to verify. In spite of its relative youth, over the following centuries Rome was able to rise, dominate and conquer its neighbouring Latin settlements, to become the region's supreme ruler.

Romulus and Remus

The uncertainty surrounding the city's origins, combined with the need of Roman writers to provide a less modest account of the origins of their mighty civilization, led to the emergence of the famous legend of Romulus and Remus.

The tale originates at the time when the ruler of Alba Longa, Numitor, had just been overthrown by his younger brother, Amulius. Alba Longa was the main city-state of Latium, and according to Virgil's *Aeneid*, the kings of the city had origins among the ancient Trojan people. Virgil's protagonist, Aeneas, was thought to have fled amidst the legendary Battle of Troy and settled in the region.

The rolling countryside surrounding Rome provided a fertile land for agriculture to support the growing population of the city.

Birth of a legend

Desperate to maintain his grip on power, Amulius sought to eradicate Numitor's descendants before they were even born. He forced his niece, Numitor's daughter, Rhea Silva, into becoming a Vestal Virgin so that she would never have children. However, Amulius' plan failed. The God of War, Mars, raped Rhea Silva and she conceived as a result. Numitor was to have not just one male heir, but two, because Rhea Silva gave birth to twin boys, named Romulus and Remus.

Anxious that Numitor's grandsons might challenge his rule, Amulius ordered that the newborn twins be disposed of. However, the servant tasked with killing the boys could not carry out the assignment and left them afloat on the Tiber, where they were spared by the river god, Tiberinus. Romulus and Remus were subsequently raised by a she-wolf on the Palatine Hill, until a shepherd, Faustulus, found them and adopted them as his own sons.

Both grew up into a life of banditry, but their noble birth meant they were natural leaders and amassed a following among fellow bandits and exiles. This brought them into conflict with authorities of Alba Longa and eventually with Amulius himself. During one of several scuffles with Alba Longa, Remus was captured, which encouraged Romulus to raise an army to free his brother and take the city. Romulus' forces were victorious, and Amulius was executed.

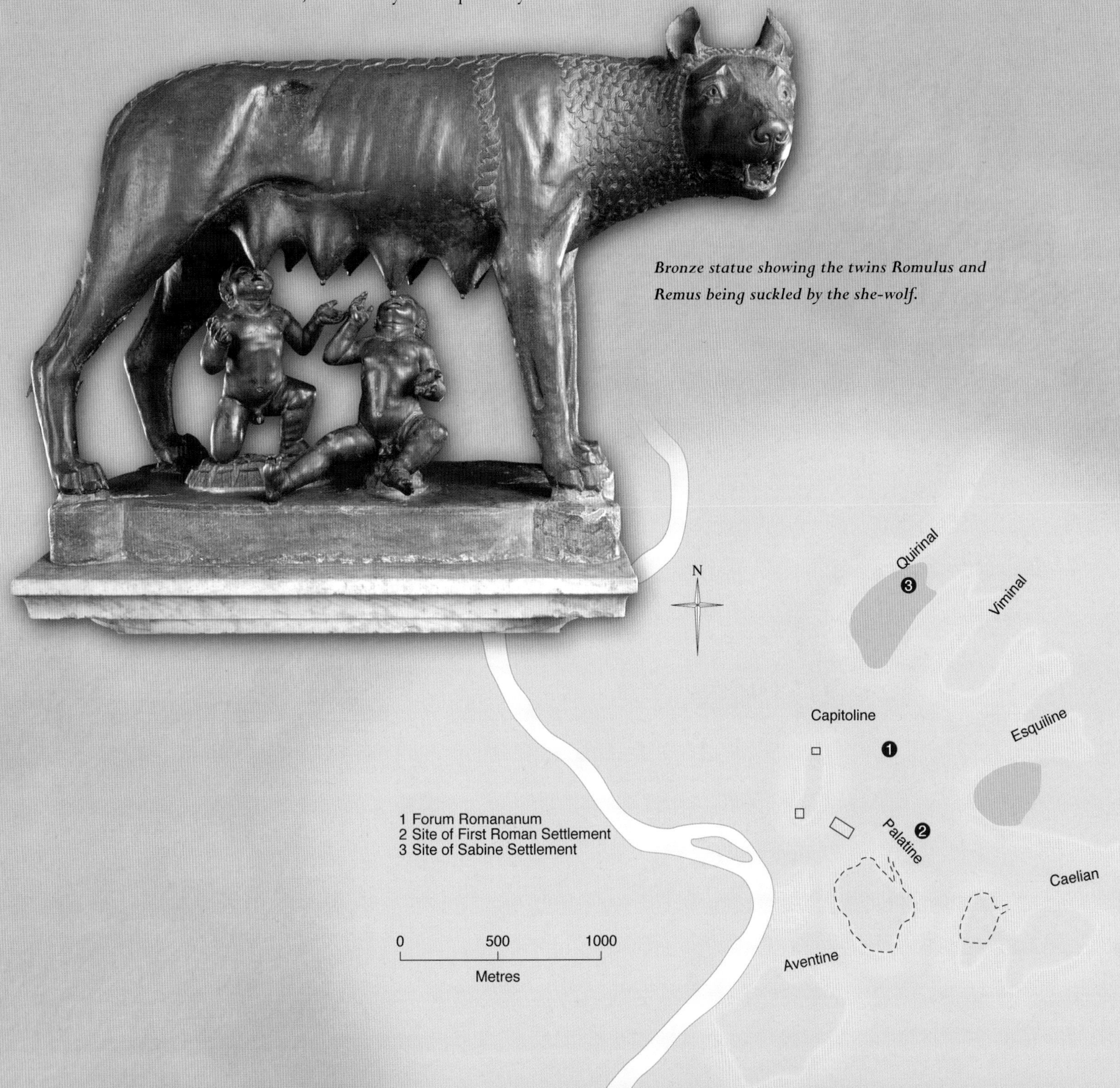

Bronze statue showing the twins Romulus and Remus being suckled by the she-wolf.

Romulus emerges triumphant

The twins were jointly offered the crown of Alba Longa, but refused, in favour of re-enthroning their grandfather, Numitor. With the threat from Alba Longa removed, the two brothers took their followers and sought to establish their own settlement close to where they had been raised. However, Romulus and Remus disagreed as to where their settlement ought to be situated. Romulus insisted on the Palatine Hill, where the she-wolf had nurtured them, while Remus stood firm to the Aventine Hill because it offered a superior strategic position. The disagreement was deferred to the gods, who found in favour of Romulus.

Work began on the Palatine Hill, but ungracious in his defeat, Remus attempted to obstruct the process and demonstrate that Romulus' location was not as defendable as his own. Angered by his brother, Romulus killed Remus and proclaimed himself king. In 748 BC the new settlement was named 'Rome' in his honour, and one of the greatest Empires the world has ever seen was begun.

The Sabine Women

Rome would not have lasted more than a generation, were it not for some underhand tactics by Romulus. Romulus' group of bandits, outcasts and exiles was, by its very nature, dominated by males, and suffered from a perilous lack of females. To compensate, Romulus invited the Sabine, a small civilization with a settlement on the nearby Quirinal Hill, to join the Romans for a religious festival. Rather than showing hospitality, the Romans stole their womenfolk and returned them to Rome to become wives for Roman citizens. Inevitably, war broke out between the Sabine and the Romans.

Ruins of a palace on the Palatine Hill. The decision to build the settlement of Rome on the Palatine Hill, where the she-wolf had nurtured the infant twins, led to a fierce disagreement between Romulus and Remus. Arbitration by the gods found in Romulus' favour but Remus continued to obstruct the building work. Angered by his brother's recalcitrance, Romulus killed Remus, and proclaimed himself king.

Tarpeia's Treachery

The Romans were thought to have been well-defended by an outpost on the Capitoline Hill, but the Sabine were able to capture the hill. According to legend, this was because the daughter of the commander of the outpost, Tarpeia, was given to greed. In exchange for payment, she opened the city gates to the Sabine. Instead of rewarding her, the Sabine army, repulsed by her treachery, brutally murdered her. The steep face of the Capitoline Hill overlooking the Roman Forum, was subsequently named the Tarpeian rock, and became an execution site, to highlight her dishonour.

War with the Sabine

Romulus marched an army to stem the Sabine advance and met his foe in the swampland between the Capitoline and Palatine Hills, the site upon which the Roman Forum would later stand. The Sabine were initially successful, but Romulus regrouped his forces ready for another attack. Just as the two sides were about to go into battle, the captured Sabine women ran onto the battlefield and implored their fathers and husbands to stop fighting. Convinced and touched by the bravery of the Sabine women, the Roman and Sabine armies not only made peace, but also agreed to unification. The king of the Sabine was to rule alongside Romulus, and Rome underwent its first expansion, stretching from the Palatine Hill to the Quirinal Hill. The Capitoline Hill, lying in the middle of the two settlements, was chosen as the political centre of Rome. A few years after unification, the Sabine king, Tatius, was killed and Romulus became the sole king of the expanded settlement.

Ruins of a structure on the Palatine Hill, the first of Rome's 'seven hills' to be settled.

The Sabine Women by Jacques-Louis David. The Sabine women who had been captured and taken to Rome, ran onto the battlefield and implored their Sabine fathers and Roman husbands to stop fighting. Convinced and touched by the bravery of the Sabine women, the armies not only made peace, but also agreed to political unification.

Roman Monarchy

King Romulus

It is difficult to verify the elements of truth in the Romulus and Remus story. However, available evidence suggests Romulus was the first king of Rome and this myth probably developed in order to provide a back-story for him, in order to ground the foundations of Rome in the grandiose world of gods and heroes.

King Romulus

Under Romulus' rule, Roman society was delineated into three tribes, Roman, Sabine and Etruscan, a civilization immediately to the north of Rome. Each of the three tribes was politically represented in an assembly, the *comitia curiata*, which was established in order to restrict the king's powers. Legislation that the king wished to pass traditionally had to be ratified by the *comitia*. However, in spite of the restrictions posed by the *comitia*, Romulus was able to circumvent the elected bodies because the king was able to monopolize the ability to interpret the will of the gods. His rule was further backed up by the creation of his own personal bodyguard called the Celeres.

Under Romulus, a forerunner of the Roman Senate was created, as one hundred patricians, or heads of noble families, were established as an advisory council for the king. This was later expanded to two hundred, as an extra one hundred patricians were brought in from the Sabine population.

The Death of Romulus

In 715 BC King Romulus vanished. Senators said they had seen him ascend to heaven, but the most likely explanation is that the Senate had him killed. In keeping with the myth that Romulus had been carried up to heaven, the senators rapidly deified him as the god Quirinus and built a temple in his honour on the hill where the ascension had reportedly taken place. This hill, the one upon which the Sabine settlement had been situated, was named the Quirinal Hill in honour of the new god.

Left: Undated engraved illustration of an ancient coin which depicts the deified Romulus as Quirinus.

Above: Remains of a street and its buildings in the port of Ostia.

Opposite right: Floor mosaic showing the head of the god Oceanus, an important god for a state with a growing dependence on trade around the Mediterranean.

Opposite left: Ruins of Ostia, the first port of Rome, established during the reign of Ancus.

Numa Pompilius

The Roman Monarchy was not hereditary; rather, the best man for the job was selected by the senators. This meant that there was a period in between successive monarchs when Rome would have had no king at all. This period was called an 'interregnum'. During this time the senators took turns at being an 'interrex'. The interrex would rule for several days before being replaced by a fellow senator until a suitable candidate could be found. After the first interregnum, Numa Pompilius was chosen to succeed Romulus. Numa was a wise choice because he was a Sabine, and thus this helped smooth the absorption of the Sabine into Rome. As Numa was such a well-respected king, it was widely believed that he was being advised by the clever water nymph, Egeria. Numa's reign was a long and peaceful one, lasting approximately forty years, until his death of old age in 674 BC.

War and Peace

After Numa, there were five further Roman kings who ruled until 510 BC. The peaceful reign of Numa gave way to the more militaristic tenure of his successor, Tullus Hostilius. His reign was marred by war with a former ally, Alba Longa, as well as with the Etruscans. So ruthless was Tullus Hostilius that he reputedly had the king of Alba Longa torn in two by chariots. This famous punishment was to highlight the perils of indecision; the king of Alba Longa had held back in Rome's war against the Etruscan city-state of Fidenae so that he could enter on the winning side. When Rome won, Tullus was so infuriated that he meted out this harshest of penalties. Fearing that too much warfare had meant that Tullus had ignored and angered the gods, the senators opted for a more serene heir, Ancus Martius. Ancus was the grandson of Numa Pompilius, and is thought to have been a similarly peaceable ruler as his grandfather. Under Ancus' reign, Rome established the first port at Ostia, where the River Tiber met the sea.

Assassinations

Ancus' appointed heir was an emigrant from the Etruscan cities in the north, called Tarquinius Priscus. Ancus' biological sons were never satisfied with his appointment as king and even forty years into his reign, they colluded to have him assassinated. The king was murdered in 579 BC but Ancus' sons were unable to get themselves elected as king. Instead, Tarquinius' wife was able to secure the succession for her son-in-law, a former slave, named Servius Tullius.

Servius Tullius undertook the first Roman census, and is widely accredited with the establishment of the class system of Ancient Rome. He replaced Romulus' *comitia curiata* with a reformed *comitia centuriata* based upon this new census information. The new *comitia* no longer excluded poorer members of Roman society, called plebs. Instead both the patrician and the plebeian classes were represented.

Although the wealthier patrician class was still able to maintain control of Roman government, they were nevertheless angered by the populist reforms of Servius Tullius. Together with his own daughter, a handful of patricians murdered the king. To dispose of the body, his daughter arranged for a chariot to drive it into the ground, and in addition conspired to have her husband, Tarquinius Superbus, named king in her father's stead.

The last Monarch

Tarquinius Superbus was the son of Tarquinius Priscus, but had been overlooked by the Senate in favour of Servius. He set about establishing absolute despotism by ignoring the *comitia* and purging the Senate of all men loyal to his predecessor. He executed Romans and embarked upon wars unimpeded, enraging not just the Senate but the general population as well.

In 509 BC dislike of the king erupted into outright rebellion. Tarquinius' son, Sextus, raped a noblewoman named Lucretia. The Romans drove Tarquinius from the city, only to have him attempt to stage a comeback after appealing for help from the Etruscan city of Clusium. Tarquinius was able to use his Etruscan roots to encourage the king of Clusium's assistance.

Desperate to avoid a resumption of the despotic monarchy, the Romans held off the Etruscan invasion and Tarquinius was doomed to die in exile in Etruria. The overthrow of the king signalled the end of the period of Roman Monarchy and ushered in the era of the Roman Republic.

Crown of golden ivy leaves.

Above: Panel painting of a Roman citizen. Under Servius Tullius, himself a former slave, the poorer classes, the plebs, gained representation. Despite these reforms, the patrician classes, who believed themselves to be descended from the original inhabtants of Rome, were still able to maintain control over the government.

The Etruscan Civilisation

Before the rise of Rome, the Etruscan civilization dominated the north and central regions of the Italian peninsula. Relatively little is known about them, but they are believed to have wielded considerable influence over Rome in its formative years.

Where did the Etruscans come from?

It was long thought that the Etruscans were immigrants to Italy. The great historian, Herodotus, claimed that they originated amongst the Lydian people of Asia Minor (modern Turkey). He believed that the Lydian king split the population in two and sent half to build a new life in Italy under the command of his son, Tyrrhenus, after whom the Tyrrhenian Sea was named. The remainder of Lydians were allowed to stay in Asia Minor under the king's control. Herodotus' theory is not universally accepted. Many historians believe that the Etruscans were native to the peninsula and that Etruscan culture simply emerged when the Ancient Greeks and Carthaginians began to influence the pre-existing bronze-age tribes.

City-states

In the eighth century BC, the Etruscans developed a series of city-states in the north west of the peninsula, in what is modern Tuscany. The cities, which included Clusium, Veii and Perusia, were first linked together by a monarch but then later by a league. Each Etruscan city retained a degree of independence, which made it very easy for its enemies to divide and conquer them at a later stage.

The Etruscans were not simply urban dwellers, they were farmers, artists and merchant seamen as well. It is believed that the Etruscans travelled large distances in the name of trade and established links across the Mediterranean.

Influence on Rome

Rome emerged at a time when the Etruscans dominated the surrounding regions. The extent of Etruscan influence over early Rome is not known because the Roman records for the period were lost when the Gauls sacked the city in 390 BC. The last three Roman kings were Etruscan, so a direct link between Rome and Etruria is almost certain. It is likely that the Romans learned a good deal from the Etruscans, from road building, sewage systems and gladiator fights to metalwork and sculpture.

Rome rapidly eclipsed the Etruscan city-states, which soon fell under Roman domination. Etruscan culture was gradually eroded and lost, but it was not until Sulla became dictator that the civilization was completely wiped out as a consequence of supporting Marius in the civil war.

The ruins of an Etruscan settlement at Cerveteri.

Roman Republic

Governing Rome

The government of the Roman Republic was founded upon the ashes of the Roman Monarchy. To avoid a return to the tyranny of King Tarquinius Superbus, a new form of leadership emerged.

Two-man rule

Rome was no longer to be led by one man, but two. They were called consuls, and by ruling together they were able to ensure that the will of one man was counterbalanced by that of the other. This was achieved through providing both consuls with a right of veto over the decisions of the other. Another way the system was designed to safeguard against despotism was to limit the terms of each consul to just one year, although they could be re-elected. This was changed in the second century BC when consuls were restricted to serving just one term. In the late Republic, however, these restrictions were flouted by powerful, ambitious men, who wanted to serve as leader for longer.

Consuls

The consuls were appointed by the *comitia centuriata*, an assembly that met annually to appoint the magistrates for the following year. It was presided over by the outgoing consuls. Decisions in the assembly were taken by a vote; citizens were organized into blocs, within which they were able to vote as a unit. There was a property qualification to be eligible to vote in this assembly and voting rights were staggered according to wealth; the most affluent citizens were given a disproportionately large influence over the assembly. The property qualification meant that the assembly was dominated by soldiers, who were expected to have a certain level of wealth to become soldiers in the first place. In addition to the consuls the *comitia centuriata* also appointed censors, *praetors* and *aediles*.

Above: Part of the Forum, at the base of the Palatine Hill that became the centre of Roman government. It was a complex of government buildings, temples and private homes.

Below: Fragment from a sarcophagus which depicts the procession of the consuls of Acilia.

Censors

Censors were in charge of enumerating the population to see who could vote in the *comitia centuriata* elections and what voting rights they would have. In addition, the censor was tasked with maintaining public morality and could also instigate public works; for example, it was the censor, Appius Claudius, who commissioned the construction of a road from Rome to Capua, called the Appian Way, as well as Rome's first aqueduct, the Aqua Appia. *Praetors* were in control of law and justice but they also performed the role of minor generals when Rome was at war. *Aediles* managed the city of Rome; their responsibilities included the running of the markets, the temples and the public games.

The Senate

The Senate managed to withstand the transition from the Monarchy to the Republic and in fact it became stronger as a result. The Senate continued to be an advisory body, as it had been to the kings, but in reality it had gained considerably more power. It set the agenda of the government and made recommendations to the magistrates who would take the executive decisions. Although the Senate was only dispensing advice, the magistrates almost always adhered to their suggestions (until the last century of the Republic). This effectively meant that the Senate had indirect executive powers. If a magistrate went against the Senate in a manner that was perceived to threaten the Republic, the Senate had the power to overturn his law. Senators were unpaid, but the position was highly prestigious and offered the opportunity for a man to carve out a power-base built upon the patronage of other citizens. This meant that senators became incredibly powerful and wealthy, but it also meant the Senate was often dogged by corruption. Senators were appointed for life, but could potentially be expelled by the censor, who was in charge of maintaining public morality. If a senator was believed to have acted indecently, the censor could remove him from the Senate.

Above: Ruins of the Capitol.

Below: A column base lies in the ruins of the Forum.

Patricians and Plebs

The patricians were the traditional elite of Ancient Rome. They were a group of several leading families who held a monopoly of power during the Roman Monarchy and the early Republican period. The word stems from the Latin for 'fathers'. They believed that their ancestors were the original inhabitants of Rome and wished to maintain the privileges they had built up over the years.

The remainder of Roman citizens were the plebeians. This term is relatively indiscriminate because plebs ranged from self-sufficient tradesmen to the urban poor who required handouts of free corn just to survive. They were marginalized from power by the patricians who frowned upon any kind of relationship between patricians and plebeians; intermarriage was strictly forbidden.

Over time the plebs sought to erode the political privileges given to the patricians and gain some of it for themselves. In the mid-Republican era, they had achieved this and the patrician class lost much of its power, although it managed to maintain its prestige.

For a time the patricians and the plebeians were both happy with the status quo, but in the second century BC, the rich began to get richer while the poor were getting poorer. This once again polarized the two groups and set Rome on a path of violence and anarchy that would eventually spell the end of the Republic.

Above: Fresco portrait of Terentius Neo and his wife found in a house in Pompeii. It is believed that the house belonged to the magistrate Terentius Neo and his brother Terentius Proculus, a baker. By the time of the first century AD, the class stystem of plebs and patricians had broken down.

Left: Pair of gold lionhead earrings.

Power to the plebs

The fact that these political institutions clearly favoured the patricians did not go unnoticed amongst the plebs. Frustrated by their relative disenfranchisement, the plebs sought to gain political equality and used their superior numbers to that end. Knowing that Rome could not function without them, they literally abandoned the city on several occasions to force the patricians into conceding to their interests. This action was known as secession and it was used as a political weapon for the first time in 494 BC. On that occasion, the patricians were forced to allow the establishment of a plebeian council to encourage the plebs to return to Rome. The plebeian council was able to manage the affairs of the plebs through so-called plebiscites, but it had no jurisdiction over the lives of the patricians. The plebs also gained political representation at this time with the creation of the post of plebeian tribune. Initially the role had little power besides bringing the interest of the plebs to the government. However, over time, the role amassed more power, and eventually the plebeian tribune was granted the power of veto over anything suggested by the Senate that was considered counter to the interests of the plebs.

In 449 BC, the plebs again withdrew from the city in protest at the arbitrary legal system. The law had favoured the patricians and the majority of the plebs were ignorant as to their rights, which had allowed patricians to gain the upper hand in trials. The patricians were left with little option but to appease the plebs; to entice them to return to Rome, the 'Twelve Tables', a codified list of laws, was displayed in the Forum for all to see. This served to make Rome a more just society than it had been, although the judicial system was still far from fair.

Above: Carved gemstone ring with Roman portrait.

Below: Panel inscribed with the names of members of the Roman Senate.

The plebs continued to knock down the barriers that prohibited them from political power. In 367 BC, the Licinio-Sextian Law allowed plebs to be appointed as consuls, the first one being elected in 366.

Plebeian consul

The law stipulated that one of the two consuls should always be of plebeian origin. In 366 BC, a popular assembly, the *comitia tributa*, was formed. It was designed to appoint the ten plebeian tribunes as well as plebeian *aediles* and *quaestors*, who were officials in charge of financial affairs. Unlike with the *comitia centuriata*, there were no financial requisites upon the electorate and all Roman citizens were each allowed an indirect vote within a unit called a tribe. There were thirty-five tribes in total and each tribe had one vote within the committee. Although this was more democratic than the *comitia centuriata*, it still had its own disadvantages; the city of Rome had only four out of the thirty-five voting tribes, which did not reflect the population distribution. This meant that the individual vote of a resident of the city was not as significant in the popular assembly as the individual vote of a rural Roman. In 339, the popular assembly was given the power to circumvent the *comitia centuriata* and pass some of its own laws, provided they were agreeable to the Senate.

Balance of power

The plebs finally achieved something near political equality in 287 BC, after a long and hard-fought campaign. In this year, the plebs once again seceded from the city of Rome and forced the patricians to give them even more powers. The resulting Hortensia Law made plebiscites legally binding on all Roman citizens, not just the plebs; furthermore it gave the plebeian council the power to make laws without the Senate's agreement.

These changes might seem revolutionary, but the reality was somewhat more conservative because the patricians continued to be deeply involved. Laws were usually drafted by patricians and the Senate's approval was almost always solicited before the plebeian council pushed ahead.

Rome had somehow struck a balance between the plebs and the patricians for the first time, leading to a golden age for the Republic's political institutions. Such equilibrium lasted for over a century, but was eventually destroyed by a social crisis, which once again encouraged the plebs to push for even more power.

Above: Statues from the House of the Vestal Virgins in the Forum.

Below: View of the ruins of the Forum.

A Roman Villa

In the second century BC the wealthy urban elite of Rome seized upon the opportunity provided by a rural depression to push the traditional Roman smallholders off the land, and carve up large swathes of countryside for themselves. These new urban landowners began building second homes on their large country estates as retreats from their hectic lifestyles in the city.

Away from the bustle

Over time Rome became even busier as ever more smallholders were alienated from their land and pushed into the city to find work. Faced with Rome's growing population and the increasingly bustling atmosphere, many more affluent Romans sought sanctuary in a second home in the countryside. A villa culture quickly emerged; soon it became fashionable for all wealthy Romans to own one, or more, such properties.

Villas were usually set in many hectares of land which the villa owner would put to agricultural use to make money. Although the farms were usually located very close to the villa, they were not always considered to be a part of the tranquil, rural idyll, and the villa was usually kept separate.

The farm would supply the villa with its food, wine and olive oil, but otherwise most landlords were quite content to keep themselves and their villa apart. Agricultural labour was left to slaves and an administrator was usually appointed to manage the farm in the owner's absence.

Above: Detail from a fresco showing a garden scene with birds. The plastered walls in the villa's interior were painted, sometimes just with colour washes, sometimes with decorative designs of pillars and geometric figures, but by the first century AD the fashion was for realistic frescoes.

Left: Mosaics on the interior walls of a villa at Pompeii.

Hypocausts

Many Roman villas had their own heating system called a *hypocaust*. The word *hypocaust* means 'heat from below'. Underfloor heating would have been especially welcome in the provincial villas in the northern provinces that were inhabited during the colder, winter months.

The way in which the *hypocaust* system worked was quite simple. The floor of the building was raised above ground level on a series of short pillars, leaving a void beneath the floor. At one end of the villa a fire in a small chamber just below floor level was maintained by a household slave. The hot air from the fire would be drawn through the void below the floors. In many *hypocaust* systems, hot air was channelled from the underground chamber into ducts between the walls of the villa, heating the walls as well.

Ingeniously, and efficiently, the same fire which heated the air for the *hypocaust* also heated water for the villa's baths and other hot water requirements.

Millefiori glass bowl from Alexandria. This may have been used as tableware or for purely decorative purposes in the villa.

Below: Diagram of a Hypocaust for heating a bath at a villa.

Below: A hypocaust at the Chedworth Roman Villa in the Cotswolds once trapped heat under the floor for use in a room or baths.

Lavish and extensive

Initially, Roman villas tended to be relatively conservative in size and decoration, but they soon became lavish and extensive as the Roman rich vied to outdo one another. Once the elite were made even richer by the plunder brought back from Rome's foreign conquests, they could afford to build larger and more extravagant villas.

Traditional Roman villas were largely similar in design to the houses that wealthy Roman families owned in the city, although they usually had much more space. Most villas were entered through an impressive tree-lined and colonnaded forecourt, which removed the need for the large atrium that townhouses would have had. The atrium was the customary place in which the family would meet guests and clients. Since most of these meetings would take place in the city home, there was less necessity for such a space in the country home and many villas would have had no atrium at all.

Al fresco dining

The villa would have all the facilities of the townhouse, including a lavish internal garden, bedrooms, kitchens and an outdoor dining room, which would be used more than the one in the city because Romans tended to visit the villa when the weather was better suited to *al fresco* dining.

Like Roman townhouses, Roman villas were sparsely furnished. The main item of furniture was a long couch, which was used for both dining and sleeping. Villas usually had very few tables on display because most were portable so that they could be moved between rooms to wherever they were needed, and stored out of sight when they were not. Roman villas were rarely cluttered; most possessions were hidden away in large wooden chests.

The property's isolated setting required it to have many additional amenities that were not common in townhouses; these included private baths, temples and bakeries. Most villas would also have a water supply and drainage system to meet the needs of the household, the baths and the farms.

Ruins of a section of Hadrian's Villa, a lavish country residence to the north-east of Rome, near Tivoli.

Seafront villas

As demand for villas grew, many were built without farmland attached or with just a sufficient amount of land to meet the needs of the villa. It became common for villas to be built along the seafront, where the cool sea breezes would contrast favourably with the stuffy heat of the Roman summer.

The Bay of Naples, to the south of Rome, became a particularly popular location for coastal villas, and a great number were discovered in the ruins of Pompeii and Herculaneum. Of all the towns in the Bay of Naples, the resort of Baiae was the one that became most linked with villa culture and the hedonism that became associated with the Roman upper classes.

Julius Caesar built a villa in the town, which encouraged many of Rome's elite to buy holiday homes there. Baiae remained popular over the years for its medicinal sulphur springs, cool climate and rich vegetation.

Villas across the Empire

Over time, villas were built across the entire Empire, as native elites and Roman administrators sought to emulate the lives of their counterparts in Rome. Provincial villas were often fashioned in the style of Roman architecture and were designed with all the amenities enjoyed by their Roman counterparts, including central heating systems, Roman artwork, bathhouses, bakeries and temples.

Outside of Italy, villa culture often had a distinctively different character, especially in the less urbanized provinces of Gaul and Britannia. In such places, villas were used less as a rural getaway and more often as a permanent residence. This meant that the villas were not usually kept separate from the surrounding farmland and were often integrated with the local economy.

Gold oil Lamp from Pompeii.

Fresco showing a seaside villa.

Mosaics

Floor mosaics have been discovered in the ruins of villas across the Roman Empire. Many have remained in excellent condition and usually prove to be among the most interesting finds at an excavated villa. Mosaics comprise many small fragments of stone or glass, called *tesserae*, arranged in intricate patterns on a bed of wet plaster.

Mosaics depended upon the personal taste of the owner of the villa, as well as the fashions of the day. A guilloche pattern of interwoven rope was especially popular, but a variety of shapes and patterns can be found. Numerous pictorial mosaics have also been discovered; most consist of a single image, often of animals or gods, but some comprise elaborate scenes, such as men hunting, gladiators duelling, or an illustration of a famous myth or legend.

Frescoes

Some Romans chose to have mosaics on their walls as well, but frescoes were more common. A fresco is a type of mural; the term is derived from the term 'fresh' because the artist would apply the paint directly on to wet plaster. This technique allowed the paint to permanently bond with the wall and has meant that several examples have lasted until this day, although many have faded over the centuries.

Unfortunately, the walls of most villas have either been demolished or collapsed over time, but volcanic ash prevented this from happening to the villas surrounding Pompeii and Herculaneum. As a result, some of the best examples of villa frescoes are to be found at these sites.

Inside a house in the ruins of Ostia. Richly decorated floor mosaics were an obvious sign of the villa owner's wealth.

War of Expansion

From the its modest origins on the Palatine Hill to its position at the heart of Italy Rome underwent several centuries of aggressive expansion, so that by 270 BC the Romans held full control of the Italian peninsula south of the River Arno.

Dominating Latium

Initially Rome had to gain domination of Latium. In 493 BC, the city joined the Latin League, a union of Latin-speaking settlements, for the purposes of common trade and protection.

Alba Longa was the chief city of the Latin League and Rome had to stand in its shadow. It was not until the reign of Tullus Hostilius, when he reputedly ordered that the Alban king be torn in two, that Rome was able to dominate the League for the first time.

The Latin War

After this time, states of the Latin League were only able to challenge Roman dominance once. In 340, they tried to exploit Roman weakness to stage the 'Latin War'. This lasted for two years until Rome was eventually successful; the Latin League was dissolved and its members were subsumed into the Roman state as *municipia*, with full citizenship rights.

Triumph over the Etruscans

In addition to dominating its neighbouring Latins, Rome faced challenges from the various small tribes which littered central Italy. During both the Monarchy and the early Republic, successful wars continued intermittently with the Etruscans and the Sabine as well as the neighbouring Aequi and Volsci. Rome's crowning achievement in these infant years of the Republic was perhaps its defeat of the nearby Etruscan city of Veii in 396 after a decade-long siege.

The city of Veii was razed to the ground, and its population killed or sold into slavery. The victory presented Rome with both short- and long-term economic gains. In the short term, there was plunder sent back to Rome, but in the longer term, Rome had removed a key trading rival from central Italy and heralded the decline of the neighbouring Etruscans.

Detail from the Palestrina Mosaic showing the Nile river delta during the flooding season. Palestrina was a town in what is now the Lazio region which fought in the 'Latin Wars' against Rome.

Humiliation by the Gauls

Roman glory was short-lived, as they suffered a humiliating defeat at the hands of the Gauls, just a few years later in 390 BC. The Gauls, a group of tribes which inhabited the region of Western Europe in the area centralized on modern-day France, had been pushing into Etruria in the preceding decades and in 391 threatened the Etruscan city of Clusium. The city appealed to Rome for assistance, an indication of Rome's new, powerful regional status.

The Romans sent a delegation to negotiate with the northern invaders, but this came to nothing when a member of the Roman delegation killed one of his counterparts from Gaul. This resulted in the ire of the Gauls who, under the leadership of Brennus, marched on Rome, defeating the Roman Army in the Battle of Allia and capturing the city.

Bas-relief from a metope (a section of a frieze) depicting a combat scene.

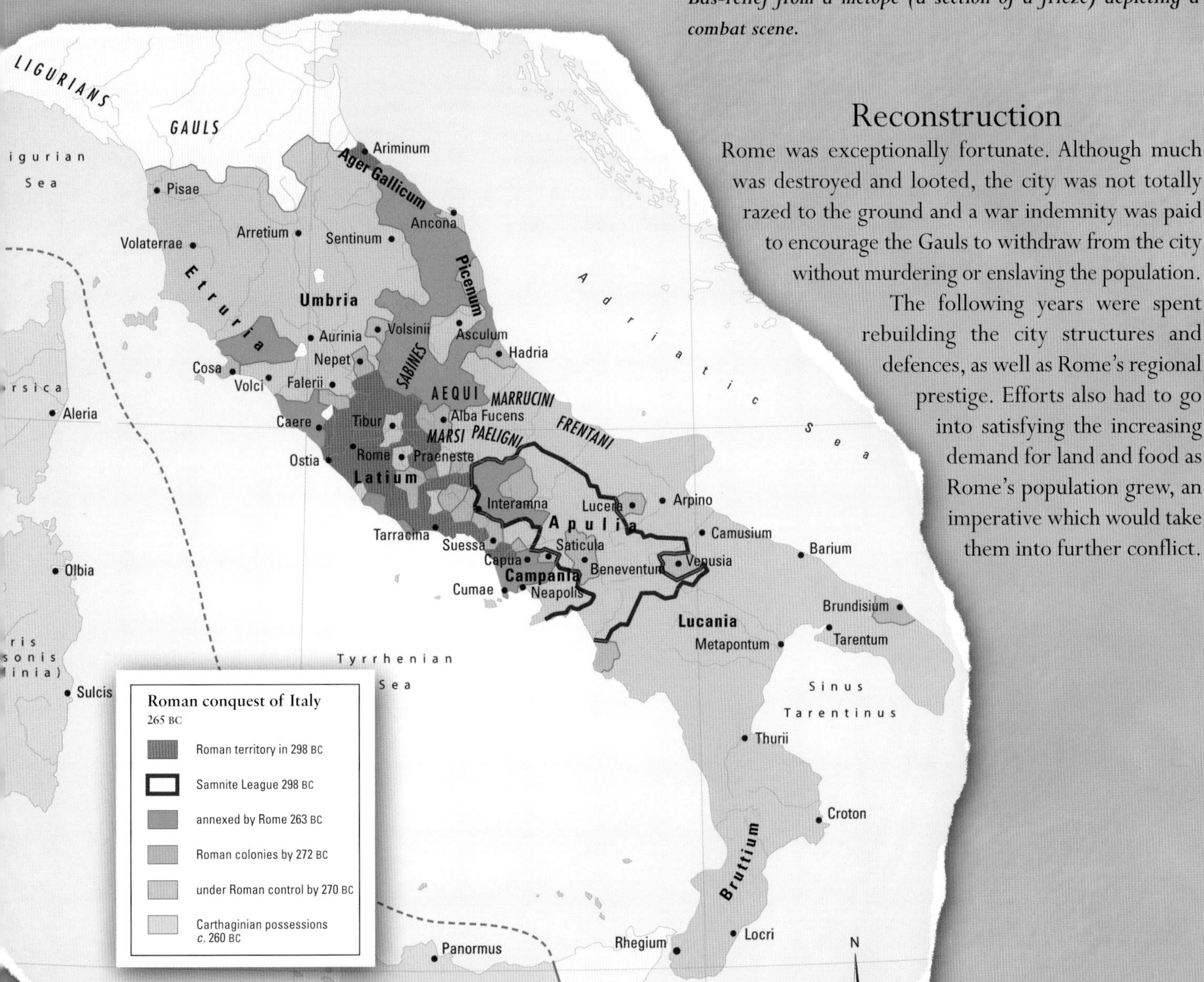

Reconstruction

Rome was exceptionally fortunate. Although much was destroyed and looted, the city was not totally razed to the ground and a war indemnity was paid to encourage the Gauls to withdraw from the city without murdering or enslaving the population.

The following years were spent rebuilding the city structures and defences, as well as Rome's regional prestige. Efforts also had to go into satisfying the increasing demand for land and food as Rome's population grew, an imperative which would take them into further conflict.

War with the Samnites

Roman expansion in the fourth century BC brought them into conflict with the Samnite tribes of the Apennine Mountains. The Samnites were a strong military nation and engaged the Romans in three prolonged wars, the first beginning in 344 BC, and the last not ending until 290.

During the Second Samnite War, in 321, the Romans suffered a humiliating defeat in the Battle of the Caudine Forks, which gave the Samnites the upper hand for several years.

The third and final war began in 298 when the Samnites enlisted help from a number of Rome's other enemies, including the Celts and several Etruscan cities.

In 295, the Battle of Sentium became the defining moment in that war. Vast numbers of men perished on both sides, but the Romans came out of the battle in the best shape, which allowed them to crush the Samnites once and for all. Victory against the Samnites handed Rome the control of central Italy.

Maintaining new territories

Rome had learned the lesson from the 'Latin War' that it was important to avoid uprisings in conquered territories when the city was distracted and appeared weak, in this case from its ongoing wars of expansion. Thus it was crucial that the Romans consolidated the land they had already conquered.

This gave rise to prudent occupation policies. Troublesome areas were totally and brutally suppressed, while less unruly occupied peoples were met with a benevolent response and were allowed to continue much as before, with the understanding that they were now subject to Roman authority.

In addition, colonization tactics were employed to dilute the native populations of a territory with Roman citizens, so as to obstruct any united uprising against Roman rule in the future.

These shrewd occupation tactics, employed during the early days of Rome, continue to be reflected in the policies of nations across the globe in our modern world.

Detail from a sarcophagus relief which shows horse chariots in use.

Expanding southward

During the third century BC, Rome began an expansion into southern Italy. This demarcates an important shift in the nation's history. Rome was no longer facing wars against the smaller tribes of central Italy, instead it moved into competition with some of the greatest powers in the ancient world, Carthage and Greece.

Among Rome's first forays into the region was a response to the request for assistance from the city of Thurii against the Greek Lucanians. Rome sent a fleet to investigate, which was promptly sunk by Tarentum, the leading Greek city-state on the Italian peninsula.

Pyrrhic victories and defeats

In 280 BC, fearing that the rise of Rome would eat away at Greek dominance in southern Italy, Tarentum paid for Pyrrhus, king of Epirus, to come to their rescue. Pyrrhus brought with him an army of 25,000 men, as well as a number of elephants, a war weapon the Romans did not have, and which proved decisive in scaring the Roman Army from the field in the initial battles.

Pyrrhus won one of the first great battles at Asculum in 279. However, Pyrrhus' victory was at a huge cost to his own army, which resulted in the phrase 'pyrrhic victory', for a victory that comes at such a high price.

In addition to fighting the Roman advance, Pyrrhus attempted to assist Greek cities in Sicily against the Carthaginians menacing from the west of the island. Dividing his troops allowed Rome time to rejuvenate its forces and march further south, eventually besieging Tarentum in 275 BC. Despite successes in Sicily, heavy losses in the south of Italy encouraged Pyrrhus to withdraw his forces back to Greece, leaving Tarentum to fall to the Romans.

Above: Coin depicting warrior with shield and hatchet.

Right: Wall fresco depicting a bust of the mythical warrior figure, Hercules. The cult of Hercules was adopted from the Greek, Heracles, early in Rome's history, perhaps as early as the sixth century BC. Hercules embodies all the masculine virtues.

The Roman Army

The Republican Army

The Army of the early and mid-Republic was not a professional one. It was raised as and when it was needed and usually only a handful of legions were maintained during peacetime. Instead, when legions needed to be raised, all property-owning Roman citizens of a certain age were expected to volunteer their services when commanded. The command to arms came from the consuls, who elected tribunes to go out and enlist the services of appropriate Roman citizens. Six tribunes commanded the entire legion and were responsible to the consuls. The tribunes were usually younger noblemen with intentions of serving in the Senate.

Legions and centuries

The Republican Army was a successful fighting force and helped Rome conquer much of the Italian peninsula, as well as defeat Carthage in the Punic Wars. The core unit of the Army was a legion, which comprised approximately six thousand men. Ostensibly, one was capable of fighting a war on its own, but this seldom happened as more than one legion was usually called into battle. Each legion was divided into sixty centuries and each century was paired with another in a unit called a *maniple*.

Each century was controlled by a centurion. The members of the legion elected thirty centurions and another thirty were appointed by those elected centurions. An elected centurion and his elected candidate together ran a *maniple*. What was termed the right-hand century was always controlled by the elected centurion, while the left-hand was controlled by the appointed centurion.

Fighting formation

The different lines of the Roman Army were comprised of different sorts of heavy infantry. The front line of the legion was fielded by ten *maniples* of *hastati*. These were the youngest men of the army. Middle-aged men in their late twenties and thirties were called *principes* and they formed the ten *manipless* of the middle ranks of the army. At the rear were ten *maniples* of *triarii*. These were veterans of previous wars and were not so much there for the fight as perhaps for the nostalgic experience of battle. If the *triarii* were engaged in fighting at all, the day would have been going badly for the Romans.

Each *maniple* was assigned a number of light infantry called *velites*. These were often boys even younger than even the *hastati* and were extremely mobile. They formed the front ranks of each *maniple* and were used for skirmishing, before retreating behind the heavy infantry.

Each legion was flanked by the cavalry called *equites*. In the early Republican era, the *equites* comprised the wealthiest members of the army, but during the mid-Republican era, the cavalry tended to be fielded by allies of Rome, rather than citizens themselves.

Men dressed as Roman centurions march through the ruins of the Forum on 21 April 2003 as part of an anniversary celebration of the founding of Rome in 748 BC.

Creating a professional army

The Republican Army had been very successful in the expansion of Rome; however, at the end of the second century BC, the Army was in need of reform. The Empire had vastly increased in size and it was no longer feasible to have only property-owning Roman citizens conscripted for a certain campaign; after all, they always returned to their land once campaigning was over. Instead Rome required professional soldiers and a standing army.

It fell to Consul Gaius Marius to bring these changes about; by introducing wages and by allowing Romans without property to join, he was able to create a professional army. The ranks swelled as poorer Romans were enticed by a military career because it offered a better quality of life for them and their families. This shift to a permanent armed force meant that more money was spent in training and kitting out the soldiers. The result was a highly skilled army, which was able to gain many victories.

In addition to reform, non-Roman citizens were increasingly used for auxiliary tasks to solve the problems of shortages of men. As well as paying these auxiliaries, Rome offered them further incentive to join the Army by allowing them the much-coveted reward of Roman citizenship upon their retirement from the forces.

Statue depicting Mithras on a bull. The male-only cult of Mithras developed in the first century AD and reached its height in the third and fourth centuries when it was particularly popular among Roman soldiers.

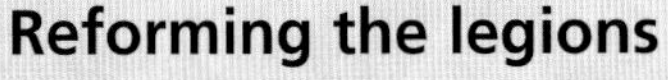

Reforming the legions

Marius also undertook reforms to the construction of the legions themselves. Between 113 and 105 BC, Germanic tribes had been able to defeat the Roman army on several occasions because the legionary composition had proved inflexible. The problem was that the line formation based upon age did not withstand counter attack from the side. Enemies were able to flank the Roman Army and forego attacking the younger soldiers in the front line, attacking instead the older, more vulnerable, *triarii* in the rear.

The reforms abandoned the linear formations of the mid-Republic and replaced them with cohorts. This mixed up the previous formation so that each group was more flexible and could face attack from the side and the rear, as well as the front.

A twelve-seater latrine in the Thermae of the Cyclops at the ruins of Dougga in Tunisia. Although they were trained to cope with difficult conditions, Roman soldiers lived with a degree of civilized comfort, especially in established garrisons throughout both the Republic and the Empire.

Legions in Imperial Rome

Marius' reforms were such that the Army had become a permanent fixture in Roman affairs. By the time of the Empire, his cohort system had emerged into the archetypal Roman Army that we imagine today. The century was reduced to eighty men, made up of eight *contubernium*, a tightly knit group that were expected to bunk together. The cohort system of Marius was maintained and six centuries comprised a cohort of four hundred and eighty men. The first cohort, however, contained ten centuries of eight hundred men in total. Ten cohorts, including the disproportionate first cohort, made up the legion. Although this totalled just over five thousand soldiers, a legion continued to contain in the region of six thousand men because a number of support staff, such as medics and chefs were attached to each legion.

Praetorian Guard: the Emperor's bodyguard

During the Empire an elite group of army officers were lucky enough to serve in the highly-esteemed Praetorian Guard. The Guard was essentially a personal bodyguard for the Emperor and his family, but was on hand to crush any unrest in Rome. The Praetorian Guard originated during the Republic when they were used to defend generals, but it was during the reign of Augustus, the first Emperor, that the Guard really came to prominence.

The position was popular among army officers because the job offered a significantly higher salary than a legionary would receive and the length of service was considerably reduced, to just twelve years. The Guard became incredibly powerful during the Empire and was the institution that could most threaten the position of the Emperor himself as Aurelian, Pertinax and Commodus, among others, were to discover.

The Guard's ability to intimidate Emperors meant that they were in an extremely privileged position, and they were known to have sold the role of Emperor to the highest bidder on occasions. Although Septimus Severus was able to marginalize the Guard during his rule, it was not until the reign of Diocletian, at the end of the third century AD, that the Guard's stranglehold was broken.

Sculpture showing Roman wrestlers. Wrestling would have been a popular sport for men serving in the Army

An aerial view of Old Sarum Roman Fortress to the north of Salisbury, England. Many members of the Roman Army found themselves serving a term in Britain, on the northernmost edges of Roman rule.

Life in the Roman Army

On the move

When the Army was moving from place to place it was expected to cover many miles in one day. Professionalizing the Army had allowed recruits to be trained at marching these long, arduous distances with heavy loads of armour, weapons and packs. After a long day on the move, the Army would set up camp for the night in tents which they carried with them.

Once a campsite was located, soldiers would make defensive ramparts by digging a ditch, reinforced with wood, around the site. The following morning they would pack everything up and begin moving again. Each *contubernium* of eight men would share the tent. Servants would usually help transport it, but sometimes the soldiers had to manage themselves.

Fortifications

The Romans built a series of fortifications across the Empire to defend the peripheries and billet soldiers. The forts were protected by walls, surrounded by moats, with heavily guarded entrances. Soldiers were given a new password each day so they could enter and exit without enemies getting in. Life in the forts was extremely regimented.

Soldiers were expected to maintain their levels of endurance through training, which involved exercises such as marches, swimming and fencing. In addition, strict levels of discipline were maintained. But the forts offered a more comfortable lifestyle than the soldiers met with when they were on the move because they were like small towns, with buildings such as a granary and a weapons' factory. Home comforts such as bathhouses, public lavatories, religious shrines were often also provided. Soldiers did not have to sleep in tents and, apart from when training, they did not need to be responsible for carrying everything with them.

Perks of the job

Life as a soldier offered many benefits. The pay was good for many men who would have earned less had they remained in Rome. Moreover, soldiers gained better medical treatment than many would otherwise have received. Most soldiers served a twenty-five-year term and afterwards received a good pension, including land and money.

There was an additional advantage in being a soldier for non-Romans because in retirement they were granted Roman citizenship. Soldiers were also honoured in death, as through the Army they were able to purchase cheaper burials than civilians.

However, there were obvious downsides. The pension could only be received if a soldier made it to retirement, and many were killed in action. Just as it is today, the Army was a perilous profession in Roman times, and when soldiers were not engaged in combat, life could be mundane and tiresome, especially with monotonous, if arduous, training.

Initially, a soldier billeted to an outlying fort was forbidden from marrying. This was another disincentive to join the Army because soldiers frequently served up to twenty- five years, making them very old before they could settle down. Although this rule was later scrapped, Roman soldiers often entered into relationships with the locals near to the fort.

Spanish Roman coin with a horseman carrying a lance.

The Punic Wars

Less than a decade after its defeat of the Greek city states of southern Italy, Rome found itself at war with Carthage, the great mercantile Empire that once dominated the western Mediterranean. Rome's ultimate victory heralded its emergence as one of the greatest powers the world has ever seen.

Dispute over Messana

The Romans and the Carthaginians had signed a treaty in 279 BC in light of their shared threat from Pyrrhus' forces. However, this treaty came under threat when a dispute broke out in the Sicilian city of Messana, a strategic settlement because of its position controlling the straits between Sicily and mainland Italy. The Mamertines of central Italy held control of the city because they had moved into the region to help the Greek city-state, Syracuse, defend against the Roman and Carthaginian threats. When Pyrrhus departed, the Mamertines did not give up control of the city, leading Syracuse to make a bid to regain the city in 264. The Carthaginians immediately moved in to take Messana in alliance with Syracuse. This crisis presented hawks in Rome with the opportunity they had been waiting for to move into Sicily. The Senate resolved to send its forces to liberate Messana from the Carthaginians. Rome was quickly successful against a smaller Carthaginian garrison. It benevolently allowed the Carthaginian and Syracuse troops to withdraw, but such mercifulness did not prevent either from declaring war.

Below: Bas-relief of a Roman warship. After losing the naval Battle of Lipari in 260 BC to the superior Carthaginian fleet, Rome embarked on a massive shipbuilding programme so that at the next encounter, the Battle of Mylae, Rome's navy triumphed and heralded a shift in power in the Mediterranean.

Opposite above: Harbour scene from a fresco in Pompeii.

Opposite below: Street in the ancient Roman port of Ostia which, while an important trading port, was also an embarkation point for military campaigns during the Punic Wars. It is now no longer on the coast and lies about eight kilometres inland.

The First Punic War

The First Punic War lasted until 241 BC and was largely a battle for the control of Sicily. (The word Punic comes from the Roman name for Carthage). The Roman Army scored some initial successes on the island, taking a handful of Carthaginian settlements and marching on Syracuse. The threat to the city encouraged its commander, Hiero, to defect to Roman side just one year into the conflict. Although the Romans scored these early victories on land, in order to challenge Carthage's power, it would need to be able to defeat the Carthaginians on water as well. This was no easy feat, because upon entering the war, Carthage was one of the most advanced maritime powers in the world with a relatively free rein in the western Mediterranean.

Rome gains naval supremacy

Carthaginian naval superiority meant that it won the first naval encounter, the Battle of Lipari in 260. But Rome did not resign itself to defeat. Instead it embarked upon an incredible shipbuilding programme, using stolen Carthaginian naval technology, to turn its navy around in a matter of months. At the next encounter, the Battle of Mylae, Rome triumphed. It was the Rome's first ever naval victory and heralded a shift in the balance of power in the western Mediterranean. Roman successes meant that it was able to capture Corsica, as well as much of Sicily.

With new territorial gains under its belt, Rome became interested in ending the war because it was placing great strain upon its finances. In a bid to force Carthage to capitulate, the Romans invaded Africa in 257, menacing the Carthaginians in their home territories. However, Rome was unable to sustain such a distant conflict because the Carthaginian defence was shored up by the arrival of Greek mercenaries and elephants.

With the Roman withdrawal from Africa the war entered an impasse and once again focused upon land battles and sieges in Sicily. Carthage was the first to succumb to the constraints of maintaining a prolonged conflict. It was forced to surrender to the Romans because of civil unrest in its African provinces.

The last battle was off the coast of the Aegates Islands. Rome emerged the clear winner and Carthage withdrew to settle its domestic strife, but not before Rome imposed a punishing treaty. The Carthaginians were ordered to pay 3,200 talents and withdraw from Sicily.

The Mercenary War

The financial indemnity imposed by the Romans, combined with the economic pinch from years of warfare, ensured that Carthage retreated from the international scene to deal with more pressing domestic concerns. A 'Mercenary War' broke out between 240 and 238 BC. It was started by mercenaries, employed by the Carthaginians during the First Punic War, who had not been paid as a result of Carthage's dire financial situation. Although the war was primarily confined to North Africa, mercenaries also became troublesome on the island of Sardinia, which was still nominally under Carthaginian control. Unable to police Sardinia as well as North Africa, Carthage could do little but watch the Romans step in and annex the island.

The Saguntum Crisis

In the 230s, with the Mercenary War won, Carthage returned to the international scene, desperate to regain its former glory and fulfil its imperial ambitions. Rather than challenging Rome for its former possessions in Sicily and Sardinia, Carthage looked elsewhere, to the Iberian Peninsula, in what is modern-day Spain. The Carthaginians had already settled the coastal regions in the south of the peninsula before the war, but between 237 and 219, they moved deeper into the interior, consolidating control over the region at the expense of the local Celtic tribes.

Carthage's resurgent expansionism was not unremarked in Rome. But the Romans were busy conquering the Gallic tribes to the north of the River Arno and expanding towards the Alps, capturing Mediolanum, modern-day Milan, in 222 BC. Therefore, the Romans resolved to make an agreement with the Carthaginians. Carthage would not expand north of the River Ebro, and Rome would not expand south of it. Ostensibly, this handed control of the Iberian Peninsula to Carthage.

However, the agreement was worth very little. Carthage's invasion of Spain had helped her recover financially and politically from the first Punic War, and Roman-Carthaginian rivalry over the Mediterranean once again began to flare up.

The flashpoint was to be the city of Saguntum, located south of the Ebro, in Carthage's sphere of influence. Rome provocatively established a protectorate over the city, and Carthage responded by laying siege to it in 219. When the city finally capitulated to the Carthaginians, Rome once again declared war.

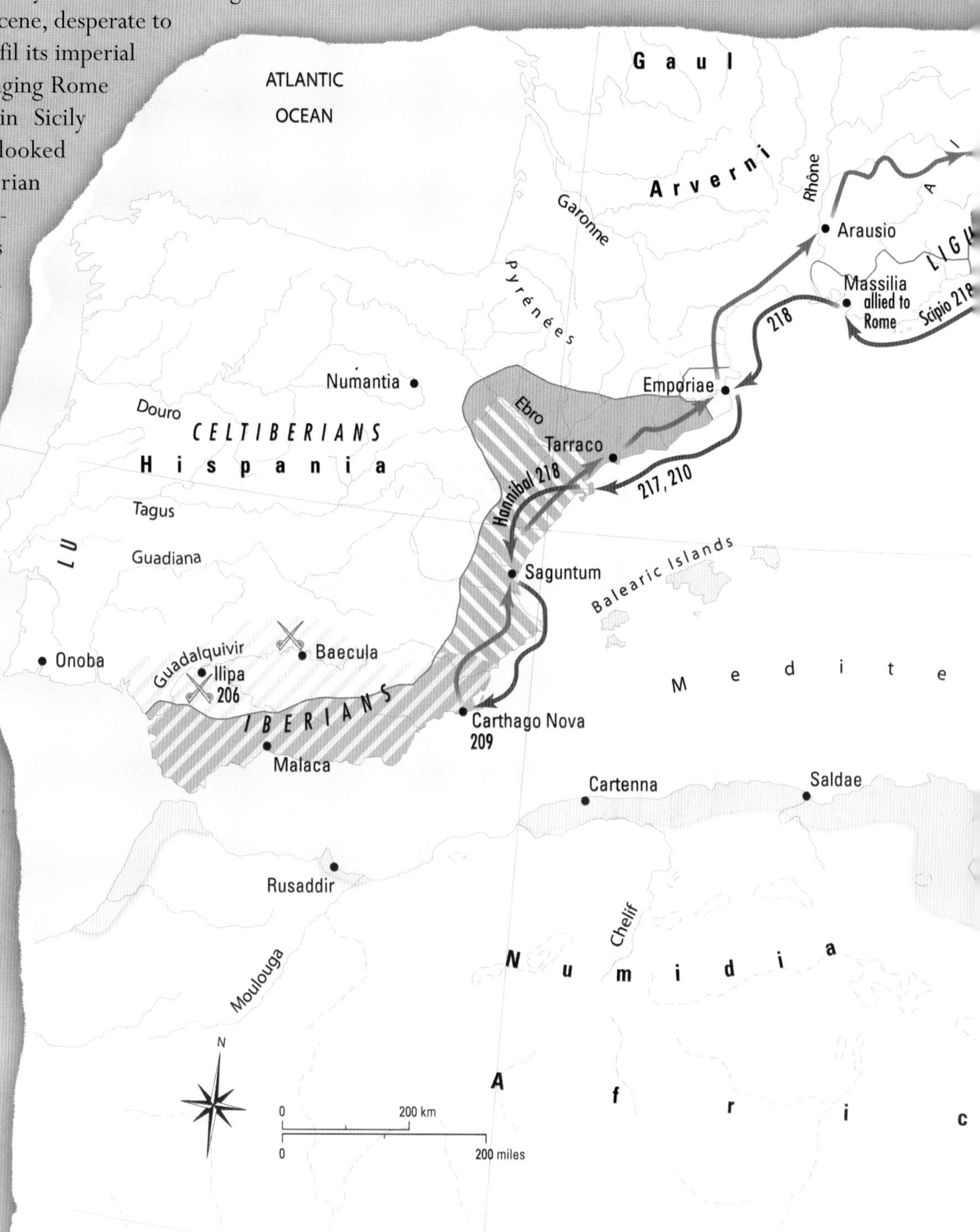

The Second Punic War

The second Roman-Carthaginian conflict was certain to be different to the first because of Carthage's new European base in Spain and also because of its new general, Hannibal Barca, who had been appointed in 221 BC. Hannibal was vehemently anti-Roman and it was said that he had sworn an oath never to make peace with Rome.

Hannibal's advance

Hannibal resolved to take the fight to the Roman heartland in the Italian peninsula. From his position in Spain, he determined to execute an overland invasion, which required his forces to traverse both the Alps and the Pyrenees, a spectacular feat that was to become legendary. In 218 Hannibal crossed the River Ebro with in excess of 100,000 men and a number of elephants. After crossing the Pyrenees, Hannibal had to fend off the local tribes that were hampering his progress, before crossing the Alps into Italy. Only three quarters of the men who had started the journey with Hannibal made it to Italy. Many had died along the treacherous route, but many had been strategically left behind by Hannibal who was unsure of the loyalty of some of his forces.

The Romans did not hinder Hannibal's advance from Spain to Italy. The Roman Army could have routed him in the Rhone valley but was distracted by rebellions in Cremona and Placentia. Desperate to halt Hannibal's remarkable progress, a Roman Army, commanded by consul Publius Cornelius Scipio, tried to defeat Hannibal's force before it had a chance to recuperate from its arduous journey across the Alps. In October 218, the Romans engaged Hannibal in the Battle of Ticinus, which resulted in a Carthaginian victory, in spite of the troops' fatigue.

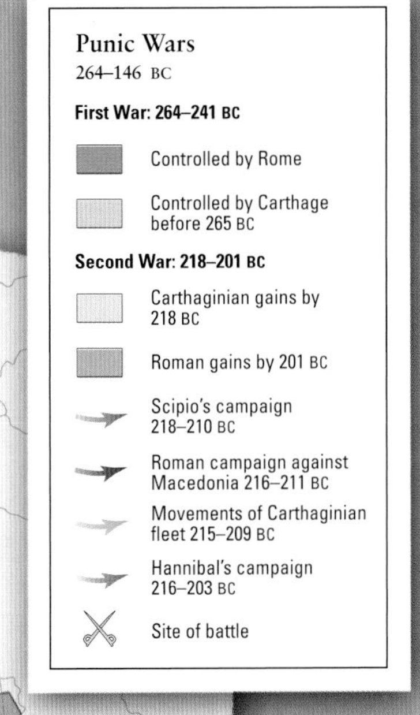

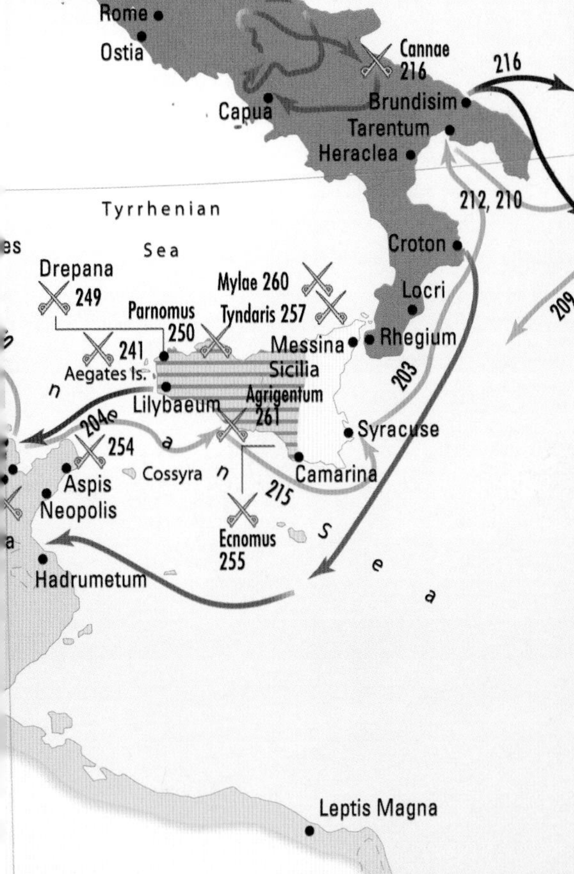

Two elephants walk below a ruined arch during a British Alpine Expedition to reconstruct Hannibal's journey across the Alps.

Hannibal

Hannibal Barca, son of the Carthaginian general Hamilcar Barca, is often cited as one of the greatest military commanders in history, most notably for his inspirational strategies and tactics. The name Barca is actually an epithet meaning 'lightning', although his descendants continued to use it as a surname.

Legend tells that at the age of nine, Hannibal asked his father if he could join a mission to create a military base in Hispania. His father agreed but only after Hannibal had sworn that he would make the Roman Republic his lifelong enemy.

Like father, like son

Hamilcar, like his son, was a great and well-respected general who had several military successes before he was finally killed in combat. After Hamilcar's death in 229 BC, his son-in-law Hasdrubal the Fair took command but was murdered in 221. Hannibal then became commander of the Carthaginian Army. He had no doubt inherited many of his father's characteristics, immediately embarking on a series of aggressive attacks that culminated in his famous journey across the mountains to fight the Romans on their home ground.

First-century BC sculpture of the head and shoulders of the Carthaginian general, Hannibal, who attacked Rome in 218 BC.

End to his career

Hannibal's military career finally ended at the Battle of Zama on 19 October 202. He then successfully transferred his skills to the position of 'suffet' or chief magistrate. To this position he brought authority and power, pushing through several important and popular reforms. In 195, after the Romans demanded his resignation from the by now client state of Carthage, he went into exile and continued to work with various military campaigns before poisoning himself in 183 in order to avoid certain capture by the Romans; he was sixty-four.

For many years after his death the name Hannibal Barca was synonymous with fear and terror throughout the Roman Empire. The expression 'Hannibal *ad portas* (Hannibal is at the Gates) was coined by Romans and used in times of anxiety or disaster.

Painting from the Renaissance period depicting Hannibal fighting a Roman legion near the Alps.

A resounding blow to Rome

Although the victory at Ticinus was only a token one, and the Roman Army was able to regroup to fight another day, it was also an important one because many north Italian tribes opted to switch sides and join Hannibal, and in doing so, replenished the ranks of his depleted army. The Roman commander Scipio's army retreated to the River Trebia where he was joined by the army of his co-consul, Sempronius, from Sicily. Sempronius insisted upon a direct attack on Hannibal, a plan which Hannibal discovered and pre-empted with his own invasion of the Roman camp early in the morning in December 218 BC. He was able to catch the Romans unprepared for the campaign, both cold and hungry, and dealt a resounding defeat; Scipio and Sempronius lost an estimated 30,000 men.

A war of attrition: 'Fabian Tactics'

In the wake of the humiliating defeat, the Senate recalled the consuls and replaced them with two new ones, Gaius Flaminius and Gnaeus Servilius Geminus, who fared little better against Hannibal. Desperate to score a victory, Flaminius allowed his legions to be lured into an ambush in the Battle of Lake Trasimene. Hannibal's Army used the lake to enclose the Romans by denying them an escape route. Once penned in, Hannibal's forces proceeded to butcher their enemy in what was another decisive Carthaginian victory. Flaminius was killed in action and the fearful Senate elected a dictator, Fabius Maximus. His response was to avoid pitched battles with Hannibal and instead try to wear down his army through a prolonged war of attrition. Maximus's strategy is still known as 'Fabian tactics' in his honour, or rather dishonour since Maximus' fellow Romans often expressed contempt for such a seemingly un-heroic strategy, especially because Hannibal was able to push further south as a result.

Funerary stele showing a warrior on horseback.

The dictatorship was ended, and Maximus was replaced with consuls Lucius Aemilius Paullus and Gaius Terentius Varro, who opted for a more active approach to Hannibal as a contrast to Maximus' unpopular policies. Their humiliation in the Battle of Cannae in 216, where Rome suffered its worst defeat of the war, seemed to vindicate Maximus' strategy. Rome had amassed a superior-sized army and the consuls thought they could defeat Hannibal.

Ruins in the port of Ostia. Although now about eight kilometres inland, this would have been an important port in the strategy against the Carthaginians.

Rome loses allegiance

In the face of the consuls' strategy, Hannibal used military genius to defeat the larger Roman Army. He lured them in to his own lines and then outflanked his enemy using a crescent formation. The Romans were encircled by the Carthaginians, who once again completely destroyed their enemy. The Battle of Cannae could have proved a decisive turning point in the war, because a number of southern Italian tribes detached from their allegiance to Rome and expressed loyalty to Carthage instead. This led Hannibal to resolve to press further south to consolidate control there, rather than march on Rome.

Scipio drives the Carthaginians from Spain

Although the Romans had stumbled from one humiliation to another during the first years of the war, there was an ongoing success story in Spain. In 218 BC, an army under Gnaeus Scipio, brother of the general at Trebia, crossed into Spain with the aim of denying Hannibal his Spanish base for future resource and finance replenishment. Battles continued in Spain until 211 when Scipio was defeated and killed. In 209 he was replaced by his brother's son, named, like his father, Publius Cornelius Scipio. Over the following three years Scipio managed to drive the Carthaginians out of Spain and returned to Italy in 205. The loss of Spain was a blow to Hannibal. He no longer had a semi-independent base and had to pay greater heed to the interests of Carthage itself. Carthage's paramount concern was defence of its heartlands and this was exploited by Scipio who resolved to send an army to conquer the capital city itself. In 204, he reached North Africa and this meant that Hannibal was recalled from Italy. He had to abandon his gains in the south and his years of campaigning became redundant as he returned to Carthage the following year, 203 BC.

Carthage sues for peace

The endgame of the second Punic War was the Battle of Zama in 202. After so many defeats in Italy, the Romans overcame the Carthaginians in this North African campaign, and Carthage sued for peace. The treaty imposed by Rome was an even greater punishment than in the first war. Carthage was forced to pay 10,000 talents and its naval capacity was restricted to just ten ships for the sole purpose of combating piracy. In addition, the treaty stipulated that should Carthage ever wish to raise an army, it would need to gain permission from Rome first. Essentially, Carthage's power had been well and truly eclipsed by Rome, but it would be another fifty years before the death blow was dealt.

Left: The remains of a Roman road crossing the Sierra de Gredos, mountains in central Spain. During the war with Carthage, Spain was an important battleground and when Scipio drove the Carthaginians out of Spain in 205 BC it was the beginning of the end for Hannibal's campaigning.

The Third Punic War

In the aftermath of the second war, Hannibal reinvented himself as a statesman, to the alarm of Rome, who demanded that he be handed over to them. Rather than giving himself up or precipitating a war, Hannibal went into exile, crossing the various kingdoms of the Middle East for over a decade until the Romans ordered the king of Bithynia to give him up. He obliged, but Hannibal committed suicide in 183 BC to deny the Romans the pleasure of humiliating him before killing him.

'Carthage must be destroyed'

Carthage itself outlived Hannibal by almost forty years. The Romans never got over their fear and mistrust of Carthage, despite its weakened status. Cato captured the popular sentiment by ending every speech to the Senate with the words 'Carthage must be destroyed'. In spite of this ingrained hostility, the die was cast by neighbouring Numidia rather than Rome itself. Numidia shrewdly antagonized the Carthaginians by attacking their cities, knowing that Carthage could not do anything about it because they first had to get permission from Rome. Numidia had helped Rome in the Battle of Zama and so Rome always favoured the Numidians in such disputes. In 150, Carthage finally rose to the bait and resolved to disregard Rome's restrictions and repel the Numidians. This placed them in violation of the treaty and Rome demanded an impossible price for peace; all Carthaginians would have to abandon Carthage and move into the African interior. Unable to comply with this unreasonable request, the Carthaginians had no option but to resort to yet another war with Rome.

Rome gains a foothold in Africa

The Third Punic War lasted from 149 to 146 and was essentially a battle for Carthage itself. In 146 when Rome was eventually successful it literally wiped Carthage of the face of the map. The city was completely razed to the ground and the whole area was sown with salt so that nothing else would ever grow and the city could never re-emerge. Most of the population was killed and the remainder sold into slavery. Rome occupied Carthage's former territories and gained itself a foothold on the African continent. However, Carthage did not entirely disappear because a new Roman settlement was eventually built upon the site and Tunis, the capital of Tunisia, stands nearby the ruins of Carthage to this day.

The Romans were so thorough in expunging the Carthaginians from history that relatively little is known about them, in spite of their crucial importance in the western Mediterranean before the rise of Rome. Much of our knowledge comes from Rome itself and therefore much is assumed to be biased and unreliable.

Above: Wall fresco of a gladiator with a lion.

Left: Detail of a gladiator and a leopard from a mosaic of battling gladiators.

Wild cats, such as lions and leopards, are recurring images in Ancient Rome. They are part of the exotic appeal of Africa and their strength and aggression being controlled by Romans is a powerful metaphor.

Romans in Africa

Rome's foray into North Africa began during the Third Punic War, when the Roman Army crushed the Carthaginian Empire and took the province for itself. Over the centuries, Rome established control of the territory sandwiched between the Sahara Desert and the Mediterranean Sea. The provinces in northern Africa proved relatively docile and provided very few challenges to their Roman rulers. As a result they enjoyed relative wealth, peace and a high degree of romanization.

Rome's ally in Africa

The kingdom of Numidia in North Africa had been allied with the Carthaginians during the Second Punic War, but when a new king, Masinissa, became leader of the tribe, he switched sides and joined the Romans. Rome considered the kingdom a valuable ally because the Numidians were willing to make sizeable contributions to the Roman cavalry in North Africa, at a time when the Empire's supply lines were heavily stretched.

Jewish Roman mosaic from Hammam-Lif in Tunisia depicting a young male figure.

Numidia had backed the winning side; after the war, the Numidians were able to eat away at the territory of the weakened Carthaginians. There was nothing Carthage could do because the peace stipulated that Rome had to sanction all of its military activities and Rome had no intention of disadvantaging its Numidian ally. When Carthage finally decided to retaliate without Rome's blessing, the third and final Punic War broke out and Carthage was utterly destroyed.

Theatre at Sabratha, one of the three cities in what is now Libya which became part of Tripoli (tri polis, meaning three cities). It was a Numidian city that was rebuilt by the Romans.

Instability in Numidia

It was in 148 BC, during the third war, that King Masinissa died and left his kingdom under Roman protection. His son, Micipsa, became ruler until his own death in 118. Micipsa left his kingdom to his two biological sons, Adherbal and Hiempsal, and one adopted son, Jugurtha. A power struggle broke out and Jugurtha killed Hiempsal, forcing Adherbal to rush to the Senate to demand protection. The Senate resolved to divide the territory between the two rulers and Adherbal returned to rule his half.

However, Jugurtha was not satisfied with this arrangement and soon invaded the portion of territory allocated to Adherbal. Adherbal's troops were quickly defeated and he was forced to find protection in the city of Cirta, amongst the Roman citizens, who, he believed, were untouchable. Jugurtha stormed Cirta, captured and executed Adherbal and took supreme control of the kingdom.

War with Jugurtha

Rome would have probably let the matter rest with Adherbal's execution, but Jugurtha made a fatal error in his pursuit of justice; he executed a number of Roman citizens who had helped Adherbal. Rome had little option but to go to war against Jugurtha in 111 to avenge the murder of its citizens.

The war against Jugurtha dragged on for several years without a Roman victory. The reactionary faction in charge in Rome were believed ineffective, so a populist general, Gaius Marius, was given control of the forces in 107. Marius brought the war to a favourable conclusion by 105 and Jugurtha was taken back to Rome, where he was paraded through the streets before being executed.

Numidia was ruled by client kings, until Julius Caesar eventually turned it into a province, Africa Nova, after the Battle of Thapsus in 46 BC. Under the rule of Augustus, the province was united with the territory around Carthage as the Roman province of Africa. A province called Numidia was created two hundred and fifty years later under the rule of Septimius Severus.

The colonnaded Cardo of Jerash.

Granary of the Empire

Northern Africa was a vital source of grain, which earned it the title 'the granary of Rome', but in reality, it exported grain right across the Empire. The grain supply was extremely important to Rome because the masses were appeased with free handouts, which thousands relied on for survival. When Vespasian overthrew Vitellius in 69 AD, he first took Alexandria in Egypt to gain command of the grain supply, prudently aware that a grip on this commodity was vital to controlling Rome.

Africa's resources

Not only were Rome's northern African territories important as a source of grain, they also provided a number of other valuable resources. Africa replaced Spain as Rome's chief source of oil, used for a wide variety of purposes in everyday Roman life. Hunting was a popular activity and northern Africa was a major source of various animals for the games in Rome and other parts of the Empire. A trade in ivory from elephant tusks also emerged in the region. North Africa also developed considerable importance in the fishing industry; not only in fishing itself, but in the salting of fish, as well as making *garum*, a popular fish sauce.

Egypt and Cyrenaica retain independence from Rome

The Hellenic rulers of Egypt's Ptolemaic dynasty maintained their independence much longer than most of their Greek neighbours. Egypt played an important role in the last civil war of the Roman Republic, when Mark Antony entrenched himself there with the Egyptian queen, Cleopatra. In 30 BC, Octavian defeated Mark Antony, forcing the suicide of both Antony and Cleopatra. Octavian murdered her son and turned Egypt into a province under the direct control of the Emperor.

Neighbouring Cyrenaica, was originally under the control of the Egyptian king, but it was turned into a separate province at the end of the first century BC for the king's son, Ptolemy Apion to rule. Ptolemy Apion bequeathed the province to Rome upon his death in 96 BC.

Although Cyrenaica and Egypt were relatively peaceful under Roman occupation, antagonisms between the Greek, Jewish and Christian population simmered beneath the surface. Fighting between Greeks and Jews forced the Romans to annex Cyrenaica outright in 74 BC and a Jewish Rebellion in 116 AD, caused great loss of life, not least during the brutal counterinsurgency launched by Trajan, and continued by Hadrian.

The Severan Forum of Leptis Magna, Libya. Leptis Magna was the birthplace of Emperor Severus who made his African hometown a flourishing metropolis. It was one of the three cities, with Sabratha and Oea, which came to make up Tripoli, Libya.

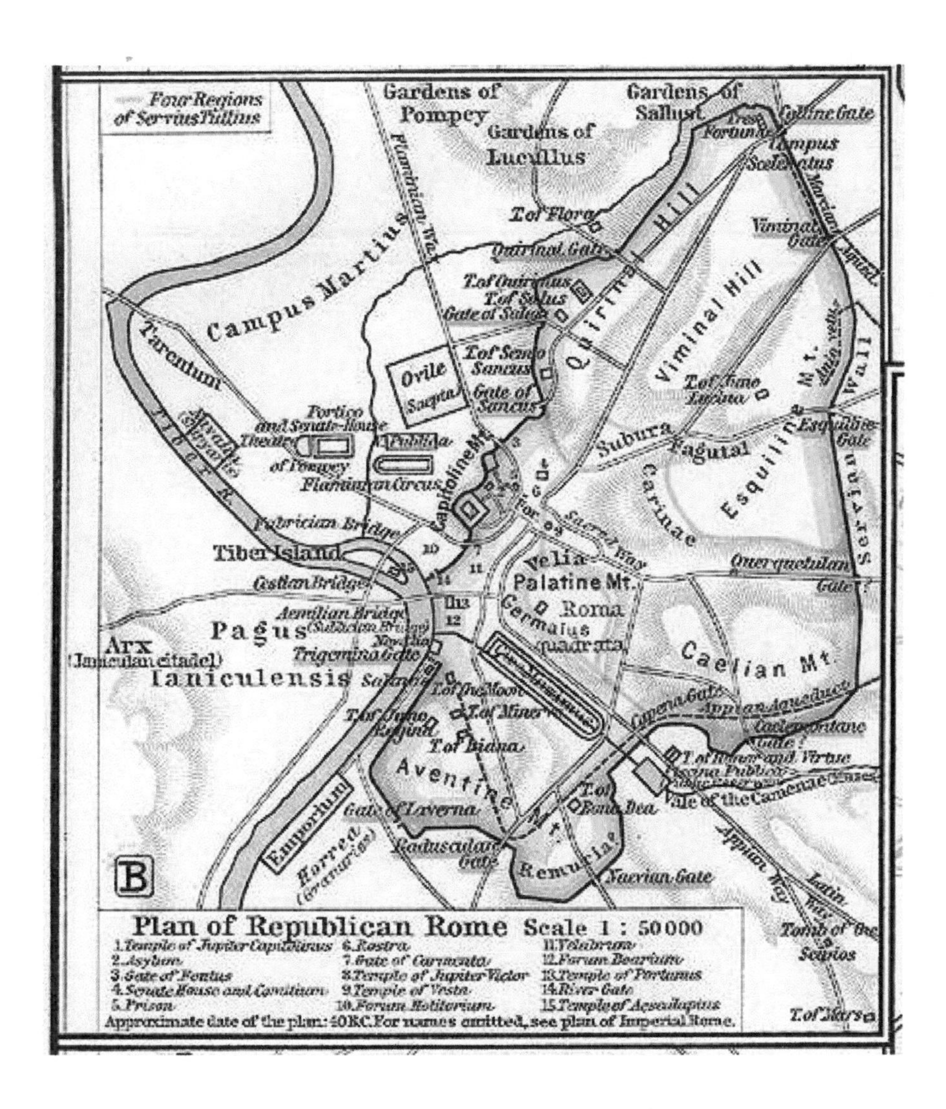
Four Regions of Servius Tullius
Gardens of Pompey
Gardens of Lucullus
Gardens of Sallust
Colline Gate
Campus Martius
Tarentum
Tiber R.
Ovile
Saepta
Flaminian Circus
Fabrician Bridge
Tiber Island
Aemilian Bridge
Arx
Pagus
Ianiculensis
Trigemina Gate
T. of the Moon
T. of Diana
Aventine Mt.
Gate of Laverna
Emporium
Horrea (Granaries)
Raduscalane Gate
Remuria
Naevian Gate
Capitoline Mt.
Velia
Palatine Mt.
Roma quadrata
Subura
Fagutal
Carinae
Esquiline Mt.
Viminal Hill
Quirinal Hill
Quirinal Gate
T. of Flora
Viminal Gate
Esquiline Gate
Servian Wall
Caelian Mt.
Appian Aqueduct
Capena Gate
Vale of the Camenae
Appian Way
Latin Way
B
Plan of Republican Rome Scale 1 : 50000
1. Temple of Jupiter Capitolinus
2. Asylum
3. Gate of Fontus
4. Senate House and Comitium
5. Prison
6. Rostra
7. Gate of Carmenta
8. Temple of Jupiter Victor
9. Temple of Vesta
10. Forum Holitorium
11. Velabrum
12. Forum Boarium
13. Temple of Portunus
14. River Gate
15. Temple of Aesculapius
Approximate date of the plan: 40 B.C. For names omitted, see plan of Imperial Rome.

African Cities

Leptis Magna: birthplace of Severus

The Emperor Septimius Severus made his African hometown, Leptis Magna, a flourishing metropolis, rivalling the Empire's many great cities. He built a new forum with a splendid colonnaded street leading up to an improved harbour.

The city's fertile hinterland had allowed Leptis Magna to thrive even before Severus became Emperor at the end of the second century AD. The city had undergone significant development during the Augustan age and Hadrian had built a vast bathing complex over fifty years before Severus became Emperor.

Carthage rises from the ruins

When the Romans defeated the Carthaginians after the Third Punic War, their city was razed to the ground and it was alleged that salt was sown into the earth so that nothing else could grow on the spot. Utica replaced Carthage as the main city in the region and became the capital city of Roman Africa. However, the ruined vicinity of Carthage proved too good a source of grain for the Romans to pass over and a new colony was founded on the site on the orders of Augustus.

Timgad and Antinopolis

The most notable cities founded by the Romans in North Africa were Timgad in Numidia and Antinopolis in Egypt. Trajan had built Timgad in 100 AD as a military colony to settle his veterans. The city was situated in a strategically beneficial area to deter an insurrection by the native Berber population. The city is remembered for its exceptionally square shape and gridiron street plan, which testifies to its functional, military origin.

Antinopolis was founded by Hadrian on the site where his lover, Antinous, drowned in the Nile. The city was developed in the Hellenic style Hadrian so adored, and functioned largely as a shrine to his lost lover. Antinous was deified and a temple was built in the city in his honour.

Mosaic which shows a reclining nude holding a basket from the entrance to the women's baths in the Musée de Timgad in Algeria.

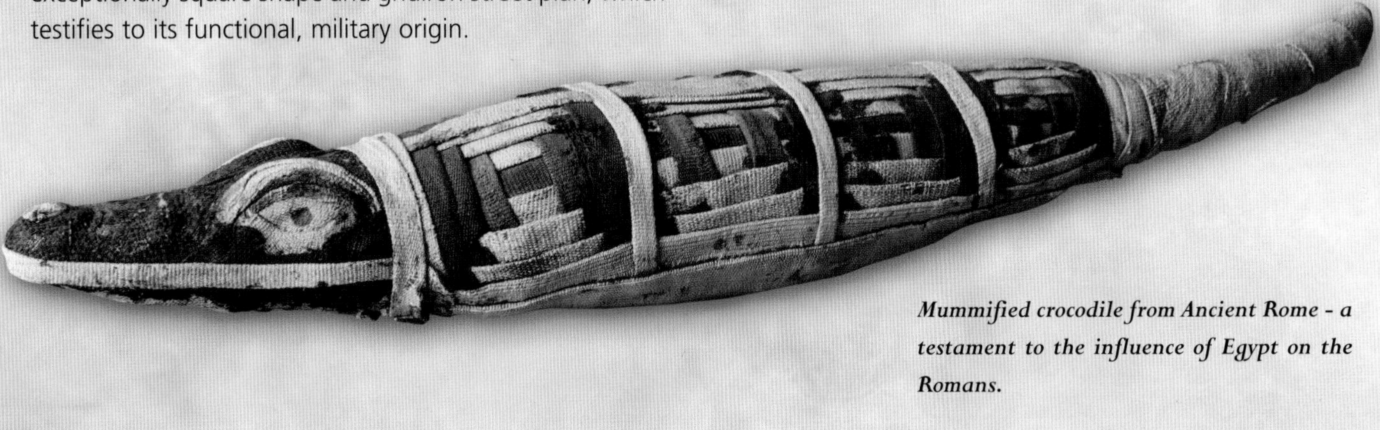

Mummified crocodile from Ancient Rome - a testament to the influence of Egypt on the Romans.

Conquest of Greece

While Rome contended with its Carthaginian rival in the western Mediterranean, politics in the East became increasingly tumultuous. After the death of Alexander the Great in 323 BC, his vast Macedonian Empire fell into decline, resulting in the emergence of a number of smaller, rivalrous Greek states.

The first Macedonian War

Rome had already expressed a limited interest in the eastern sphere during the interlude between the first and second Punic Wars when it conquered Illyria, which lay on the opposite coast of the Adriatic to Italy. Roman expansion into the region alarmed the Macedonian king, Philip V, who entered into an alliance with the Carthaginians against Rome during the Second Punic War in 215 BC. The alliance meant that Rome and Macedon were now at war, but with Hannibal running amok across the Italian Peninsula, Rome responded by allying with Macedon's rival, the Aetolian League. This was a shrewd move because it kept the Macedonians in check without Rome having to deflect troops from the defence of Rome. In 206, however, the weary Aetolians agreed to a peace and the first Macedonian War ended, with very little Roman involvement in the process.

A second war with Macedonia

Macedon was not spared direct Roman involvement in the Second Macedonian War, which lasted from 200 to 196 BC. With the war in the West won, Rome would have probably begun looking to expand into the prosperous East at some point, and a call for assistance from smaller Greek states provided a pretext. Philip V had attempted to reassert Macedonian control over the eastern Mediterranean in order to regain something of the former glory Macedon enjoyed during the days of Alexander the Great. Fearful of such Macedonian expansionism, two smaller Greek states, Rhodes and Pergamum, appealed to Rome for help, and the war began. There was one decisive battle in the conflict, in 197 at Cynoscephalae. The Romans won, and imposed a heavy indemnity, which was to mark the eclipse of the once great Macedonian Empire for ever.

With Macedon pacified, Rome withdrew its troops out of respect for its Greek allies, but this did not mean that Rome had no political interests in the region, as the king of the Seleucid Greeks, Antiochus III, discovered to his misfortune. With the decline of Macedon as a regional hegemonist, Antiochus decided to expand into the region. This brought him into conflict with Rome who returned to the region and expelled the Seleucids in the Battle of Thermopylae in 191. The Romans may not have maintained an army in Greece, but Rome was there to stay.

In 333 BC Alexander of Macedonia (Alexander the Great) won a great victory against the Persian king, Darius III at Issus, a site close to present-day Iskenderum in Turkey. Alexander was revered in Rome as a great military strategist. At the Battle of Issus Alexander's men were outnumbered by three to one. The defeat was the first for Darius, pictured here in his Battle chariot, and marked the beginning of the end of Persian power in the region. This mosaic was found in the House of the Faun in Pompeii.

Macedonia challenges again

After Philip V of Macedon died in 179 BC, his son, Perseus, became king. Perseus, like his father, had delusions of Macedonian grandeur and attempted once again to reassert Macedonian control over Greece. He went on a charm offensive with neighbouring Greek states, but this aroused the suspicion of Pergamum, which again called upon Rome. In 171 BC, the Romans declared war for the third time, fearing that Macedon might be able to resume its position and wrestle political domination of Greece from Rome. The decisive battle was in 168 at Pydna. In the aftermath of another Roman victory, Rome ensured that Macedon would not be able to challenge it again by dividing the territory into four and enslaving thousands, including the Macedonian elites.

Rome crushes Macedonia and its allies

Two decades later, while Rome was distracted, an imposter pretending to be the son of King Perseus, claimed the Macedonian throne. Rome invaded and saw off the challenger by 148, but its patience with Macedon had evaporated and it was incorporated as a province of Rome. With a permanent Roman settlement to the north, other Greek states were alarmed and the Achaean League in the south declared war. This act achieved nothing; it gave Rome cause to expand its control even further to the south in crushing the League.

By 146 Greece was essentially overrun by Rome. The Romans ensured the compliance of the remaining Greek states by making an example of the wealthy city of Corinth in that year. Corinth was a member of the Achaean League and in retribution for declaring war the Romans burned the city to the ground, killed all the men and sold all the women into slavery. Brutal as it was, it was an effective symbol that ensured obedience from Greece for many years.

***Above:** A large marble head sits near the Baths of Hadrian in Aphrodisias, an ancient Greco-Roman city in the Anatolian uplands of Turkey.*

***Right:** Marble relief sculpture with scenes from Cumae. In the eighth century BC, the Greeks had established the colony of Cumae, in the area around the Bay of Naples.*

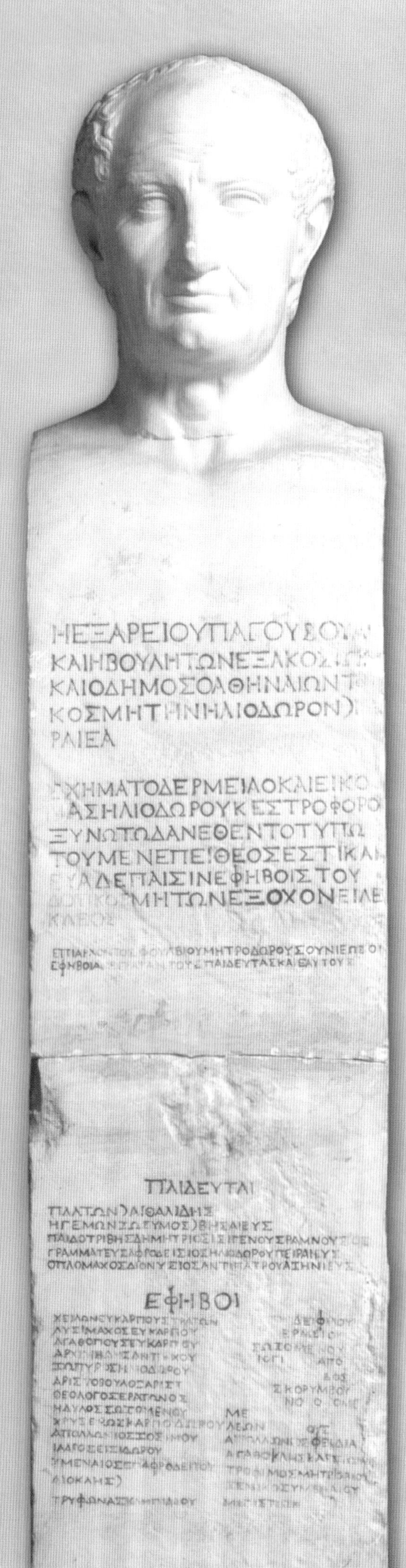

Hellenization of Rome

Greek culture, education and values began to have a direct impact upon Rome. The invasion of the Greek city states of southern Italy had begun this process of Hellenization, but it was not until the invasion of Greece that the impact became profound. Greek culture was more extravagant than the Romans were used to; Romans had traditionally emphasized qualities such as duty and frugality. For example, one of the early Republic's great figures was a Roman named Cincinnatus who responded to the call of duty, stopped farming during a time of crisis and became dictator for a few weeks. When the crisis was resolved he returned to his farm to live a simple life. In contrast to Cincinnatus' example, the invasion of Greece ushered in an era of ostentatious living that was to define Rome during the Empire.

New fashions and foods

Greek life infused into Roman life in many different ways. Romans sought out Greek art and treasures for their homes and Greek architectural styles became increasingly popular, especially Greco-pillars. Greek foods and fashion began replacing Roman foods and fashions and it was around this time that Roman men, in line with their Greek counterparts, preferred not to sport beards.

Greek intellectuals find a home in Rome

Rome was also a magnet for Greek intellectuals who were in demand as tutors for young Romans, or welcomed into Roman academic and political circles. In addition, Greek doctors found ready employment; for example, the Greek physician, Galen, moved to Rome during the late Republic and his ideas on medicine became sacrosanct for hundreds of years.

Left: Directional pillar with the bust of the Greek writer Heliodorus.

Below: Roman fresco painting depicting the Greek story of the sacrifice of Iphigenia. Roman life became increasingly influenced by Greek culture and lifestyle.

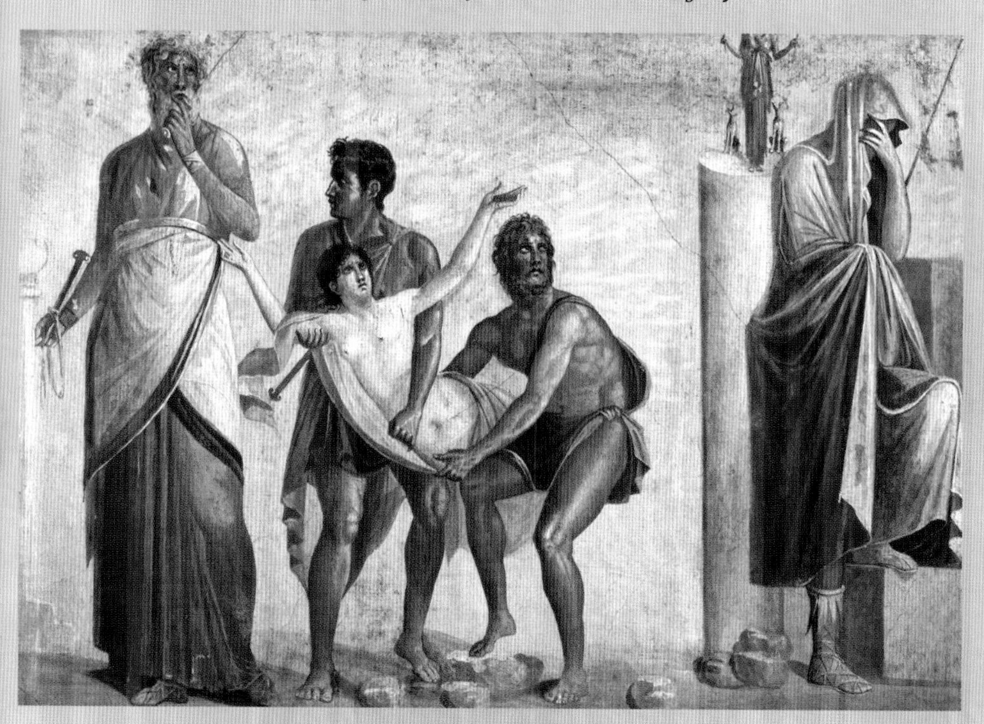

Alexander of Macedonia

Alexander III of Macedon, who lived between 356 and 323 BC, is remembered as one of the most successful generals of all time. He conquered a vast Empire, spanning from Greece all the way to the Himalayas in northern India.

Formidable enemy

The Persian Empire, which had hitherto been the leading power in the Middle East, was Alexander's most formidable enemy. After crossing into Asia Minor, his army won a score of battles and sieges, which brought Judea, Egypt and the area of modern Turkey quickly under Macedonian control.

In 331 Alexander and his men pushed eastwards, soon overrunning Mesopotamia and Babylon before capturing the Persian capital, Persepolis in 330. He maintained his eastward momentum into the Hindu Kush until the Himalayas prevented him from marching further east. Thus, he turned into India, maintaining that southward advance until 325 when he started tracking back to the west.

Untimely death

Alexander died unexpectedly in 323 AD at just thirty-two years old. With his passing, his vast Empire was fragmented among his various generals and friends; the all too brief glory days of Macedon were over.

Revered by Rome

Alexander the Great was a contemporary of the early days of Rome. While he was invading much of the known world, Rome was engaged in a war with the Samnites for dominance of the southern Italian peninsula.

Throughout the Ancient Roman civilization, Alexander became a revered icon, especially for the Emperors, who sought to emulate both his success and the magnitude of his legacy.

The historian Suetonius records that Julius Caesar was jealous of Alexander's accomplishments and that the Emperor Caligula took to wearing Alexander's breastplate, which he had taken from the dead king's tomb at Alexandria. In the second century AD, the Emperor Trajan was encouraged by Alexander's triumphs to push into the East, until old age forced him to halt his ambitions at the Persian Gulf.

Medicine

Roman Medicine was greatly influenced by the Ancient Greeks. Based upon a mixture of limited scientific knowledge and religious convictions, many of their ideas seem ridiculous today. Nevertheless, Roman medicine continued to dominate its field for more than a century after the collapse of the Empire.

Faith Healing

Religion played an important role in Roman medicine. Many Romans believed that illnesses were an indication of the disapproval of the gods and therefore many treatments involved a patient attempting to regain favour with the gods through worship and piety.

It was also believed that ill-health was caused by evil spirits and thus sufferers would resort to alms and spells to drive them out. Many illnesses would eventually subside and it would appear that the spiritual treatment had worked.

The god Asclepius was particularly revered by the sick. He was originally the Greek god of healing, but his cult was adopted by the Romans. People would make a pilgrimage to one of his temples, called *Asclepions*. At these sanctuaries it was believed that Asclepius would visit and cure the patient in a dream.

Evidence suggests that the *Asclepions* had many successful cases – of course unsuccessful patients would have been less readily recorded, but the strength and endurance of the cult is testament to the widespread belief that this method of healing worked. Initially, Romans would visit the more established Asclepions in Greece, but later a temple was built on the island in the River Tiber, in Rome.

Statue of the god, Asclepius who was revered by the sick. He was originally the Greek god of healing, but his cult was adopted by the Romans.

Brass balance scales found at the ruins of Aphrodisias, an ancient Greco-Roman city in the Anatolian uplands of Turkey. These could have been used by a doctor to weigh out 'medicines' for a patient.

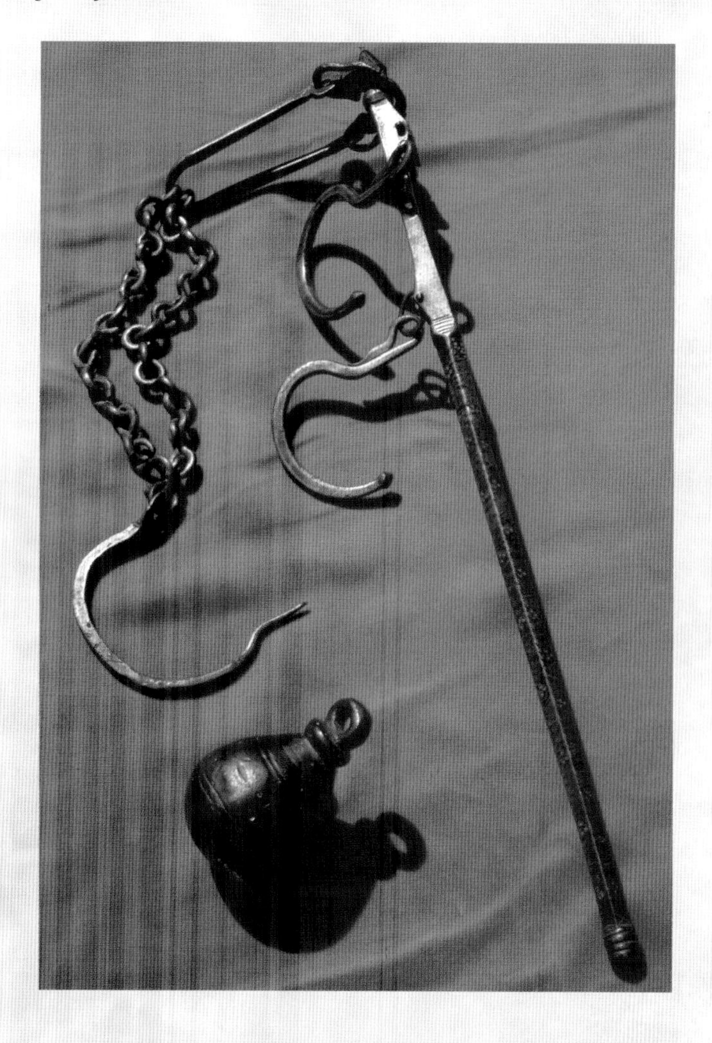

Visiting the doctor

Asclepius was not the only Greek import; most doctors working in Ancient Rome were of Greek origin. During the Republic, medicine was not a highly regarded profession because most doctors were slaves or freedmen. The onset of the Empire elevated their position because doctors gained the support of Augustus. He kept a personal physician and professionalized their role in the military.

Wealthy Romans could afford to call a doctor to their house, but the poor – if they could afford treatment – would have to visit the doctor. Without free healthcare, a number of 'quacks' established practices in Rome to provide a cheap service, to poor Romans, that was of little or no help whatsoever. This unfortunate state of affairs was redressed in 100 AD, when the government assisted the poor in paying for healthcare.

A scientific approach

Doctors emphasized a variety of preventative measures to maintain public health. They recommended balanced diets, exercise and clean living, much the same as a doctor would today. However, when it came to treatments, the doctors were not so well informed; they subscribed to the Greek notion of four humours. The idea, begun by Empedocles and applied to medicine by Hippocrates, argued that the body comprised four fluids, (blood, black bile, yellow bile and phlegm), that were in harmony with the four elements of nature, (air, earth, fire and water). Those who favoured a scientific approach to medicine believed that all disease was caused by an imbalance in one of the four fluids in the body. The symptoms the patient exhibited would explain which fluid was in excess – for example, flu was the result of too much phlegm. Doctors would prescribe treatments designed to restore balance, such as blood-letting, which aimed to reduce the amount of blood in the body.

Galen

Many Greek ideas were translated into Latin by the famous doctor, Galen. He mixed Hellenic medicine with the concept of a single Creator, which later made his theories palatable to the Christian and Islamic faiths. Supported by these two powerful religions, Galen's work meant that Greco-Roman medicine was able to dominate its field for more than one thousand years.

Surgery

While Roman medicine was relatively primitive, Roman surgery was exceptionally advanced. Galen pioneered the field and encouraged students to take whatever opportunity they could to see the inside of the human body. Although dissection was discouraged, the Romans were able to gain a working knowledge of anatomy by studying human skeletons without dissecting the body first. However, because Romans were very strict about burying their dead, only the unburied corpses of executed prisoners were readily available, which made the study of anatomy particularly gruesome. Galen also advocated other, less sinister methods, such as dissecting the body of an ape, rather than a human, and looking at the inside of the body through the wounds of gladiators and soldiers.

Roman surgeons met with a reasonably good success rate. They could perform basic operations such as amputations, but were also adept at more skilled procedures, such as trephination and cataract surgery. In a trephination operation, a hole was bored into the skull using a small drill to relieve pressure on the brain; records would suggest that this painful-sounding operation met with relative success.

Many Greek ideas were translated into Latin by the famous doctor, Galen. Galen mixed Hellenic medicine with the concept of a single Creator, which made his theories palatable to the Christian and Islamic faiths. Supported by these two powerful religions, Galen's work meant that Greco-Roman medicine was able to dominate its field for more than one thousand years.

The Late Republic

Social Crisis

Impressive victories, expanded territories and accumulated wealth had transformed Rome by the time of the late Republic. The city itself had become a busy metropolis with the largest population in the world, but such rapid change was threatening the very existence of Roman society.

Although victory in the Second Punic War set Rome on a path to longer-term greatness, in the short term, it created problems for the state. The army used in the war came from the *adsidui* class. This was a Roman citizen classified as a landowner because they owned in excess of a given amount of land. In the fighting against Carthage, Rome sustained heavy casualties, which decimated the numbers of the *adsidui*. Not only did this class have to face the loss of a substantial number of men, but the war itself ravished much of the land in Italy, exacerbating the problem confronting rural Romans.

Rome's rich treasury

While the Roman countryside was entering crisis, the city itself was entering something of a golden age. Plunder, trading monopolies and hefty war indemnities had glutted Rome's treasury. The prosperity of Rome acted as a magnet to people wishing to escape the rural depression and the city was flooded with people, and the population boomed. However, Rome offered little salvation to these newcomers because its affluence was narrowly distributed.

Opposite above: Gold fibula, or pin, from Pompeii. This type of decorative broach would have been worn by the wealthy. While it has a functional purpose, to secure clothing, the richness of the material and the design would have been a statement of status.

Opposite below: Via Appia, *the Appian Way, was seen as a symbol of the Republic. The road began in the Forum and ran all the way to Brindisi on the south-east coast of Italy. Begun at the end of the fourth century BC, it was an important factor in establishing and maintaining Roman order and control.*

Growing gulf between rich and poor

The gulf between rich and poor citizens was growing, and the situation was only getting worse. Rome's new super-rich were able to buy up vast swathes of the countryside, amassing large estates. In doing so, they alienated many of the remaining *adsidui* from the land, and brought in slaves to work on these farms, with the result that the landless Romans had to migrate to the city to find work. But the city was not always a saving grace for these Romans because Rome's conquest had resulted in the acquisition of huge numbers of slaves. The slaves did all the menial jobs leaving the poor Romans plunging even further into destitution.

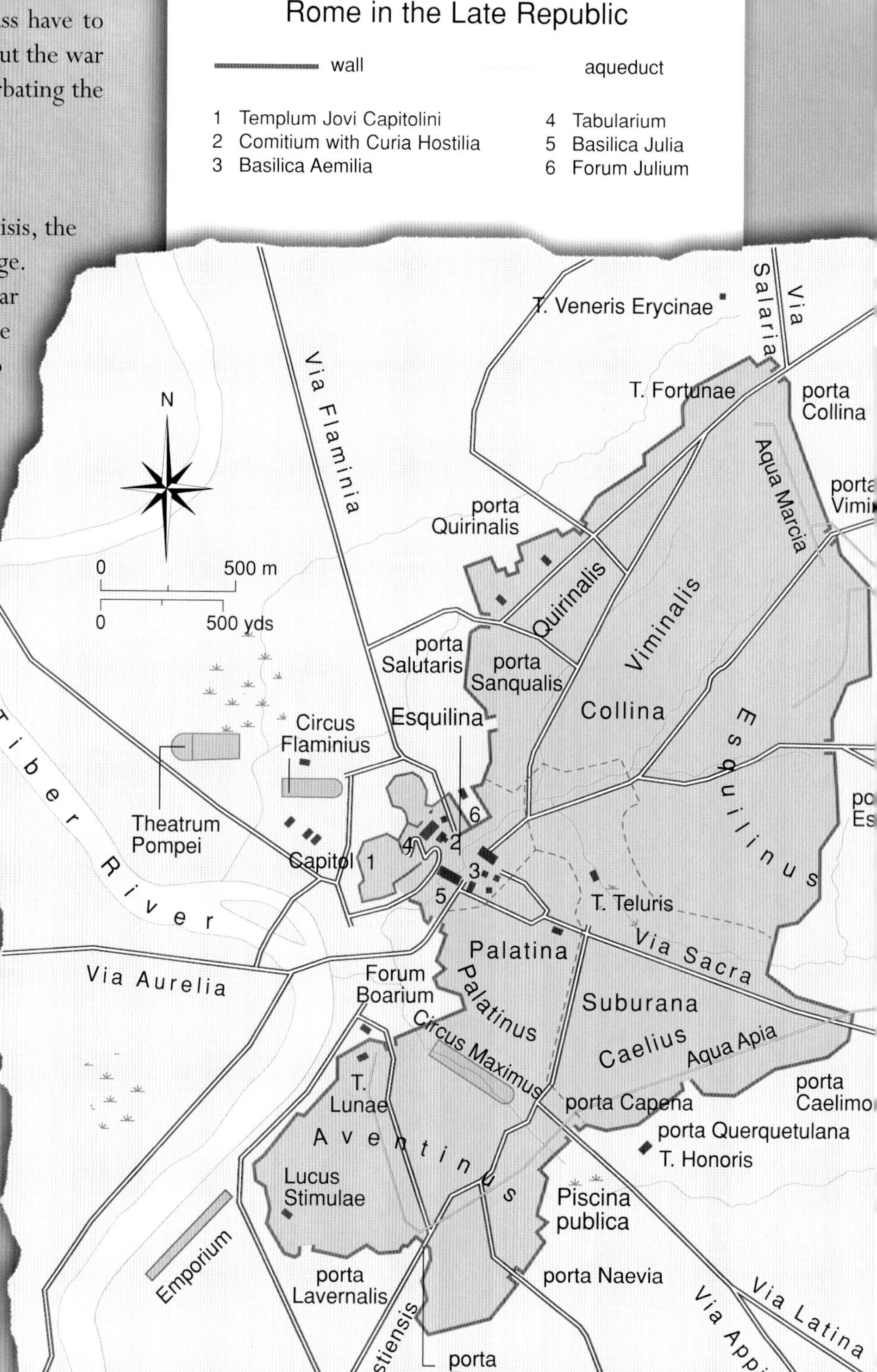

Social reform

As Rome's society became increasingly polarized, so too did Rome's political scene. The *Populares*, or popular faction, advocated policies to help Rome's new poor residents. The members of this faction were still aristocratic but they took a populist stance, either because they were genuinely interested in social reform or because they were trying to secure a popular support base outside the Senate. Their political opponents were known as *Optimates*, meaning the 'Big Men', who were more reactionary in outlook and did not wish to see the progressive policies of the *Populares* implemented. These men were often senators who wished to extend the power of the Senate to control of the popular assemblies.

Tiberius Gracchus' plans

The immigration and poverty problems facing Rome did not go unnoticed by these factions. In 133 BC, an ambitious plebeian tribune, Tiberius Gracchus, proposed agrarian reforms to put the former *adsidui* back on the land by redistributing the large estates. Many of the senators were owners of these properties and responded to Tiberius' agenda with outright hostility. Tiberius marched ahead with his plans, using the power of the plebs to circumvent the Senate and land reform got underway.

The senators got their revenge through a smear campaign against Tiberius; they convinced the people that he held the ulterior motive of becoming king and was simply using land reform as a means to that end. Fear of monarchy had been ingrained in the Roman psyche since the days of Tarquinius Superbus and huge numbers of people turned against Tiberius. The Senate was able to mobilize the people to its advantage on this occasion and Tiberius was killed, but he had already opened 'Pandora's Box', unleashing social discontent and upsetting the delicate equilibrium that had existed between the people and the Senate; this was the beginning of the end of the Republic.

The herald of turbulent times

Reform did not cease with the death of Tiberius; in 126 BC, his brother Gaius assumed the role of tribune and pursued a similar agenda. Gaius Gracchus attempted to introduce a grain subsidy so that poorer Romans could afford food, but this, together with his other populist policies, incurred the anger of the senators and reactionary Roman aristocrats. However, they could do little about his threat because Gaius had a strong popular base; he was even re-elected as tribune in 122.

His downfall came when he alienated that base by proposing to extend Roman citizenship to other Latins. The senators were able to find common cause with the plebs, as neither wished to see Roman citizenship expanded. Gaius' attempts to win another election were thwarted and the Senate, alleging that Gaius would mount an imminent coup, established a state of emergency. The Senate encouraged its followers to give Gaius the same treatment as had been extended to his brother, and he and thousands of followers were duly murdered. Such political violence heralded the dawn of one of the most turbulent periods in Rome's history.

Rural Life

Initially, most Romans lived in rural areas as smallholder farmers, but over time, they were pushed off the land and into the city as wealthy landowners amassed vast estates. While this meant that most Romans were urban residents, across the Empire, the vast majority of people continued to live in rural settings.

Mosaic showing workers using horses and cattle to thresh wheat.

Early Republic smallholders

In the early days of the Roman Republic most landowners were smallholders who grew just enough food for the needs of their family. Any additional produce could be exchanged or bartered with neighbouring farmers. There was no necessity to provide Rome with vast quantities of grain because the city's population was relatively small, and most people had access to their own farms close to the city.

Whenever Rome went to war, the Army was made up exclusively from the ranks of these landowning Romans; army recruitment was not open to the landless, urban class that emerged over time. As soon as a campaign or war was completed, a landowner was demobilized and could return to his duties at the farm.

The loss of a generation of farmers

At first, Rome won many of its wars and the system seemed to work well, but when Rome lost, the pitfalls inherent in its recruitment system quickly emerged.

When Hannibal invaded Rome through the Alps in 218 BC, his army wrought such havoc over Italy and killed so many Roman soldiers, that an entire generation of landowners was lost over the course of the war. This resulted in a sea change in the countryside; bereaved families found life extremely difficult without the help of their husbands or fathers and were often forced to sell their farms to ensure survival. They found willing buyers as a new class of super-rich emerged in Rome, made wealthy by the plunder from defeated cities in Carthage and Greece.

Large estates

Over time, more land was concentrated in fewer hands as most of the remaining smallholders were forced to sell to the large landowners. The old smallholdings gradually disappeared as the countryside was divided up into large estates called *latifundia*.

The new landowners were absentee owners, who spent most of their time living and working in Rome. As the land was simply a means of income the owner would appoint a manager to run the farm in his place. When the landowner did visit, it was usually to spend time in his villa, away from the city, and not to do any faming.

With the establishment of these large estates, agriculture underwent a degree of marketization. Agricultural produce was no longer grown simply for personal use, instead it was destined for the marketplaces of Rome, where the population had swelled as the dispossessed smallholders had converged on the city.

Mosaic from a Roman villa in Piazza Armerina, Sicily, depicting a man restraining an ostrich.

Emerging capitalist economy

With the new landowners desiring to see a profit from their estates, a capitalist economy emerged in the countryside. To keep the cost of production low, slaves were brought in for farm work. The abundance of slaves meant very little investment was made in labour-saving devices.

The exceptions to the rule were the use of oxen-driven reapers to mow the harvest and a mechanical wine press. However, both of these processes still required considerable input from the slaves. Rural slaves were less well treated than their urban counterparts because household slaves could build up a close relationship with the family they served. In the countryside, by contrast, the slave was under the control of the farm manager, usually a freedman or a highly-regarded slave, whose concern was to impress the landowner with his management skills. This meant the manager usually prioritized production levels over the wellbeing of his expendable workforce.

Slave labour

This use of slave labour on absentee landlord farms effectively spelled the demise of the traditional Roman farmer, who could not compete with the cheaper slaves for jobs on the estates. The handful of remaining smallholders who had held out against the onset of the *latifundia* were eventually forced to sell out because they could not contend with the new, capitalist environment of the countryside.

Smallholder farming was not entirely lost to Ancient Rome because army veterans were granted small plots of land upon their retirement as a bonus for good and loyal service. During the Republic many of these soldiers were given land in Italy, but over time, as space became limited, most were settled in the provinces instead. Cities such as Timgad in Numidia and Italica in Hispania were set up for the purpose of accommodating veterans, where they could act as a supplementary army in case of any provincial unrest.

Ram's head wine press in the Villa of the Mysteries at Pompeii

The main crops grown on the latifundia *were fruit, vegetables and cereals, most of which went directly to the markets in Rome. However, olives and grapes were first turned into wine and olive oil.*

Winemaking became a particularly lucrative industry, with many large estates desperate to own and grow their own vines. Wine was consumed on a great scale in Rome, where it was the staple drink. It was drunk throughout the day because most Romans preferred it to the water (although they usually diluted their wine with water anyway).

Most wine was grown from wild grapes, which grew naturally across the Mediterranean at the time. The grapes were collected and then sent to be pressed; most farms used a mechanized press, called a torculum, *but some opted to use the more traditional method of trampling the grapes with bare feet.*

The grapes were stored and fermented in ceramic containers called amphorae. *To give the wines individual tastes, a variety of flavours would be sought by adding herbs, spices, honey, or even salt.*

Winemaking became such a popular enterprise that the Emperor Domitian was forced to legislate against it, to encourage the estates to invest in other produce.

Army recruitment reformed

The reform offered by the brothers of the Gracchi family had not lifted Rome from its crisis, and after the death of Gaius Gracchus the reactionary *Optimates* dominated the Roman political scene for over a decade. During this time, Rome was busy in wars against Numidia in Africa and Germanic tribes, the Teutones and the Cimbri, to the north. Soldiers for the Army still came from the *adsidui* classes, but their declining numbers meant that the Army was denied many new recruits and the wars in Africa and Germany were dragging on.

It fell to Gaius Marius, an aristocrat affiliated with the *Populares*, to raise Rome out of its quagmire, both at home and abroad. He did this by creating a standing army and opening recruitment to all Romans. In the short term this helped the Romans to defeat their enemies in Numidia by 105 BC and in Germany by 101 by replenishing the Army with better-skilled, new recruits. In the longer term a career in the armed services offered a way out of destitution for the poor Roman citizens.

Gaius Marius' foreign victories helped him to amass a popular following leading him to an unprecedented sixth consulship in 100. Although ostensibly allied to the *Populares*, it is clear that Marius' foremost concern was his own power. When popular reforms, such as further reducing the price of grain, were called for by the plebeian tribune, the Senate refused and violence between the factions broke out. In spite of his allegiance, Marius favoured the Senate in this instance. By opposing the plebeian tribune, Marius alienated his support base and prudently chose to retire from political life in 100.

The Social War

Marius was not gone for long; nine years after he disappeared from the political scene, he re-emerged to fight in the Social War. The conflict was effectively a civil war because it was fought between Rome and its allies on the Italian Peninsula.

In addition to the strife associated with the proletarianization of the rural Romans, there was growing discontent amongst Rome's Italian allies because they had to pay all the taxes, while Roman citizens were exempt. This anger was compounded by the fact that while Roman citizens had a say in how that revenue was spent, as non-Romans, the allies had no say whatsoever.

In line with the interests of Rome's allies, and picking up where Gaius Gracchus had left off, the tribune in 91 BC, Marcus Livius Drusus, had suggested that citizenship rights be extended to these long-time allies. But just as had happened to Gracchus, few Romans, rich or poor wished to extend citizenship rights and the proposal was rejected.

The majority of the allies broke with Rome and formed their own independent confederacy with its seat of government in the town of Corfinium. A war was inevitable. Rome budged on the citizenship issue, prudently offering it to any ally that did not take up arms against it. This helped to isolate and weaken its enemy and handed Rome victory by 88 BC.

Lucius Cornelius Sulla

The war heralded the emergence of Lucius Cornelius Sulla. Sulla had so distinguished himself in the war that he earned the grass crown, one of Rome highest military honours. An additional reward was his election as consul in 88 BC. This appointment enraged Marius who believed he should have been given the consulship instead. Sulla had served under Marius but the pair had fallen out during the campaign against the Numidians in Africa. Marius evoked his old alliance with the *Populares*, getting the plebeian assembly to name him consul in Sulla's place. This political uncertainty sparked a wave of violence in the city and Sulla, with fewer loyalists on hand, was forced to flee the city.

Opposite: Ruins of the Forum where the tribunes and senators met.

Left: Directional pillar with the bust of the Greek Sosistratus.

Below: Amphitheatre at Leptis Magna. In about 23 BC the Punic city became part of the Roman province in North Africa. It is the site of some of the most lavish and best-preserved remains from the Roman period.

Sulla marches on Rome

Sulla's forces were not in the city because they had just finished campaigning in the Social War. However, this meant that they were easy to group and Sulla was quickly ready to march on the city. Marius fled to Africa leaving the city open for Sulla to reclaim the consulship, where he exacted a brutal retribution on Marius' followers and thousands of people were killed.

With his reign of terror complete, Sulla left the city to embark on a campaign against Mithridates in the East. Mithridates was the king of Pontus, who had made successful gains in Roman Asia and had been treated as a liberator by the local tribes. While Sulla's back was turned Marius returned with the help of Lucius Cornelius Cinna, and began a reign of terror of his own against Sulla's followers. Marius regained the consulship in 86 BC but died soon after. However, Marius' friend, Cinna, became consul and ensured that Sulla's supporters were kept out.

Pompey 'the Great'

After exacting heavy-handed retribution in the East, Sulla made a quick peace with Mithridates so that he could return to Rome and regain his power. His return was not easily achieved as Marius' supporters had ruthlessly purged Sulla's support in the city, but was aided by the help of two young generals, Marcus Licinius Crassus and Gnaeus Pompeius Magnus (Pompey). Pompey gained his title 'the Great', during Sulla's second march on Rome, in honour of his pacification of Marius' supporters in Sicily and North Africa.

The death of Sulla

In a bid to end the violence and chaos Sulla was appointed dictator. From this position he exacted one of the most brutal purges Rome had seen to date. Many thousands were killed and their assets went to the state, making Sulla even wealthier. As an affiliate of the *Optimates*, he extended the ranks of the Senate at the expense of the popular assembly and doubled the number of senators. In 81 BC, with his enemies disposed of, Sulla announced an end to the dictatorship and arranged for his appointment as consul in 80. At the end of his one-year term he went into retirement and died in 78 BC. However, the political violence did not end once Sulla and Marius were off the scene. On the contrary, it had only just begun

The First Triumvirate

When Sulla retired from the dictatorship it seemed that the *Optimates* had won the war. Sulla's reforms had severely undermined the plebeian tribune, a key support base for his rivals, the *Populares*. In contrast, the Senate now stood as the most powerful governing body in Rome.

Resistance against the *Optimates*

The *Populares* were much weakened during Sulla's reign of terror, but Marius' supporters still existed. Quintus Sertorius, a Marian by virtue of his animosity towards Sulla, refused to acknowledge the Senate's authority and joined with the native Lusitanian tribe in the west of the Iberian Peninsula against Rome. He ruled much of the peninsula during the 70s and, together with exiles and natives, he held off the Roman counterinsurgency. Pompey was sent to crush his rebellion in 76 BC, but did not succeed until 72 when Sertorius was assassinated. In spite of his lucky break, Pompey was lauded as a hero in Rome.

Challenge to the Senate

The supremacy of the Senate was challenged more directly in Rome itself, when Marcus Aemilius Lepidus, the consul in 78 BC, tried to undermine the political arrangement and reinstate the tribunate's powers using his army. This attempt was also thwarted by Pompey, and Lepidus was forced to flee to Sardinia. With Marius' supporters unable to restore the powers of the tribunate, it fell to three powerful individuals, Marcus Licinius Crassus, Gnaeus Pompeius Magnus (Pompey) and Gaius Julius Caesar to balance the power of the Senate.

Left: Marble statue from the ruins of the port of Ostia.

Far Left: Roman bridge at Alcantara in the province of Caceres in Spain. It was from Spain that the Marian resistance to the power of the Senate came. Pompey failed to put down an uprising by Quintus Sertorius who refused to acknowledge the authority of Rome.

Opposite: Mosaic, depicting a hunter fighting a lion, from the Piazza Amerina in Sicily. The island of Sicily and northern Africa, like Spain, were regions where it was difficult for the authority of the Senate to hold sway.

Crassus and Pompey

The oldest of the three men was Crassus. Born in 115 BC, he had become incredibly wealthy as an ally of Sulla's and a participant in the confiscations of land and riches that accompanied the reign of terror. He was not as well known for his military skill as Pompey but he had successfully put down a slave rebellion in 71.

Spartacus

The rebellion began in 73, when gladiators broke out of a school in Capua. They were led by Spartacus, a slave from Thrace, and in their quest for liberty camped out on Mount Vesuvius before destroying two Roman legions. Success brought ever more slaves to their side but they were held in the toe of Italy by Crassus' forces. Although the slaves were able to break out of the siege, they were routed by Pompey's legion which had just returned from Spain. It was Crassus who dealt the final blow and Spartacus was probably killed in battle. Thousands of slaves were captured and Crassus made a brutal example of them, having each one of them crucified along the Appian Way, the Roman road from Rome to Capua.

Both Crassus and Pompey were credited with their victories on behalf of Rome and jointly offered the consulship in 70. The two men openly disliked one another, but they were the richest and most powerful men in Rome and had to work together if they wanted to succeed. To challenge one another would have been extremely costly.

Caesar emerges

For much of the 60s Pompey was away campaigning in the East, engaged in the third war against Mithridates of Pontus. During this time Julius Caesar emerged on the political scene. Caesar had a privileged early life, but as a child his family had lost its wealth and as a result Caesar developed frugal habits, which later helped ingratiate him with the poor.

His background meant that he did not have sufficient funds for a dazzling political career but he tied himself to the wealthy Crassus, who valued Caesar as an orator. Crassus was linked with the *Optimates* but Caesar was clearly allied to the *Populares*; Marius was his uncle by marriage and his wife was the daughter of Cinna, Marius' closest ally. In addition to Crassus' backing, Caesar was able to establish an independent political and economic base of his own when he was elected *pontifex maximus*, chief priest, in 63, and to a governorship in Spain in 62.

Pompey returns

In 62 BC, Pompey returned from the East. He had successfully defeated Mithridates and his popularity became unassailable. Crassus and Caesar were anxious as to how his return would affect their positions in Roman politics and society. Fortunately for them, the Senate was also concerned for Pompey's return; they feared that he might re-establish a dictatorship like Sulla. As a result, the Senate tried to weaken Pompey by failing to grant land for his veterans.

A frustrated Pompey decided that the only way of circumventing the Senate was to ally with the two other most powerful individuals in Rome, Crassus and Caesar. Together they were able to challenge the authority of the Senate by using Caesar's popularity to gain a support base amongst the plebs.

The Triumvirate gains power

Although their authority was never official, this Triumvirate, or rule of three, was able to undermine the Roman government, weaken the Senate and pave the way for the age of the Emperors. The Triumvirate was always an icy arrangement because of Pompey and Crassus' dislike of one another, but this was to some extent smoothed over by Pompey's marriage to Caesar's daughter.

The Triumvirate's power was increased with Caesar's appointment as consul in 59, but with Caesar away conquering Gaul in the early 50s, the Triumvirate began to break down as the antagonism between Crassus and Pompey began to re-emerge. Caesar called the men together at Luca and agreed that they should both stand for the position of consul once again in 55. The meeting thinly patched over their differences until 54 when Caesar's daughter, who was also Pompey's wife, died in childbirth and the familial bond between the two men was broken.

Death of Crassus

In 53 BC the final blow was served to the Triumvirate when Crassus was captured in battle against the Parthians in the East. Legend has it that he was executed by having molten gold poured into his mouth, an end perhaps befitting a life of incredible wealth.

The united power of these three titans helped to erode the power of the Senate and remove it from the perch upon which Sulla had left it. With the Senate weakened and Crassus dead, the future of Rome was to be decided by Caesar and Pompey.

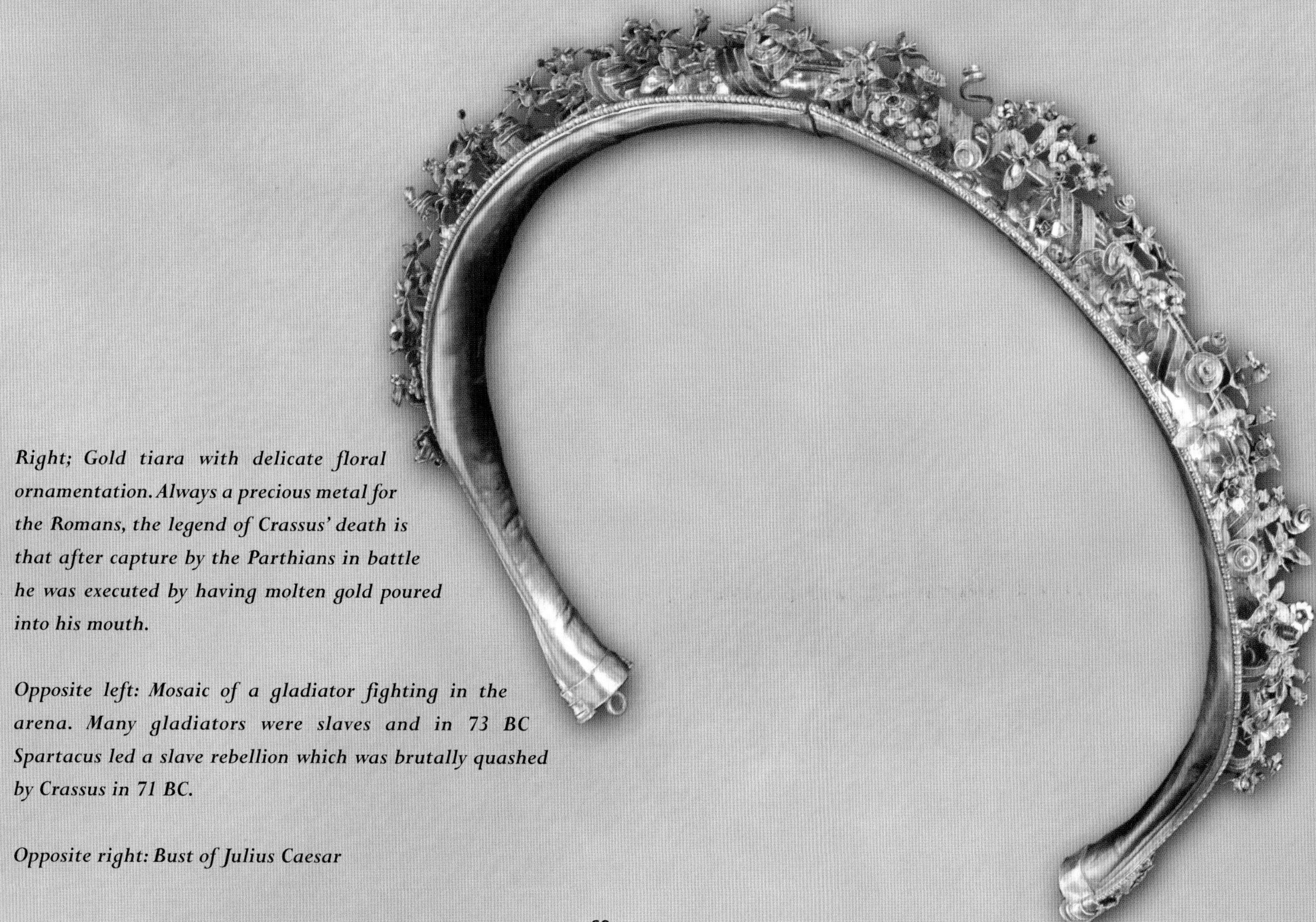

Right; Gold tiara with delicate floral ornamentation. Always a precious metal for the Romans, the legend of Crassus' death is that after capture by the Parthians in battle he was executed by having molten gold poured into his mouth.

Opposite left: Mosaic of a gladiator fighting in the arena. Many gladiators were slaves and in 73 BC Spartacus led a slave rebellion which was brutally quashed by Crassus in 71 BC.

Opposite right: Bust of Julius Caesar

Germany under the Romans

The Romans did not have any substantial contact with the Germanic tribes of north eastern Europe until the end of the second century BC, when the Cimbri and the Teutons migrated south-westward towards Gaul. The German migration caught the attention of Rome because it caused displacement among the settled Celtic tribes of the region. Rome finally decided to deal with the threat when the Germans invaded the lands of the Taurisci, a Roman ally.

Battles with the Germanic tribes

The Germanic invaders won the first two encounters, crushing the Roman Army at the Battle of Noreia in 112 BC and completely annihilating them at Arausio in 105. Arausio provided Rome's greatest military defeat since the Battle of Cannae against Hannibal, more than a century beforehand.

The tables were turned when Gaius Marius was put in charge of the campaign. Fresh from defeating Jugurtha, the king of Numidia, and with an army which he had professionalized, his fighting force swiftly defeated the Teutons in 102 and then the Cimbri in 101. The two tribes were almost wiped out; the men were slain in battle and the women and children committed mass suicide to avoid being sold into slavery.

The Roman advance

After the defeat of the Cimbri and the Teutons other Germanic tribes made incursions into Gaul. During Caesar's Gallic campaign, he was forced to deal with these menaces and undertook punitive expeditions against the Usipi, Tencteri and the Suebi.

It is thought that Caesar had hoped to establish a more permanent Roman presence in Germania, but he believed the task difficult because the Germans were warlike and could not be civilized – unlike the Gauls, who he thought were warlike, but could be civilized. The civil war with Pompey and his subsequent assassination scotched any plans to invade Germania, and the Roman border remained at the Rhine.

Roman coin depicting a female head with a crown of oak leaves.

The remains of a fourth century Roman city gate, the Porta Nigra, stand near the centre of Trier in modern Germany. Trier, known as Augusta Treverorum, the capital of Roman Belgica, became an important town after Diocletian's division of the Empire.

Augustus takes control

When Augustus came to power, he rearranged the Roman provinces, creating Germania Inferior and Germania Superior on the west bank of the Rhine. Germania Inferior was the territory at the mouth of the Rhine, in the location of the modern Netherlands. Germania Superior was upstream in what is today western Germany and eastern France. The capital of Germania Superior was based at Moguntiacum (Mainz).

Augustus was not content to maintain the status quo and dispatched his stepsons, first Drusus and then Tiberius to push further into Germany. Drusus arrived in 12 BC and succeeded in advancing across the Rhine to the River Elbe by 9 BC. Tiberius then consolidated the new Roman position.

Massacre forces a retreat

However, the local tribes resented the Roman occupation and conspired to repel the invaders. A romanized German, Arminius, of the Cheruscan tribe befriended the governor, Quinctilius Varus and convinced him of a rebellion in a remote part of the province. Varus set off with three legions to defeat the insurgency, but in reality, it was a trap. The Romans were led into an area of hills and marshes in the Teutoburg Forest, where an alliance of German tribes completely wiped them out. The destruction of three legions shocked and wounded Roman pride and forced Rome to abandon the Elbe frontier for safety behind the Rhine.

Rhine border

By 16 AD, the Romans had recovered their lost territory and re-established the border at the Elbe under the command of Tiberius' highly popular adopted son, Germanicus, under whom they took back much of the territory they had lost earlier.

These victories reinvigorated Roman morale, but Tiberius considered operations in Germany too costly. He withdrew Roman forces to the Rhine, which was established, for the most part, as the permanent border for the remainder of the Empire. The Romans did continue to occupy some territory on the eastern bank of the River Rhine; without the natural defence of the river, they fortified their positions with an extensive series of man-made defences called *limes*.

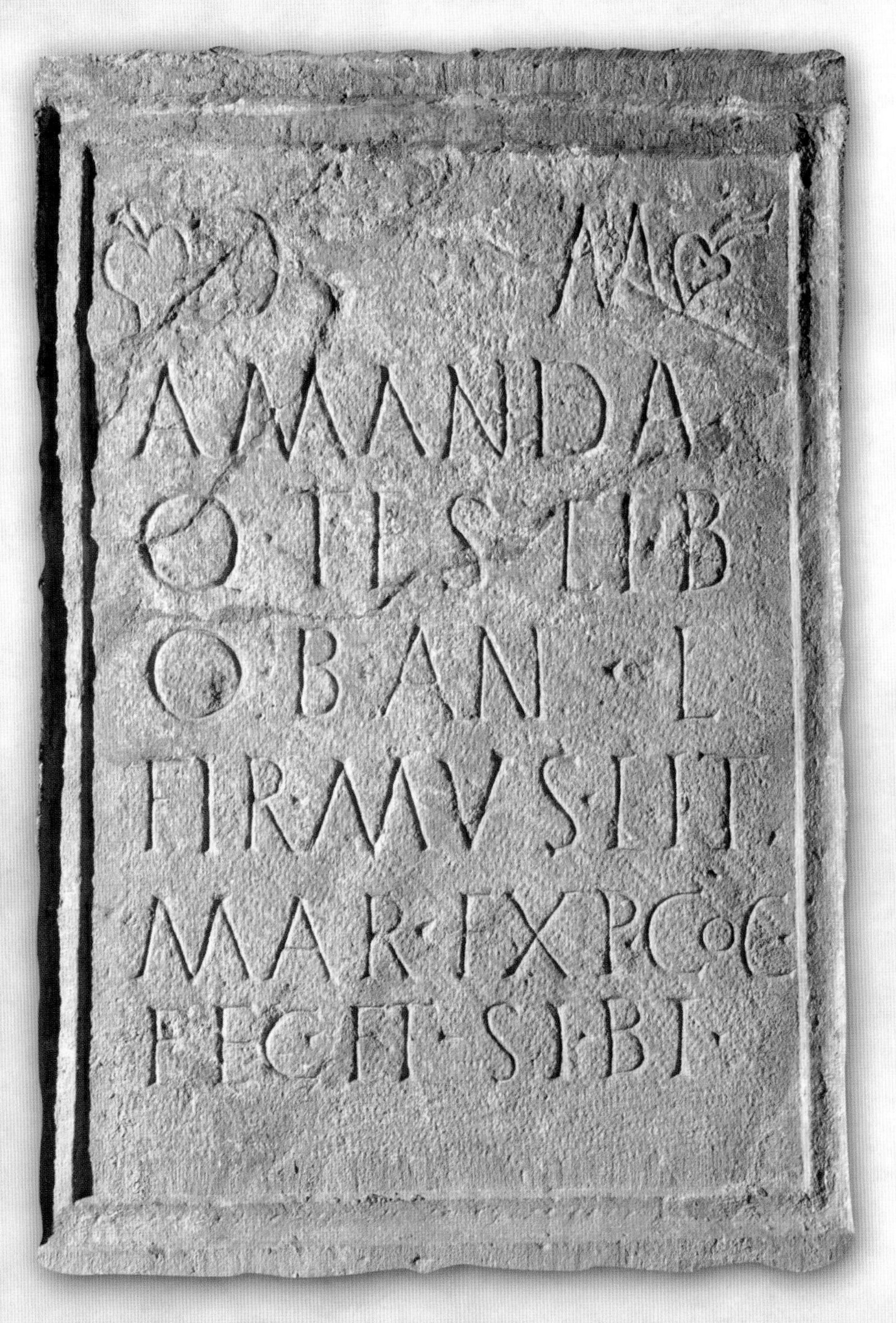

Carved Roman tombstone from Chiemgau in Germany.

The Invasion of Gaul

Caesar sought military glory in order to improve his own standing within the Triumvirate and within Roman politics as a whole; pacifying the supposedly hardy Gallic and Germanic warriors to the north provided the perfect opportunity for him to achieve this.

Caesar makes his name

After his stint as consul in 59 BC, Caesar became the governor of three of Rome's northerly provinces, Cisalpine Gaul, Illyricum and Transalpine Gaul. The influence of the Triumvirate over Roman politics was so great that it was able to secure Caesar an exceptionally long period as governor. Throughout the 50s, Caesar was handed control of the border provinces between the Roman Empire and Gaul; a perfect springboard for a campaign to make his name.

Caesar's pretext to intervene in Gallic affairs was delivered to him when the Helvetii planned a massive migration into Gaul. The Helvetii were a Gallic tribe, who lived in the south of Germania, where they were terrorized by the local Germanic tribes. Hemmed in by the Romans to the south and the Germans to the north, the Helvetii resolved to migrate to Gaul. Caesar refused to permit this migration because he feared it would destabilize Gaul and remove a very important buffer between the Roman Empire and the Gallic Tribes.

In spite of Caesar's orders, the Helvetii began their migration through Geneva, in Transalpine Gaul. This was routed by Caesar's forces and the Helvetii were forced to find a route that did not pass through Roman territory. The Helvetii passed through the land owned by the Aedui, who appealed to Caesar for help. Caesar obliged and decisively defeated the tribe in the Battle of Bibracte, where he slaughtered the majority of the tribe; those who survived were forced to return to their homeland.

Rome's increasing influence in Gaul

Caesar's defeat of the Helvetii pleased several of the Gallic tribes, who requested his help against another menace: the Germanic Suebi tribe. The tribe had been intervening in Gallic politics by shoring up the Averni tribe against the Aedui. Caesar obliged this request and marched on the Suebi, encountering them in the Battle of the Vosges in 58 BC. The result was another Roman victory and the Suebi were forced back across the Rhine into Germania.

Ruins of a necropolis in Alyscamps, just outside the ancient city walls of the French town of Arles. Roman cities usually forbade burials within the city.

The Dying Gaul. This is a Roman copy of a lost Greek statue but serves the purpose of making the enemy seem both noble and brave, thus emphasizing the might of the Romans' victory. The figure shows the Gaul naked, apart from his neck torc, with his weapons beside him. Julius Caesar, governor of Gaul for several years, records that the Gauls went into battle in just such a manner.

Caesar invades Britain

Caesar's increasing influence over Gaul caused concern in a number of tribes in the far north. Communally known as the Belgae, from the region of modern-day Belgium, they intended, in early 57 BC, to mount a surprise attack on the Romans, but Caesar pre-empted them and destroyed the tribes one by one before they could join forces against him. In 56, Caesar moved in to attack the Veneti of modern-day Brittany, before crossing the *Mare Britannicum* (English Channel) in 55, and again in 54, to upset supply routes to northern Gaul and dislodge the Belgae tribes who had settled there.

Insurrection in Gaul

Caesar's foray into Britannia was halted as insurrection once again reared in Gaul. A Belgae tribe, named the Eburones, under the leadership of Ambiorix, had risen up against the local Roman garrison. The Eubrones exacted a humiliating defeat over the Romans and, buoyed by their success, many other natives joined the rebellion against Rome. Caesar was furious; he brought in new legions and brutally suppressed the uprising, such that the Eburones were completely destroyed. Although peace had been forcibly returned to Gaul, it was short-lived as a new insurrection was brewing.

In early 52, taking advantage of the distraction caused to the Roman Army by revolt in the north, tribes in the south-central regions of Gaul rose up against Roman dominance. The insurrection was led by a chieftain of the Averni named Vercingetorix. The rebellion enjoyed several successes owing to the insurgents' use of guerilla tactics, scorched-earth policies, and superior knowledge of the local terrain.

Each victory encouraged more tribes to join the uprising. Caesar grouped his forces in the north and marched on the rebels, taking the town of Avaricum, which had not been razed by the rebels; once inside, the Romans slaughtered the entire population. The Romans scored ever more victories in minor engagements that took place across the region and Vercingetorix lost a number of his key men and the rebels were forced to regroup at Alesia.

Built in the late first century BC by the Roman general Agrippa, this temple sits in the town of Nîmes in France. Its rededication as a Christian church in the fourth century AD probably helped in its preservation.

Battle of Alesia

Alesia was a stronghold for the Gallic insurgents because it was a hilltop fort surrounded by rivers, making it easily defensible. When Caesar arrived in pursuit, he discounted a direct attack because the fort was so well defended; instead he opted to besiege the fort and starve the Gallic rebels out. Vercingetorix's men held on for a time but were forced to try and break the siege to escape the fort. This was a failure, as the superior Roman Army and cavalry were able to rout the breakout and slaughter thousands of the rebels, forcing the remainder to retreat to the fort. Vercingetorix was left with little option but to capitulate to the Romans. Most of the rebels were sold into slavery, and Vercingetorix was kept in prison for five years so that he could be paraded in Rome upon Caesar's victory against Pompey. After this five-year wait, he was executed.

Gallic rebellion ended

Although the rebellion continued, Vercingetorix had proved to be a unifying figure and without him, the insurgents were divided. This made them perilously weak and allowed the Romans to isolate individual tribes and destroy them. Although Caesar was exceptionally ruthless, he did use a mixture of benevolent policies to co-opt the strategically important tribes. By 51 BC, the Gallic rebellion was over because the natives were exhausted; towns and villages were destroyed and it is estimated that at least one third of the population of Gaul was killed in the fighting. Back in Rome, Caesar was not seen as a butcher; his popularity was rising meteorically, to the concern of his old ally, Pompey.

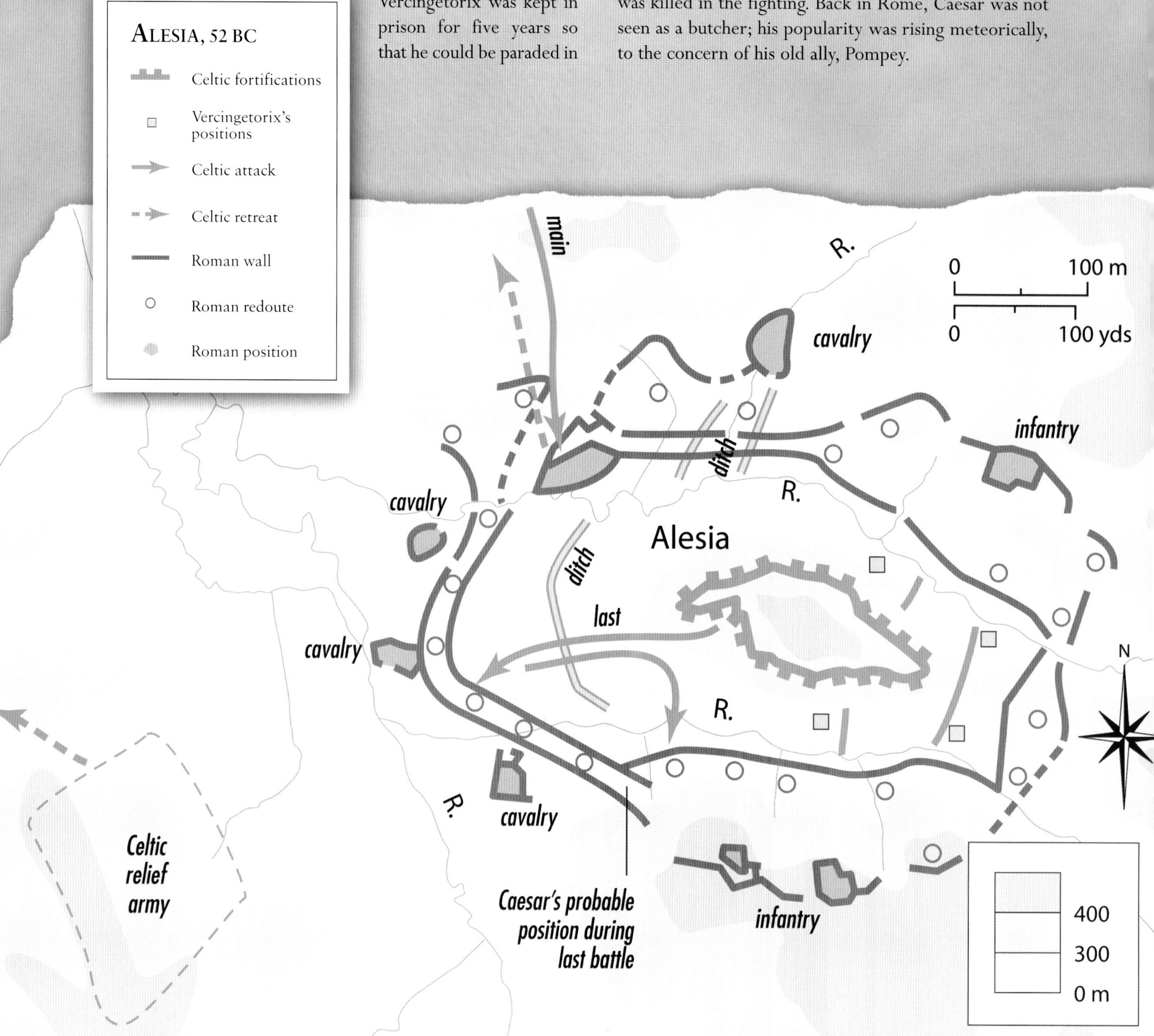

Apollo

It was from the Greeks that the Romans adopted the god Apollo. The cult of his worship appears in Rome as early as the fifth century BC, and during the Punic Wars the Apollonian Games was instituted.

Augustus develops the cult

Under the reign of Augustus, the importance of Apollo as a Roman god developed. Following the Battle of Actium, at which Augustus defeated Mark Antony, he built and dedicated a new temple to Apollo. The temple, on the Palantine Hill, was dedicated in 28 AD, although the exact site is uncertain because there are no extant remains.

Head from a statue of the god Apollo found at Pompeii.

The myth of Apollo

In mythology, Apollo was the son of Jupiter and Leto, and Diana's twin brother. He was god of the sun, archery, music and poetry, and is often depicted playing a lyre. As father of Asclepius, he was also seen as the god of healing who taught medicine to mankind.

It was believed that one of his most important roles was to harness four horses to his chariots, with which he would then drive the sun across the sky each day. Mythological symbols for Apollo include the laurel tree, the crow and the dolphin.

Athleticism

Images of Apollo show him to be a beautiful, eternally youthful man, athletic in build and action. The Greeks held the Pythian Games every four years at Delphi, in honour of his slaying of Python. While these games stemmed from Greek mythology and culture, the Romans also held games in Apollo's honour.

Although its precise site is unknown, Augustus built a temple in honour of Apollo on the Palatine Hill. There are no remains of the temple, which was dedicated in 28 BC. The area has been developed over the years, including the Farnese Gardens (pictured here), designed in the Renaissance by Vignola for Cardinal Alessandro Farnese.

Roman Gaul

Before Caesar's campaigns in Gaul, the Romans had already established a presence in the former Gallic territories surrounding the Alps. At the end of the second century BC, territory in southern Gaul was turned into a province called Gallia Transalpina (Transalpine Gaul) meaning 'the far side of the Alps'. The name was to distinguish the territory from Gallia Cisalpina (Cisalpine Gaul), a province on the nearside of the Alps, between the mountains and the River Rubicon.

Mirror with an image of a winged man on the handle.

A separate state

In the first century BC, Augustus incorporated Gallia Cisalpina into Italy, but Gallia Transalpina remained a separate province. It was renamed Gallia Narbonensis after the provincial capital, Narbo Martius (Narbonne); however, the Romans frequently referred to it as 'the Province'; hence the modern name Provence for the region in south-west France.

Narbo Martius was the first Roman colony in Gaul. It was founded in 117 BC at the junction where the Via Aquitania spurred off from the strategic Via Domitia. The Via Domitia was the Roman road which led from Italy to Spain and the Via Aquitania led to the Atlantic Ocean.

Nîmes comes to prominence

Narbo Martius was quickly eclipsed as Nemausus (Nîmes) became the main Roman city in Gaul. During the reign of Augustus, the town was significantly developed and subject to romanization. The town's temple, the *Maison Carrée*, was built on an imposing platform by Augustus' general, Marcus Vipsanius Agrippa, shortly after he oversaw the completion of the Pantheon in Rome. It remains in spectacular condition and is one of the best-preserved Roman temples in the world. The town also had a circus for chariot races and a large amphitheatre capable of seating over 20,000 spectators. The circus has been destroyed, but the amphitheatre remains in good condition, and is still in use today.

The water in Nîmes was supplied by a 50-kilometre-long aqueduct, which was also built by Agrippa. A spectacular bridge, the Pont-du-Gard, was constructed where the aqueduct needed to cross the Gardon river. The fifty-metre-high bridge was built over three tiers and remains in excellent condition.

Arcades in the impressive amphitheatre in Arles.

Birthplace of Antoninus

In 86 AD, the future Emperor, Antoninus Pius, was born in Nîmes. However, Antoninus was frugal and fiscally austere, meaning he did not lavish attention on the city as his predecessors, Hadrian and Trajan, had done to their own hometown in Spain. Without subsequent redevelopment, much of the Roman architecture dates back to the time of Augustus, and a good deal of it remains remarkably well preserved, earning Nîmes the title, 'the Rome of France'. This title is also coveted by nearby Arles, which is also home to a magnificent amphitheatre.

Caesar's Gaul

The territory to the north of Gallia Transalpina was conquered by Julius Caesar between 58 and 50 BC and turned into three provinces, Gallia Lugdunensis, Gallia Aquitania and Belgica. The economy was predominantly agricultural and mining.

Roman visitors used to note the distinct lack of towns and cities in Gaul, with most of the natives preferring to live in smaller villages. Of the few towns Lugdunum (Lyon) and Augusta Treverorum (Trier) were the principal ones.

Major towns of Gaul

Lugdunum was founded the year after Caesar's assassination to settle refugee tribes. It developed as a key administrative centre for Gaul and western Europe, and was frequently used as a rear base for generals fighting in Germania, who rewarded the city for its hospitality with various public works. Lugdunum thrived until the end of the second century AD, when the city was partly destroyed in the civil war that ensued when Septimius Severus installed himself as Emperor.

Augusta Treverorum, as its name suggests, was founded by the Emperor Augustus in 19 BC. Augustus made his new town the capital of Belgica province and began to adorn the city with the construction of a variety of public buildings. He was copied by Constantine more than three hundred years later, who added imperial baths and a vast throne room, which was subsequently used as a basilica.

Trier became the capital of the breakaway Gallic Republic in the third century, and an important residence of the Western Roman Empire after Diocletian's division of the Empire.

The Roman amphitheatre in Arles is still in use today.

Slaves

Slavery was commonplace in Ancient Rome. As the Republic won ever more wars, increasing numbers of slaves from all over the Roman world filled the city of Rome and the surrounding countryside. Rome's greatness was founded on the back of many of these faceless individuals who struggled to build glorious public works, toiled in the farms or performed household functions for Roman citizens.

A wide range of duties

Slaves performed a wide range of duties; they were not simply labourers and cleaners, but were also tutors, nurses, cooks and gladiators. The worst job a slave could have was to be sent to work in the mines, where the work was gruelling and life expectancy was short. The best job for a slave was to work in a family home, but this of course depended upon the nature of the family; some owners were exceptionally harsh, including Cato the Elder, who publicly advocated showing little compassion to slaves, but many were reasonably compassionate and a slave would be able to establish a friendly relationship with a family over the years. In fact, household slaves were treated as the masters for the duration of the Roman festival of Saturnalia. The extent of the role reversal varied, some masters simply waived punishments, while others got fully involved and waited on their slaves.

The Servile Wars: slave rebellions

For the most part, slaves acquiesced to their lot; however, there were three unrelated uprisings by slaves in the later Republic, called the Servile Wars. The third Servile War is the most famous of the three. It was led by Spartacus, a slave-gladiator, originally from Thrace.

The rebellion began in 73 BC, when Spartacus and fellow gladiators decided to fight for their own freedom and overran the gladiator school in Capua where they were held. After killing the guards, they broke out and ran amok in the south of Italy. The rebellion quickly spread as the story of the self-emancipation of the gladiators inspired other slaves to abandon their owners and join the uprising. With a growing force, the rebels occupied Mount Vesuvius and managed to destroy two Roman legions sent to subdue them. These successes encouraged yet more slaves to join their cause.

Above: A gladiator fights a leopard. Most gladiators were slaves. Spartacus was a slave who in 73 BC led a rebellion by slave-gladiators which lasted for two years, before being brutally crushed by Crassus.

Below: Panel painting depicting dancers. Slaves also took on roles as entertainers.

Spartacus' revolt is crushed

Spartacus' initial plans had been to escape across the Alps outside Roman territory, but as his army scored ever more victories against the Romans, he was encouraged to stay in Italy and fight.

The Senate sent Crassus to deal with Spartacus once and for all, but his forces did not perform well against the rebels. Crassus, desperate for victory and glory, employed one of the most brutal disciplinary methods to get his army into gear: decimation. Decimation was when every tenth soldier was killed as an example to the rest of the troops.

With a newly disciplined fighting force, Crassus was able to hem the rebels in to the toe of Italy. The slaves managed to break out of the siege, but they were marching headlong into Pompey's forces, who had come all the way from Spain. Trapped between Pompey and Crassus, the slaves had little choice but to fight. It was Crassus' army that dealt the final blow and Spartacus was probably killed in the battle.

Thousands of slaves were captured and Crassus made a brutal example of them, having each one of them crucified along the Appian Way, the Roman road from Rome to Capua.

Better treatment

In general, slaves were treated better during the Empire than during the Republic. Claudius introduced new laws to prevent inhumane treatment of slaves and later in the Empire slaves were even allowed to take their masters to court.

Slaves were not necessarily condemned to lifelong service; they could be emancipated. Manumission could occur in several ways: they could buy their freedom from their owner; the owner could release a slave from service upon the master's death; or the owner could choose to willingly free the slave while he was still alive, perhaps as a reward for good service.

An emancipated slave was called a 'freedman'. There were relatively few restrictions on freedmen; they could own land and their children were granted Roman citizenship. In fact, freedmen became an important part of Roman society. During Claudius' reign, freedmen held the most senior posts in his civil service.

Below: Captured Dacian workers as depicted on Trajan's column. Most slaves came from Roman-occupied lands throughout the Empire.

ASTYANAX VIC

Death of the Republic

Twilight of the Republic

The Triumvirate had undermined the control of the Senate and the death of Crassus had left just two rival contenders to fill the vacuum. The ensuing battle between Caesar and Pompey was to be the endgame of the Roman Republic.

An alliance of convenience

Caesar and Pompey's alliance had largely been one of convenience. Caesar had been a traditional ally of the *Populares*, while Pompey was affiliated with the *Optimates*. Nevertheless, both men had found common ground in opposing the intransigence of a bloated Senate, and Pompey joined Caesar in drawing support from the general population of Rome. However, at the end of the 50s, Caesar's successes in Gaul were beginning to eclipse Pompey's support amongst the masses, forcing him to fawn on the Senate in order to shore up his own position against Caesar's rocketing popularity.

The Senate did not trust Pompey, but in 52 BC he was appointed the sole consul so that he could deal with civil unrest and factional fighting that had been getting worse since the time that Marius and Sulla had begun undermining Roman government. By successfully restoring order, Pompey was able to get back into the Senate's good graces and undermine Caesar from within the system.

Sculpture head of Pompey the Great whose head was offered to Julius Caesar on a plate by Ptolemy of Egypt.

'The die is cast'

The opportunity to do just that came in 50, when Caesar's tenure as proconsul expired. Caesar wished to continue his popular and successful war in Gaul and therefore he needed to be granted another consulship. This placed him at the mercy of Roman politics, and therefore provided the Senate and Pompey with a chance to undermine their mutual rival. They insisted that Caesar could not apply for the consulship in absentia and must return to Rome. This meant abandoning his army, which would have placed him in a perilously weak position. Caesar decided upon a compromise, but illegal, solution; he would return to Rome, but bring his army with him. In January 49 Caesar ordered his troops to cross the Rubicon, a river demarcating the border between Gaul and Italy, and war between Pompey and Caesar was begun.

This well-preserved Roman building on the Nile-island temple complex at Philae in Egypt was left unfinished.

Civil War

As Caesar marched on Rome, Pompey decided his best option was to abandon the city so he could group his forces and present a more formidable challenge. He went first to Brundisium and then fled across the Adriatic to Dyrrhachium. After capturing Rome, instead of going straight for Pompey, Caesar went to Spain to defeat Pompey's army stationed there. This was a shrewd move because Pompey's Spanish army might have advanced on Italy while Caesar was dealing with Pompey in the East.

After overcoming Pompey's army in Spain, Caesar travelled to Dyrrhachium to face his rival directly. The first battle against Pompey did not go well for Caesar; Pompey had amassed as many as 45,000 men and was able to fend off Caesar's attack in January 48 BC. Pompey, however, failed to consolidate his gains and Caesar's army was able to escape to fight another day.

During 48, Pompey had naval superiority in the Adriatic, meaning that Caesar's supply lines were stretched to near breaking point and his troops went hungry and thirsty. Pompey was happy to let Caesar's armies run themselves down, but his senatorial colleagues were spoiling for a fight and encouraged him to attack Caesar prematurely. The result was the Battle of Pharsalus in August 48 where Caesar correctly anticipated Pompey's tactics and won. Caesar believed that Pompey would try to flank to the right of Caesar's forces with his cavalry, so Caesar simply took a gamble by shoring up the defences on his right wing, but leaving the rest of his line gravely weak. The gamble paid off; Pompey attacked to Caesar's right, handing Caesar victory in the most important battle of the conflict.

Pompey flees to Egypt

In defeat, Pompey fled Greece for Egypt with Caesar in pursuit. As soon as he arrived, the Egyptian Pharaoh, Ptolemy, had him murdered to curry favour with Caesar. He hoped that Caesar might help him solve a dynastic conflict between him and his co-ruler, Cleopatra, who was both the Pharaoh's sister and wife. Ptolemy believed Cleopatra was overshadowing him and wished to dispose of her.

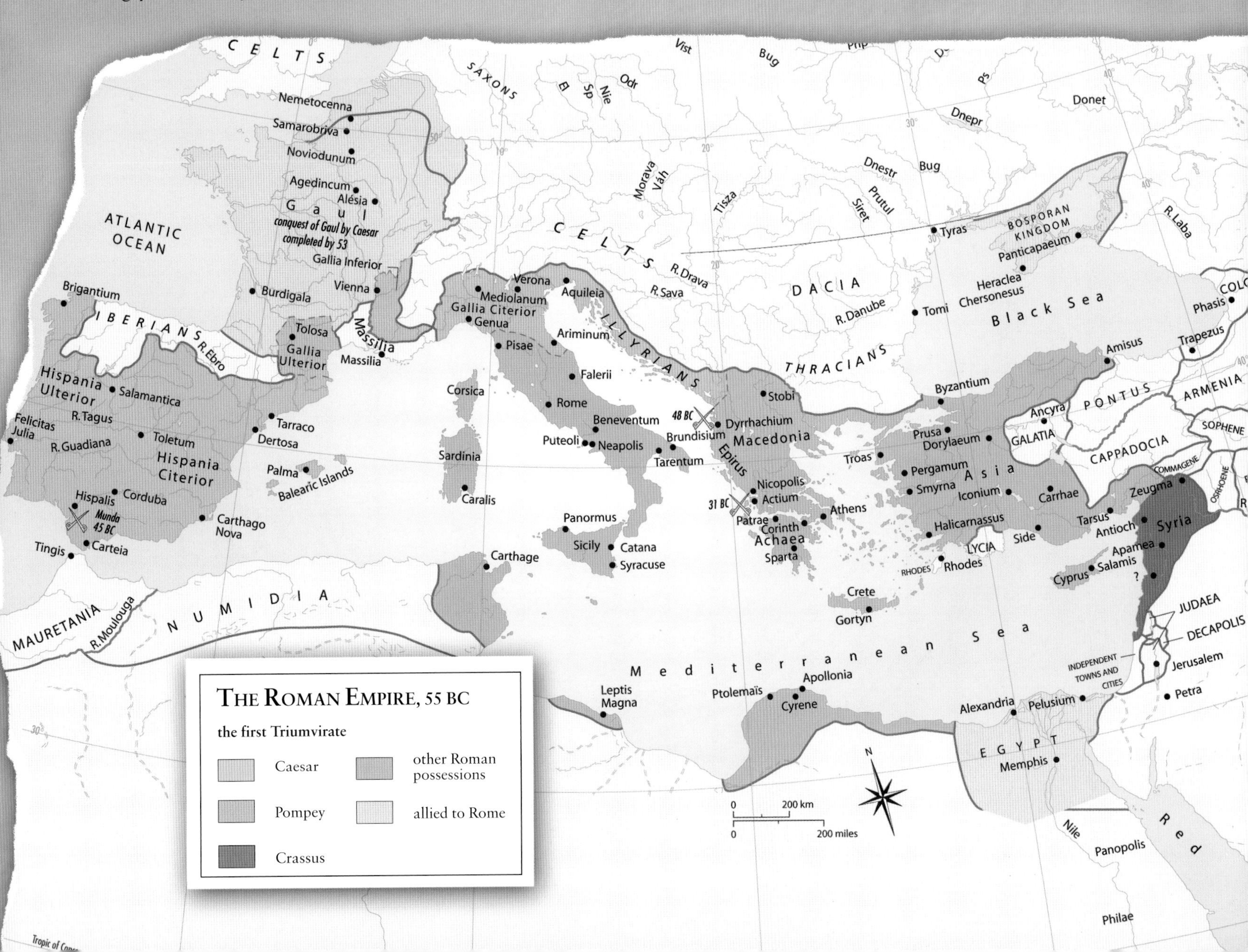

Pompey's head on a plate

When Caesar arrived in Alexandria in pursuit of his enemy, Ptolemy had Pompey's head presented to him as a gift. This gesture not only shocked Caesar, but deeply upset him as well; after all, despite their recent differences, Pompey was his one time colleague and father-in-law. As a result of Ptolemy's barbarity, Caesar sided with Cleopatra in the dispute between the warring Egyptian siblings and Ptolemy was ousted.

Soon after, with Cleopatra as sole ruler of Egypt, she and Caesar began an affair. Cleopatra claimed to have to have borne a son by Caesar, whom she named Caesarion. He later became co-ruler of Egypt with his mother, and it was Cleopatra's intention that he would succeed his father as ruler of Rome. However, when Octavian, Caesar's adopted son, defeated Cleopatra, he ordered Caesarion's execution because he viewed him as a potential rival.

Caesar triumphant

In 47 BC, after leaving Egypt, Caesar went to the Middle East to challenge Pharnaces, the son of Mithridates, in the battle of Zela. Pharnaces had exploited Rome's distraction with the civil war to seize more territory in the East. Caesar's victory over Pharnaces was so swift that he boastfully coined the phrase '*veni, vidi, vici*' (I came, I saw, I conquered). Caesar scored another success at Thapsus the following year. He faced the remainder of Pompey's allies who had fled to North Africa after the battle of Pharsalus and the death of their leader. Caesar won at Thapsus and forced the opposing general, Cato the Younger, to commit suicide. Thapsus had almost wiped out the opposition to Caesar, but Pompey's sons had been able to escape to Spain for one last stand. The battle, which took place at Munda in 45, was yet another success for Caesar. It was to be the last military challenge posed to his rule; Caesar had won the war.

Pompey's Pillar in Alexandria stands surrounded by Egyptian statues of female sphinxes. The pillar was erected in 300 AD in honour of the Roman Emperor Diocletian, who saved Alexandria from famine. The pillar's name was given by medieval travellers under the misapprehension that Pompey's head was buried beneath it.

Board Games

Ivory dice excavated from Pompeii.

Romans played a variety of board and dice games including *Latrunculi*, a tactical chess-like game played out on a board grid and using sixteen pieces. The aim was to capture the opponent's pieces, the game concluding when all the pieces had been taken. Excavated *Latrunculi* pieces have been made from stone and coloured glass. The boards themselves were mostly made from wood, and occasionally stone or marble.

Dice, or *Tesserae*, played by adult Romans, proved to be a favourite form of gambling. Despite the fact that games of chance were forbidden by Roman law, except at Saturnalia, they appear to have been widespread, with gambling houses, brothels and taverns playing host to these activities. Most dice were made from bone or ivory, or more commonly wood.

The Lines of the Twelve Philosophers

Duodecim Scriptorum (also known as *XII Scripta*) was a board game thought to be a predecessor of modern backgammon. The board was marked out with three rows of twelve spaces and the aim was to move all one's pieces to the final square on the opposite side of the board. As three dice were used, the game was considered to be gambling by the Roman authorities and therefore illegal. In an effort to disguise the true game, it is thought that some boards were made with letters replacing the squares on the board. This game was then known as 'The Lines of the Twelve Philosophers', although it was almost identical to *Duodecim Scriptorum*. Tabula is thought to have evolved from this game as it uses the same number of pieces and three dice.

Bones and stones

Calculi, or *Ludus Calculorum*, was a simple game, similar to the game 'five in a row'. Played by two people on a board of any size, the winner was the first person to make five stones in a row, horizontally, vertically or diagonally.

Tali is the Latin name for knucklebones, and is so called because the pieces would originally have been made from the knucklebones of sheep and goats. The game originated in Ancient Egypt and was played in Greece as *Astragali*. Romans played with pieces made from a variety of materials, including gold, silver, marble, ivory and wood. Four pieces would be thrown in the air and fall onto one of four sides, each of which would have a value. *Tali* was a form of gambling; it was superseded by dice as the preferred game in later Imperial Rome.

A third century AD Roman mosaic from El Djem, Tunisia, shows three men seated at a table, playing dice.

Julius Caesar: Dictator for Life

Like Sulla, Caesar ostensibly adhered to the pre-existing governing structures of Rome. But in reality, the Republic was in tatters. Caesar was appointed dictator for life and took to wearing purple robes, a tradition previously upheld only by the old Roman kings.

Roman crown with ivy and berries. Although Julius Caesar refused the title of 'King', in the senate he sat on a throne wearing a laurel crown.

Below: An inscribed tablet lies in the ruins of the Forum.

Refuses title of 'King'

He may have refused the actual title of king, which would have been an obvious deathblow to the Republic, but he did sit on a throne wearing a laurel crown while in the Senate. During 45-44, Caesar's cult of personality blossomed; coins were marked with his face and the month of July was named in his honour. Caesar's power began to know no bounds when he began appointing people to government positions rather than have them elected.

Caesar controls the Senate

Given his affiliations with the *Populares* and his military campaign against senatorial forces, it might have been expected that a victorious Caesar would have castrated the Senate as Sulla had neutered the Tribunate. But Caesar did not have to resort to the political machinations of his

predecessors because he had dealt the decisive blow to his rivals on the battlefield. This meant that Caesar believed he could maintain the Senate as a governing institution but replace reactionary senators who had once sat in it.

Although he appointed some of his own men to these positions, he also allowed many of the pre-existing senators to keep their jobs; this was adroit because it meant the Senate did not need to be rebuilt from scratch. With the Senate seemingly compliant, Caesar even resolved to increase its membership from six hundred to nine hundred because he argued that an Empire the size of Rome's required a larger assembly.

Populist reforms

The quest for personal power was not Caesar's only goal; after capturing Rome in 49 BC, he embarked on a series of social reforms in line with his populist views. For example, the wealthy were to be held more accountable for crimes against the plebs and a quarter of debts for all Romans were to be cancelled because interest rates had spiralled out of control during the civil war.

In addition, Caesar instigated a number of public building works, which provided employment for a number of poor Romans. However, Caesar did not get carried away with social reforms, and many of his policies were distinctly moderate in character; he stopped short of cancelling all debts and slashed in half the number of the population receiving corn benefits. Such policies were not necessarily designed to be popular, but rather to be of wider benefit to the health of the Roman economy.

Benefits to the legions

Caesar also ensured his legions were well cared for. At the time of his victory, he gave each soldier a massive cash bonus and ensured that land was found for his retiring veterans, by establishing new colonies across the Roman world. Among the most famous of these were the rebuilt cities of Corinth and Carthage, the two cities most harshly treated by the Roman Republic. In addition to Caesar's veterans, poorer Romans and emancipated slaves or 'freedmen', came to settle in these new frontiers.

Alarm at Caesar's autocratic rule

In hindsight, Caesar's biggest mistake was to assume that the Senate, purged of the elements that outwardly opposed him, could be made compliant. But this was not the case; members of the aristocratic Senate became increasingly alarmed by Caesar's autocratic rule with its monarchical trimmings.

A group known as the 'Liberatores' plotted to murder Caesar, and on the Ides of March, (the fifteenth day), they succeeded. The senators lured Caesar into the trap on the pretext that they wished him to read through a petition they had written and the dictator was stabbed to death. Chief among the conspirators were Marcus Junius Brutus and Gaius Cassius Longinus, both conservatives who had originally been affiliated with Pompey but had been magnanimously, if foolishly, pardoned by Caesar.

Upon Caesar's death Brutus proclaimed the regained freedom of Rome, but this was highly premature; the struggle had not been won and in many ways it was only just beginning.

Bust of Julius Caesar. After winning the civil war, Caesar returned to Rome and began to amass substantial personal powers. Alarmed senators plotted and carried out his assassination on the Ides of March 44.

Measuring Time

One of Julius Caesar's most enduring legacies was his introduction of a new calendar, the Julian calendar. The traditional Roman calendar had fallen out of step with the solar year (the amount of time it takes the sun to return to the same place in the sky) and the priests, for whom the marking of time was important to know when religious festivals fell, had traditionally compensated by introducing random leap days or weeks.

Julian Calendar introduced

Caesar, in his role as *pontifex maximus*, sought a more long-term solution than adding random days here and there, and introduced a brand-new calendar as a result. A year in the Julian Calendar was fixed at three hundred and sixty five and one quarter days – the length of a solar year. The quarter day was compensated for by introducing a quadrennial leap day.

The new calendar began on 1 January 45 BC, but to correctly align the new calendar with the solar year and make sure the seasons were in their correct place, the year 46 BC was extended to four hundred and forty five days.

Caesar's calendar was maintained until the sixteenth century when the Pope acknowledged a slight adjustment; the solar year was found to be just short of three hundred and sixty five and one quarter days, meaning that the new 'Gregorian Calendar' occasionally omits a leap year.

Zodiac calendar

The zodiacal calendar was also employed, with the constellations of the heavens representing each of twelve divisions of the year. The zodiac probably came to the Romans through the Greeks, the source of many aspects of Roman understanding of astronomy and measuring time.

Temple of Apollo in Pompeii showing the altar and sundial.

Sundial

It was probably also through the Greeks that the Romans came to use the sundial to measure daily time. A simple device, the sundial uses a gnomon to cast a shadow on a dial which is calibrated to show divisions of time.

Pliny the Elder records that in the third century BC it was a plundered sundial from Sicily, then under Greek influence, that was the first used in Rome. He also notes that, until the inscriptions on the dial were adjusted to take account of the difference in latitude between Rome and Sicily, it failed to give an accurate time.

Sand and water clocks

The obvious drawback to using a sundial is that it is only useable in daylight. It is likely that the Romans would have used a number of different devices to measure the passage of time when the sun was not present. Sand clocks, whereby time is measure by the time it takes for a given quantity of sand to trickle from one vessel to another would be one.

However, the most accurate timekeeping mechanism in the Ancient World was the water clock, or *clepsydra* as it is known in Greek. The Greeks developed mechanized water clocks, an idea which the Romans borrowed and developed.

Roman zodiac wheel.

Mosaic depicting a calendar with days of the week and zodiac signs.

Antony and Octavian

Mark Antony, who had stuck by Caesar throughout the campaign against Pompey, manoeuvred to take charge immediately after the assassination of his colleague. However, Caesar's will revealed that he had had another heir in mind: his nephew and adopted son, Octavian.

Octavian challenges Mark Antony

After the assassination of his uncle/father, Octavian returned from his studies in Illyria to Rome. Upon his return he discovered an ambitious Mark Antony planning to shore up his position by occupying Cisalpine Gaul and ingratiating himself with Cleopatra in Egypt.

The Senate feared that Antony was attempting to make himself dictator and encouraged the eighteen-year-old to challenge Antony so they could play the two leadership contenders off against one another. Their first encounter came just a year after Caesar's assassination, when Octavian joined the Senate's forces and the two consuls in the Battle of Mutina against Antony. The senatorial forces were victorious, but the two consuls were killed in the fighting and Octavian all of a sudden found himself at the head of an army.

The death of both consuls meant that the consulship had come up for grabs and Octavian demanded his own appointment. His demand was refused by the Senate which was not willing to see him become a dictator. With his new army, Octavian simply marched on Rome and took the consulate by force.

New alliances

Like Pompey, two decades earlier, Octavian's initial support for the Senate was destroyed because the Senate was unwilling to see him become too powerful. His solution to the intransigent Senate was the same as Pompey's; to build an independent power base outside the Senate by throwing in his lot with his powerful rivals. In Pompey's case this had been Julius Caesar; in Octavian's it was his former enemy, Mark Antony, and also Aemilius Lepidus, a close associate of Caesar, with a large army.

Antony and Lepidus had already joined forces and added to Octavian's strength, as well as his status as Caesar's adopted son; the three could dominate Roman politics and marginalize the Senate. The result was that a Second Triumvirate was formed at a meeting in Bononia (Bologna) in 43 BC.

***Right:** Cleopatra had relationships with both Julius Caesar and Mark Antony. With Caesar she had a son, Caesarion, whom she intended would succeed his father. Her relationship with Mark Antony was a personal affront to Octavian whose sister, Octavia, was married to Antony.*

The Second Triumvirate

Unlike the first Triumvirate, the second gained official status because the Senate, too weak from years of fighting and purges, was unable to challenge the combined will of the three men. The second Triumvirate was restricted to a five-year tenure, although there seemed little anyone but the triumvirs could do to police such terms. Although consuls continued to be appointed, their role was marginalized by the triumvirs and at various times one of the triumvirs doubled up in the position of consul.

Avenging Caesar

The three men had their close personal links to Caesar in common and therefore the first task of this three-man dictatorship was to hunt down Caesar's assassins and avenge his death.

An angry mob had forced the chief culprits, Brutus and Cassius, to flee Rome because they did not share the opinion that Caesar's death had liberated the population. The assassins settled in the East where they were hunted down by Antony and Octavian, while Lepidus had remained in Rome in a dual role of triumvir and consul.

Revenge was served in the Battle of Philippi, in Macedonia, in 42 BC. In the first encounter, Antony's forces defeated Cassius', but Brutus was able to overcome Octavian. However, disaster struck for the assassins when incorrect intelligence led Cassius to believe that Brutus had also been defeated. Cassius duly took his own life, leaving Brutus to face Antony and Octavian on his own. In the second encounter Brutus was defeated and forced to commit suicide before being captured.

Death of Cicero

The conquest of Brutus and Cassius was not the end of the retributions; back in Rome, the triumvirs were content to use their hunt for co-conspirators as a pretext for purging their political enemies. Obvious foes such as the famous philosopher and political theorist, Cicero, who had openly and very publicly opposed Caesar and Antony, were hunted down and killed.

However, the triumvirs were not particularly discriminate in the purge; even Antony's uncle, Lucius Julius Caesar, an ally of Julius Caesar, was killed. In total, well over one thousand enemies of the triumvirs were proscribed; the majority faced death and only the lucky few managed to survive. Not only did the purge shore up the Triumvirate in itself, but the confiscated wealth of the proscribed men lined the triumvirs' pockets giving them an even stronger base against the remnants of Roman government.

The second Triumvirate, like the first, was largely a marriage of convenience. The three men were not the best of friends, and the dislike between Antony and Octavian was particularly palpable.

Above: The famous philosopher and political theorist, Cicero, who had openly and very publicly opposed Caesar and Antony, was hunted down and killed as part of the second Triumvirate's plan to avenge Caesar's assassination. Left: Bust of Mark Antony.

Division of the Empire

The triumvirs did try to patch over their differences. For example, in 40 BC, when Octavian arranged the marriage of his sister, Octavia, to Mark Antony, but mutual antagonism meant that conflict was always around the corner. To keep each other at arm's length, the triumvirs divided the Empire into three spheres of influence. Octavian took the West and Antony the East, while Lepidus acquired North Africa. Infighting was largely averted and the Triumvirate was given a second five-year term in 38.

Octavian and Lepidus clash

During the second term the second Triumvirate quickly came undone. Octavian's and Lepidus' relationship was immediately severed when Octavian believed that Lepidus was conspiring to take control of Sicily. Lepidus had brought his legions from Africa to assist Octavian in dislodging Pompey's son, Sextus, who had based his armies there. Octavian feared that Lepidus' assistance was a ruse to bring his own legions to Sicily and keep them there. To pre-empt this eventuality, Octavian encouraged Lepidus' legions to switch loyalties to him.

This was not an easy task but Octavian was able to win the legions over because he was the son of Caesar, and moreover, because Caesar was in the process of deification, Octavian was even able to claim that he was the son of a god. Octavian cast Lepidus, now bereft of his armies, out of the Triumvirate, but was merciful with his colleague; Lepidus was allowed simply to quietly retire and even keep his post as *pontifex maximus*.

Preparation for war

The relationship of the remaining two dictators also soured, although it had never been very good in the first place. Antony's ambition once again flared when he married and had children with Cleopatra of Egypt. This move was a political threat to Octavian because Antony had become the king of Egypt, and had additionally gained important influence over Greece, owing to the Hellenistic origins of Cleopatra's dynasty.

Concurrently, Antony tried to weaken Octavian by asserting that Caesar and Cleopatra's son, Caesarion, should become ruler in Octavian's stead. Besides the political threat, Octavian also had a personal gripe with Antony; his marriage to Cleopatra was humiliating to his Roman wife and children, who were also Octavian's sister and nieces. The personal and the political combined to make Octavian prepare for war. To convince the Senate to support him, he illegally read Antony's will, which indicated that he would divide the East up among Cleopatra's children and wished to be buried in Alexandria instead of Rome. An outraged Senate gave Octavian the necessary backing for a war.

Left: The temple site on the island of Philae in the middle of the River Nile was associated with the Egyptian goddess Isis, who was associated with the Greek goddess Aphrodite, whom the Romans worshipped as Venus.

The last civil war of the Republic

In 32 BC, Octavian declared war on Cleopatra and, by extension, on Antony. Although he had the backing of the Senate, not all senators were on Octavian's side and a number went to join Antony in Egypt. Both sides amassed vast armies of men but the decisive encounter was to happen at sea in the Battle of Actium in 31.

Octavian's forces had naval superiority and won the day, in part due to Octavian's competent general and lifelong friend, Marcus Vipsanius Agrippa. Antony's ship managed to escape back to Egypt but his legions in Greece were left behind. They had little choice but to defect, but the mastery shown by Agrippa at Actium was encouragement for many generals to do so willingly. Octavian found himself in charge of the vast majority of the Roman Army and began his march on Alexandria overland.

Octavian allied with his cousin, Lucius Pinarius, who was governor of Cyrenaica, the Roman province immediately to the west of Egypt. Together, the two armies pinned Antony's forces in Egypt and eventually trapped Antony in Alexandria.

Antony and Cleopatra commit suicide

In 30 BC, Antony committed suicide by falling on his sword and soon after Cleopatra followed suit, allegedly allowing an asp to bite her, but it has not been ruled out that Octavian actually murdered her. What is known is that she outlived Antony by a few days, during which time she tried to negotiate with Octavian to spare the life of her son by Caesar, Caesarion. However, the negotiations failed because Octavian feared 'too many Caesars' and had Caesarion, a potential political rival, pre-emptively murdered.

With the death of Caesarion, who had reigned jointly with his mother, the Egyptian throne was presented to Octavian who became not just the ruler of Egypt, but the master of the entire Empire.

Above: Roman coin, depicting a crocodile, marking the defeat of Cleopatra.

Right: Bronze head of Augustus at about the age of 30. The sculpture was found in Meroe in the Sudan. Augustus, meaning 'majestic', was the name given to Octavian by the Senate in 27 BC.

Food and Drink

Mosaic depicting creatures of the sea, many of which would have graced the tables of the rich.

Food for the rich

In the early Republic, Romans, rich and poor alike, ate similar foods. Meals were frugal; breakfast, for example, usually consisted simply of gruel made with grain. It was during the period of the late Republic, when wealthy Romans began to develop Greek habits, that the cuisine of the poor and the rich began to differ. Wealthy Roman citizens began to eat a wider variety of imported and luxurious foodstuffs, which the poor could not afford.

The breakfast of prosperous Romans usually consisted of bread, cheeses, fruits, eggs and honey. It was followed by a second breakfast, or lunch, comprising leftovers from the previous evening meal.

Most wealthy Romans did business in the morning and went to the baths in the early afternoon. Therefore the main meal of the day would be taken in the early evening. Although, when guests were coming, or when many courses were to be consumed, dinner was often started in the late afternoon.

Exotic imports

Initially, no matter how rich they were, Romans were confined to eating foods that were native to Italy. But as the Republic expanded into new territories, a variety of new foods became available to them.

A range of different fruits such as cherries, pomegranates, apricots and lemons were found in the East, and exotic meats such as flamingo and ostrich were brought back to Rome from Africa.

Despite their acquisition of a range of foreign food products, the Romans never enjoyed many of the foods that are considered commonplace today. They had no potatoes, chocolate, tomatoes or maize. Additionally, sugar was unknown in Ancient Roman cuisine; instead, honey was used as a sweetener.

Bone spoons and bowl from Pompeii.

A meal becomes a banquet

Wealthy Romans would often eat their evening meal in the company of friends or colleagues, either as the host in their own home or as the guest at someone else's. As hosts sought to outdo one another by providing the best evening, these dinners were frequently turned into lavish banquets.

Dinner was usually eaten in a very leisurely fashion. It would last several hours, during which time the guests would be served a huge array of dishes that would be eaten with their hands. As the meal progressed, guests were often treated to entertainment from musicians, actors, poets or dancers between courses.

Rather than be seated at a table, people would lounge on long couches when they ate at such banquets. It was conventional for three people to lie on each couch and for three couches to surround one table of food. If the guests were particularly intimate, or if some of the guests were children, then four people might have been squeezed on.

Unusual tastes

Slaves would spend all day preparing a variety of foods for the banquet. As well as a range of fruit and vegetables, fish and meat were almost always served. The most commonly available meat was pork, but most wealthy Romans preferred to cater to more exotic tastes and served anything ranging from peacock to dormouse.

In addition to prizing outlandish dishes, the Romans loved their foods to have unusual tastes, so hosts would often go out of their way to give a dish an unanticipated flavour. A range of herbs, spices and sauces were used for this purpose, one of the most common, and highly prized, was liquamen, a sauce made from olive oil and fermented fish intestines.

Fresco painting depicting the beginning of a Roman banquet.

Dealing with excess

As there was so much food served at the banquet, it was usual for much of it to be uneaten. It was commonplace for guests to take food home with them at the end of the evening for the second breakfast the following day.

However, not all Romans stopped eating when they were full; although it was not a common practice, some purged their stomachs during the meal, by inducing vomiting, and then carried on eating.

Whether they took home the leftovers, or carried on eating, it was polite for a guest, upon finishing the meal, to show appreciation of the food by belching.

Slaves' jobs

Slaves were worked hard during a banquet, not only would they prepare the meal, but they would also attend to the diners' needs during the meal. When the guests first arrived, in preparation for eating, their hands would be washed by slaves. As Romans usually ate with their fingers, this hand-washing process was repeated between each course.

Slaves were also responsible for bringing dishes to and from the table as well as pouring the wine. In some houses, slaves were expected to fan the guests throughout the meal, which would have been a long and tedious job.

Amphorae storage jars from Ostia. Romans stored many foodstuffs in amphorae - large, conical vessels - which were often buried in the ground to help preserve the goods.

Seafood was usually eaten by wealthier Romans, but a sauce called liquamen made from fermented fish was popular with all classes.

Food for the poor

The majority of Romans were not wealthy enough to afford the lavish banquets and extensive cuisine enjoyed by the rich. Breakfast and lunch usually consisted of bread made from the free grain handed out to all citizens by the government.

As with their wealthier counterparts, poorer people would take their main meal of the day in the evening, although it consisted only of bread and vegetables. Ordinary Romans seldom ate meat or fish because it was very expensive. The poorest only usually ate meat when an animal was sacrificed to the gods; as only the internal organs were required for the religious ceremony, the meat from the animal was distributed among the needy.

Hunting was a favourite occupation among the rich and in many cases would provide food for the table. Here a hunter with a dog kills a boar.

Street vendors

Most Romans lived in crowded, multi-storey tenement buildings which, to reduce the risk of fire, were not equipped with stoves. Instead of cooking at home, Roman women had to go out and buy the evening meal from vendors on the street. Any leftovers from dinner were eaten for breakfast or lunch the next day.

There were exceptions to these norms; some people chose to buy lunch or an afternoon snack from a food vendor, especially the ones surrounding the entrances to the public baths. Some families even opted to cook in their own apartment, disregarding the risks and often sparking dangerous fires.

Public fountains

Ordinary Romans mostly drank water from public fountains throughout the city. These fountains were connected to an aqueduct, which brought fresh water through a system of underground pipes.

In addition to drinking water, most Roman men also drank wine throughout the day. Roman women were forbidden from drinking wine but, for wealthier women this rule became slightly relaxed over time. The wine consumed by the rich and the poor differed sharply in quality, but all classes shared the opinion that it was uncouth not to dilute their wine with water.

Julio-Claudian Emperors

Augustus

Octavian emerged as the great winner after more than a century of turmoil. Following his defeat of Antony and Cleopatra in 30 BC, he ruled for a long period over a relatively serene Empire and laid the foundations for a new golden age.

Octavian becomes Augustus

To all intents and purposes Octavian was the first of the Roman Emperors. In 27 BC he ostensibly restored the Roman Republic but this was more of a token gesture because he continued to amass more power for himself. In the same year the Senate honoured Octavian by renaming him 'Augustus', meaning 'majestic' and gave him the status of *princeps* or 'first citizen'. This gave him a specific position in Roman government, whilst superficially adhering to the overarching Roman Republic. In fact, the Emperors were to continue to pay lip-service to the Republic and disguise their despotic rule until Diocletian came to power in 284 AD.

Augustus was very quickly made a dictator and a consul for life and accumulated even more functions when he was granted the powers of a tribune, allowing him to set the agenda of the Senate and wield an absolute veto against all laws. He was handed control over all proconsuls, which gave him the right to manage the affairs of the entire Empire and he was also given exclusive *imperium*, or authority, over the city of Rome. After the death of his former colleague in the Triumvirate, Lepidus, in 12 BC, Augustus also acquired the role of *pontifex maximus*.

Creation of the Praetorian Guard

Although Augustus created a ruthless personal bodyguard, the Praetorian Guard, to ensure his own safety and authority, his success in gaining absolute power was largely a result of his relative moderation. After generations of civil wars and anarchy, Romans were happy to accept Augustus' rule in exchange for stability and the rule of law that he offered. The streets of Rome were cleared of the gangs that had menaced them for so long, and Rome regained its peace and prosperity.

Gold coin with portrait of Augustus.

Statue of Augustus as pontifex maximus, ***the head of the state religion.***

A return to 'family values'

Augustus' emphasis on frugality and a return to family values also chimed well with ordinary Romans, who had detested the ostentatious lifestyles that the city's rich had enjoyed during the late Republic. Such was his stress on modesty that he even had his own daughter exiled from Rome as punishment for her hedonistic lifestyle.

The Senate, which had traditionally been reluctant to accept any curbs on its own power, also provided very little resistance to Augustus because purges and warfare had transformed it into a relatively benign institution. Octavian further benefited from the support of the Army, whose continued loyalty was assured by generous offers of land to veterans. Moreover, the size of the Army was greatly reduced and the legions dispersed across the Empire so that it would not have been easy to mount an effective challenge to Augustus' rule, even if the Army had wished to do so.

Marble pillars lie within a ruined room in the Forum. Augustus famously boasted that he found a city of brick and left it a city of marble.

Rome regenerated

With increased stability and security in Rome, a regeneration of the city got underway. Augustus famously boasted that he found a city of brick and left it a city of marble. This might have been an exaggeration but he did make a number of upgrades to the city.

One of his first works, the Forum Augustus, was begun in 42 BC after the Battle of Philippi but not completed until 2 BC. The Forum was complete with a temple to Mars, the god of war, an offering to thank him for victory against Caesar's assassins.

During Augustus' reign, the Campus Martius underwent particular development; Augustus had the Senate build the peace altar to commemorate the return of peace in Rome and additionally he convinced his general, Agrippa, to build the Pantheon on the site. The original building was destroyed in a fire, but its replacement, built during the reign of Hadrian, still stands to this day.

Another prominent addition to the city was the temple of Julius Caesar, built by Augustus to honour his deified adoptive father. Not only did Augustus oversee the construction of a number of buildings, he also set a fashion for later Emperors, who took to building grandiose public works, especially forums, which were usually named after the Emperor who had commanded their construction.

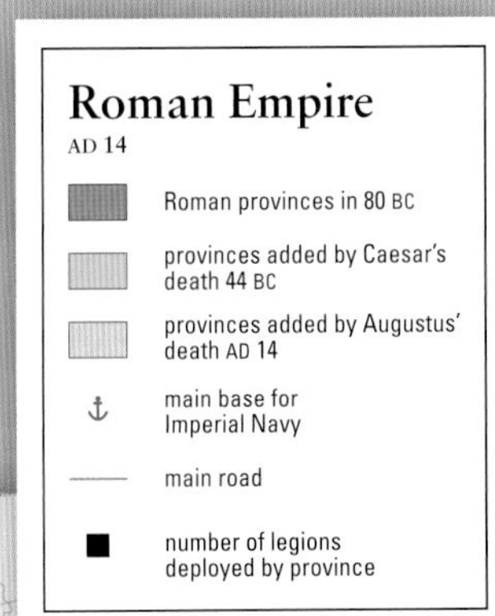

Ostia: the port of Rome

It is believed that Ostia was founded in the seventh century BC by the fourth King of Rome, Ancus Martius, although so far remains have only been excavated dating back to the fourth century BC.

Series of walls from Ostia showing different styles of brickwork.

The town was located at the mouth of the River Tiber, 30 kilometres west of Rome, and almost certainly developed to defend the capital from anyone entering via this waterway.

A naval base

In the third century BC it was mainly used as a naval base where the quaestor classici (officer taking care of the fleet) operated during the Punic Wars against Carthage. It was from Ostia that Scipio sailed in 211 BC when he set off to defeat the Carthaginians in the Second Punic War. Inhabitants of the town were not involved in the fighting, as they were needed to keep the harbour running.

Ruined entrance to a house, domus, *in Ostia.*

The second century BC saw it emerge primarily as an important commercial harbour with many goods from the colonies passing through the port on their way to Rome. The quaestor was now responsible for the import of grain.

Independence and renovation

The town was attacked by Marius in 87 BC and again by pirates in 67 BC so was rebuilt by the statesman Marcus Tullius Cicero, with additional protective walls. Also around this time Ostia ceased to be governed by Rome but was able to have its own government.

Under Augustus and his son Tiberius much of the renovation of the town began. During the reign of Claudius (41-54 AD) a new port was built at Portus. It was constructed about two kilometres north of Ostia and therefore created a new, separate settlement. Trajan later enlarged Portus with the construction of a hexagonal basin designed to withstand erosion from the waves. After the harbour was completed there was a great building boom in the city, with much of this work supervised by Hadrian and Antoninus.

Rise and decline

Local government in Ostia consisted of two magistrates called duoviri who were in power for a year and presided over the city council. Two quaestores aerarii handled the city's finances, the curator operum publicorum et aquarum looked after the public buildings and water supply, and the quaestor alimentorum helped poor children. These served a population in the first century AD which had risen to fifty thousand, a figure that included seventeen thousand slaves, who came mainly from Egypt and the Middle East.

However, in the second half of the third century, along with the rest of the Western Roman Empire, Ostia began a slow decline. Buildings that collapsed were not rebuilt, and Portus was beginning to gain in importance. The town was now mainly a residential area with some expensive habitations built between the third and fifth centuries, probably for merchants working in Portus.

Interior of a bakery at Ostia, showing the bread ovens.

In the eleventh century, marble and other materials taken from Ostia were used for magnificent new buildings, including the Leaning Tower of Pisa, which gives a clear indication of how neglected the city had become. In 1461 Pope Pius II visited the city and commented on the vast areas of ruins; it was in this condition the city remained until the end of the nineteenth century.

Uncovering Ostia

Occasional and spasmodic excavations of the city began in the 1700s with the Roman archaeologist Rodolfo Lanciani starting his work in the 1800s.

Dante Vaglieri began to systematically excavate the city in 1907, although he died six years later. Guido Calza took over, but unfortunately, during the age of fascism, the buildings were uncovered too quickly, without a systematic study of the layers that would have provided a greater understanding of the history of the town. During this time some of the ruins were rebuilt or renovated, so it is the case that some buildings, such as the Theatre, are largely 1930s reconstructions.

Excavations have, however, shown an urban structure typical of Roman town planning, with the Forum at the centre, crossed by the Cardo and Decumanus. Close by is the Temple, built under Tiberius and dedicated to Rome and Augustus. The Basilica, used for the administration of justice, and the Curia, normally used for council meetings (although Ostia's was probably used as a temple) were constructed at the beginning of the second century when Hadrian was responsible for building the Capitolium. This was the largest temple in the city, with impressive Corinthian columns, dedicated to Jupiter, Juno and Minerva. There were also many cult buildings, dedicated to the different divinities located around the town.

Nowadays Ostia is actually eight kilometres from the shoreline as major silting of the Tiber estuary took place between the Middle Ages and the nineteenth century.

Carved stone sarcophagus from Ostia.

Tiberius

The ultimate death blow to the Republic was Augustus' longevity. He ruled Rome for more than forty years, during which time his autocracy was accepted as the norm and the days of Republican control gradually slipped from the living memory of most Romans.

Augustus' succession

Despite, or perhaps because of, his long reign, Augustus had gone as far as appointing a successor in his stepson Tiberius. Tiberius had not been the first choice of heir; Augustus had earlier chosen to adopt his grandsons. However, his longevity meant that he outlived several of these potential heirs, and it was Tiberius who ended up in pole position at the end of Augustus' reign.

Accusations have been made with regard to Augustus' wife, Livia Drusilla. It has been suggested that she had a number of rival heirs disposed of so that her son, Tiberius, would inherit. Tiberius had shored up his position by marrying Augustus' widowed daughter, Julia, after the death of her first husband, Agrippa.

The reclusive Emperor

Tiberius had large shoes to fill, and although he did a competent job, he is seen as a rather lacklustre emperor. He did not like public life and had a history of reclusive behaviour; before he became heir apparent he had secluded himself on the island of Rhodes and even as Emperor, after 26 AD, he retreated from Rome to live the rest of his days on the island of Capri.

With the Emperor out of the city, the ambitious head of the Praetorian Guard, Lucius Aelius Sejanus, tried to gain power for himself. Early in Tiberius' reign, Sejanus had convinced him to build a large camp to concentrate all the Praetorian Guard in one location, which was, in part, a ruse to allow Sejanus to secure his own power base. He spent the 20s purging Rome of his personal opponents, and is even the chief suspect in the murder of Tiberius' son, Drusus in 23.

Bust of Tiberius, a largely unpopular Emperor who spent much of his reign away from Rome, secluded on the island of Capri.

Tiberius acts to secure his position

Sejanus was becoming so powerful that he began to worry the Emperor, who became convinced of a conspiracy against him. Tiberius secretly replaced Sejanus as head of the Praetorian Guard with Naevius Sutorius Macro, who assisted the Emperor in organizing the execution of Sejanus in 31 AD. What followed was a plethora of treason trials, which amounted to more than just a purge of Sejanus' allies.

After the relative calm of Augustus' rule, Tiberius was beginning to return to the terrifying political tactics of the late Republic, hinting at the brutal despotism that would plague Rome in the not too distant future.

Family intrigue

Another intrigue that plagued Tiberius' reign was that of the family of his adopted son, Nero Claudius Germanicus. Germanicus was the son of Tiberius' older brother who had died relatively young. When Augustus had adopted Tiberius, he instructed that Tiberius in turn must adopt Germanicus.

Germanicus was quite different in character to Tiberius; he was exceptionally popular, brave and handsome. He was a successful general, and in 16, restored the Roman frontier in Germany at the River Elbe, earning him the name Germanicus. The border had been catastrophically lost in the Battle of Teutoburg Forest in 9 AD, where almost three legions were completely wiped out. Germanicus' success in 16 was seen as glorious retribution for Rome's humiliating defeat, making him ever more popular with ordinary Romans, such that calls for him to replace Tiberius as Emperor began to emerge.

Mysterious death of Germanicus

In 18 he was transferred to Asia, where he died under mysterious circumstances that led many Romans to believe in a conspiracy theory that Tiberius had murdered his adopted son.

Germanicus' widow, Agrippina the Elder, allowed this conspiracy theory to blossom across Rome, seriously damaging Tiberius' reputation. When she returned from Asia to Rome, she proved more of a nuisance to the Emperor by joining a group of senators opposed to both Sejanus and Tiberius.

Tiberius as tyrant

The Emperor eventually had Agrippina exiled from Rome, together with her two eldest sons. The three of them died in exile, probably through suicide, but many Romans chose to believe Tiberius had murdered them.

The fate of the popular Germanicus and his family, combined with treason trials and his lengthy absence from Rome, did little to endear ordinary Romans to their Emperor with the result that Tiberius is remembered as a tyrant.

***Right:** Arch of Germanicus. This triumphal arch in the French town of Saintes was built at the entrance to a bridge where the main Roman road crossed the Charente. The arch was moved and rebuilt on its present site in the nineteenth century when the old Roman bridge was demolished.*

Caligula

Agrippina's youngest son and three daughters were deemed less of a threat to Tiberius and they escaped death by being sent to live with their grandmothers. After 31 AD, the only surviving boy, Gaius Germanicus (Caligula), was then taken to live with his adoptive grandfather, the Emperor, on Capri.

'Little Boot'

Caligula got his nickname, meaning 'little boot' from his father's soldiers during the German campaign of 16 A D. He was so called because his mother used to dress the boy in a little soldier's outfit, complete with little boots.

On Capri, the boy was reared as an heir, but faced competition from Tiberius' biological grandson, Tiberius Gemellus. Gemellus was the son of Drusus, who had been murdered by Sejanus. Gemellus' mother was also dead, having been implicated in the plot to kill his father and executed. Like his orphaned cousin, the parentless Gemellus was also raised on Capri as a potential heir.

Caligula becomes Emperor

When Tiberius died in 37 AD, he did not choose between them and appointed both as his heirs. However, any uncertainty was swiftly overcome by Naevius Sutorius Macro who had become powerful since helping Tiberius defeat Sejanus. He found in favour of Caligula, whom he believed would better suit his own career plan. Caligula duly became Emperor in 37, but Macro had made a mistake; a paranoid Caligula later had both him and Gemellus murdered.

Initially, for the Romans, who had tired of Tiberius' absentee rule and treason trials, Caligula had shown promise. His popularity was assured as a member of the admired and much-pitied Germanicus family and he was able to bask in the reflected glory of his father's military success. He was welcomed to Rome by citizens yearning for change and initially he did not disappoint; he reduced taxes, he offered amnesty for political prisoners and put on grandiose public events.

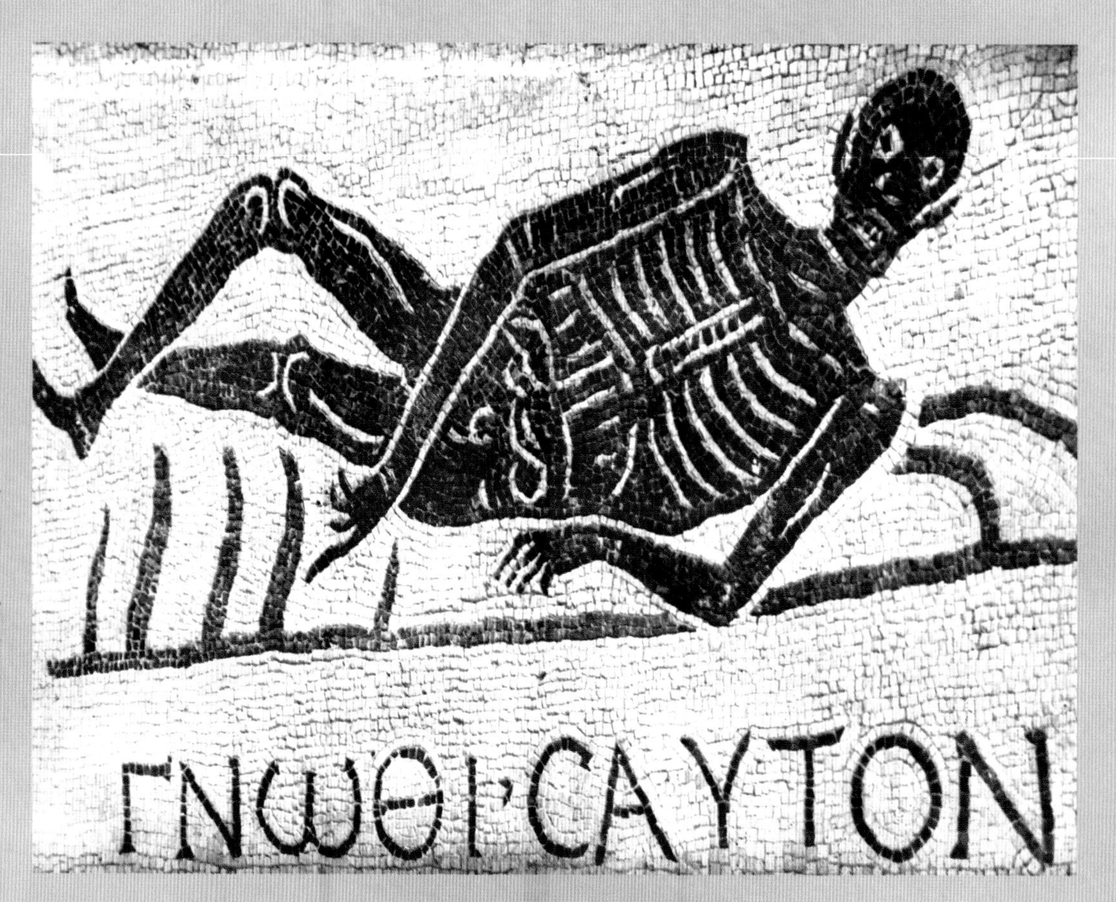

Right: Mosaic depicting death as a skeleton with scythe, from the floor of a Pompeian villa. The motto reads 'know thyself'.

Opposite below: Sculpture bust of Caligula. After contracting a mental illness, Caligula became a cruel and capricious Emperor, prone to humiliating his Senators, and proclaiming himself to be a living god.

Reign of Terror

However, that was all set to change by the end of the first year of his reign when Caligula contracted a mental illness. After this time, Caligula became a depraved and capricious Emperor who exacted a heinous reign of terror against his people. He famously remarked, 'Let them hate me, so long as they fear me', and he kept to his word.

He shunned Augustan frugality in favour of lavish spending, which meant he was always short on money. To compensate he insisted that all wealthy Romans had to appoint him as their heir and then ordered them killed to get his hands on their fortune faster. When this did not cover his expenditure, he placed the burden on ordinary Romans by raising taxes on absolutely everything.

Caligula was a megalomaniac; he believed that he was a living god and had a total disregard for the rule of law. He intimidated and humiliated people for his own amusement. His senators suffered his whims the most, for they were arbitrarily ordered to commit suicide or run alongside his chariot and their wives were even forced into prostitution.

The Arch dedicated to the Emperor Caligula in Pompeii.

However, the plebs did not escape; it was rumoured that whenever there were insufficient prisoners to fight lions in an arena, he would arbitrarily throw spectators in to make up the numbers, and was not averse to beating ordinary Romans who had mildly irritated him.

Of all his crazed acts, the one most remembered is that he made his horse a senator, and even tried to get the Senate to grant it a consulship.

Assassination of Caligula

Caligula's outrageous behaviour left severe discontent brewing beneath the surface. A conspiracy to murder the Emperor was swiftly underway and found a willing and able executioner in Cassius Chaerea, the commander of the Praetorian Guard. Cassius had been a colleague of Caligula's father Germanicus, but Caligula saw this as no reason to show respect. Instead, Caligula always mocked and degraded Cassius by insinuating that he was a eunuch. As head of the Praetorian Guard Cassius was an ideal candidate because he could get up close to Caligula. In 41 AD, at his wits' end, Cassius, in league with the conspirators, assassinated Caligula and his entire family.

Family Life

Romans lived in a patriarchal society and this was reflected in family life, where the father's word was final. During the early Republic his power was absolute, but over time, such supremacy was eroded, as social values shifted and women and children began to gain greater independence.

Patriarchal power

The male head of the household, the *paterfamilias* or 'father of the family', wielded absolute power over every person in his house. Such control was called *patria potesta*, or 'paternal authority', and gave him supreme control over his wife, children, slaves, extended family and anyone who lived in his home. Several generations of one family often lived under one roof, which meant that even adult sons were legally accountable to the *paterfamilias*. However, in practice, sons were usually given more freedom, especially in patrician families, where they were expected to make their way in politics or the army.

Patria potesta gave a father extreme powers; he could sentence any member of his household to death, sell them into slavery, or expel them from the family. The control of the *paterfamilias* was greatest in the early Republic, as over time legislation was introduced to curb his powers. For example, one of the laws of the 'twelve tables' drawn up in 449 BC, gave a son freedom from his *paterfamilias* if he had been sold into slavery three or more times. These excessive powers were probably used sparingly, but the father certainly meddled in the business of the members of his household.

Below: Interior of a villa at Ostia. Several generations of a family would live in one house, under the authority of the paterfamilias.

Opposite below: Wind instruments from Pompeii. While Rome had a wealth of entertainment, families would also have entertained themselves at home.

Opposite above: Strongbox. Roman households would keep their money and valuables in the home.

Changes in paternal authority

During the late Republic, the power of the *paterfamilias* was weakened in practice as Rome became wealthier and the stricter social norms of the early Republic began to break down. Many men tried to react against the demise of their traditional authority, especially Cato the Elder, but nevertheless, changes were afoot, as women gained more independence and children were slightly freer to choose whom they would marry. Such social transformations were more true of the upper classes; the authority of the *paterfamilias* remained relatively strong among ordinary Romans.

When Augustus came to the throne, he emphasized a return to the old-fashioned family values and the control of the *paterfamilias*, but never to the extent he had enjoyed in the early Republic. Augustus once again insisted that the head of the household should have a say in whom his children married, but he ought to have a very good reason to forbid a union.

Marriage as a business arrangement

Marriage amongst the patrician families of Ancient Rome amounted to more of a business arrangement than a love match. Political and economic alliances were sealed through marriage, which was considered a gesture of goodwill. Pompey married Julia, the daughter of Julius Caesar to seal the Triumvirate – the fact that she was besotted by him was simply an added bonus. When Julia died in childbirth, the union between the two men quickly broke down.

Women were usually married between the ages of twelve and fifteen to men who were older than them. They were transferred straight from the authority of their father to their husband, but gained a greater degree of independence in the late Republic.

Wedding rituals

The wedding ceremony commenced when a priest sacrificed an animal and read its insides to see whether the gods approved of the union.

The day before, the bride would have sacrificed all her childhood possessions to the household gods and her *paterfamilias* would have provided a dowry for the groom.

Weddings usually took place in the atrium of the bride's house, where the betrothed couple would have to join hands in front of witnesses and the groom would present the bride with an engagement ring for the third finger of the left hand. A marriage contract was also signed, highlighting how the Ancient Romans looked upon the institution.

After the ceremony, a procession would make its way from the bride's house to the groom's house, where the groom would carry his wife over the threshold of her new home. The festivities would continue and were known to go on for several days.

In the early Republic, intermarriage between patricians and plebeians was strictly forbidden. However, as the plebeians fought for more rights, they were eventually entitled to legally marry members of the patrician class, but any offspring would adopt the social status of the father. Similarly, if a Roman citizen married a non-citizen, the citizenship rights of the children depended strictly upon the father.

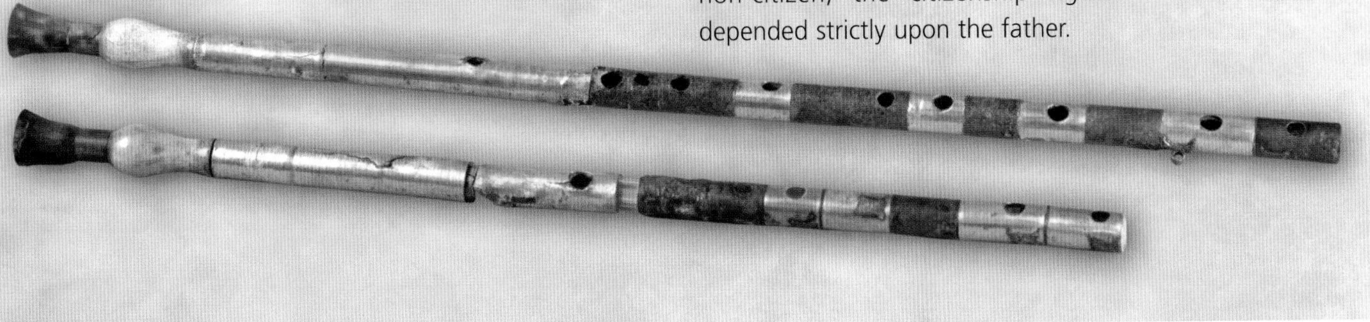

Divorce

In the early days of the Republic a husband could divorce his wife without providing just cause. In the mid-Republic, husbands were expected to give greater justification, but it was still relatively easy for them. If a husband decided to divorce his wife, he would have to return her and her dowry to her former *paterfamilias*.

During the reign of Augustus, the husband no longer had to issue grounds for a divorce, but by this time, the wife could also break with her husband. These changes came about because it was expedient for the Emperor to introduce them; he wished to marry Livia Drusilla, who was married and pregnant by another man. In spite of Augustus' increased toleration, women were made to feel greater consequences of a divorce; they could not expect the return of a complete dowry and unfaithful wives were forbidden from remarrying.

Above: Detail of a fresco painting from the Oplonti Villa, depicting a birdbath and foliage.

Children need to be accepted

Soon after the birth of a child, the *paterfamilias* had to officially welcome the baby into the family by taking it into his arms. If he refused then the child had to be disposed of; a slave would leave the baby on the roadside, where it would die of exposure. It is unknown how prevalent such infanticide was, but it was commonly practised with disabled children.

Given the high infant mortality rate, it is unlikely that many healthy children would have been killed, but if a poor Roman household had too many mouths to feed, they may have been faced with little option but to reject the baby.

If the baby was accepted, the birth was celebrated for eight days with feasts, prayers and visits to the temple. Over the course of the celebrations, the baby would be given a name and presented with a lucky charm to ward off evil spirits during its childhood. The Ancient Romans suffered from an incredibly high infant mortality rate, which meant that couples had as many children as possible to increase the likelihood of one or more surviving.

At the age of seven most children were sent for some form of elementary schooling, but before that much time would be spent in the home. During these formative years, Roman children would enjoy a variety of pastimes, such as leapfrog, hopscotch, seesaw and hide and seek, which still give pleasure to children today. The toys of Roman children also resemble modern toys: miniature carts, hoops, board games, balls and rag dolls made from papyrus; all seem to have been popular.

Coming of age

A Roman boy came of age at fourteen and was recognized as a citizen in his own right. The boy would have had considerable practice at adulthood before the age of fourteen, because fathers were expected to take their young sons under their wing and show them how to behave and how to operate in the family business.

To mark his passing in to adulthood, the boy would sacrifice his childhood lucky charm and don the toga of an adult male. He would then march toward the forum to add his name to the list of citizens and visit the temple. On the march, he would be accompanied by all the available adult males his family knew, to give the impression that the boy was strong and supported. The celebrations would continue into the evening, when a large banquet would be held to mark the occasion.

The client system

A wealthy Roman male usually had a wide network of clients, for whom he also had acted as their patron. This was an additional family of sorts, based on loyalty rather than blood and was a fundamental social relationship, especially during the Republic. It was a mutually beneficial arrangement; a patron could command loyalty, while a client would be rewarded with food and money for his support.

Each morning, before starting the workday, a client would put on his finest clothes and go to his patron's home to salute him in the atrium of the house. In exchange for his troubles, the client would be given food and money for the day.

There were also longer-term benefits to be had by clients; patrons would ensure that he and his family received a proper burial, legal aid and financial help from destitution. This, in part, made the client system a social welfare network, whereby a wealthy private citizen would provide the services that most governments supply publicly today.

Mutually beneficial

However, the motivations were not necessarily altruistic; for his part, a patron received a good deal of support in exchange for his patronage. Clients provided a ready and loyal support base in case a patron decided to run for office or was undertaking a military campaign. The patron could mobilize his clients to go onto the streets and support him for whatever purpose he required.

Often patrons would be the clients of an even wealthier man themselves, which meant that in the event of civil war, Rome could be quite quickly polarized along the lines of the client system; the would-be ruler could count on the support of not just of his client, but of his client's clients as well.

The bond between a client and patron was not broken upon the death of either man because his heir was expected to continue the link. This meant that the client system endured for centuries and a wealthy family could retain their status in society for many generations.

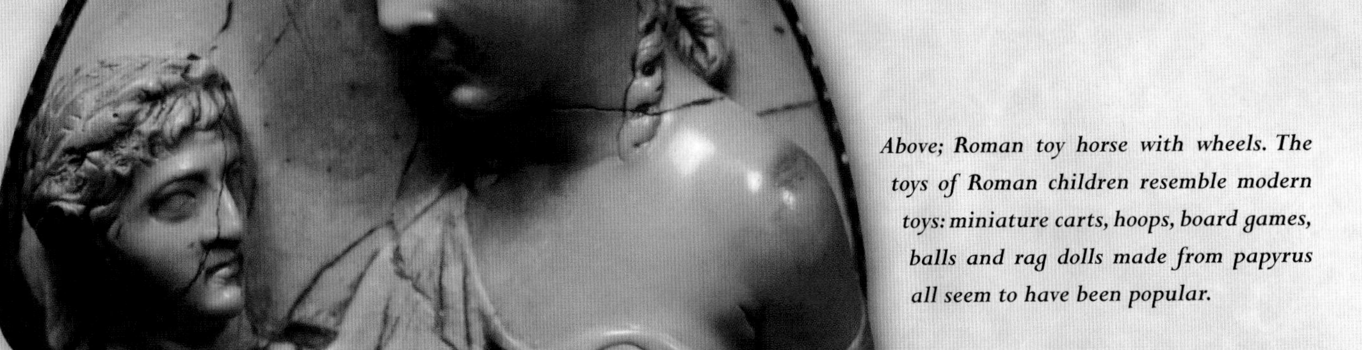

Above; Roman toy horse with wheels. The toys of Roman children resemble modern toys: miniature carts, hoops, board games, balls and rag dolls made from papyrus all seem to have been popular.

Left: Imperial cameo of Livia, wife of Augustus and her son, Tiberius.

Death Rites

The ruins of a Roman necropolis at Carmona, Spain.

Death was a commonplace occurrence in Ancient Rome: infant mortality was high; contracting illnesses and diseases that are considered easily treatable today could result in death; and for women, death in childbirth was not unusual. Thus, the fear being unmourned was probably greater than the fear of death itself.

Family duties

It was considered imperative to give the dead a proper send-off. Families had a duty to organise at the very least decent funeral for the deceased. Trades and craftsmen, as well as soldiers, could pay into a group fund which would provide for a fitting funeral when they died.

Preparing the body

Professional undertakers would prepare the funeral, which began with the dead body being washed and covered in oil. In some cases embalming was also part of the preparation. The deceased was then dressed in what had been, in life, their finest clothes, and a coin was placed under the tongue as a payment for Charon, the ferryman, who took souls across the River Styx into the underworld.

After the body had been prepared it was put on display for people to come and pay their last respects; if the person was particularly popular or high-ranking, the body could lie on display for a number of days.

Once everyone had paid their respects, a funeral procession made its way to the burial site, with family, friends, clients and even hired mourners in tow.

Roman law forbade the burial of bodies or cremated remains anywhere within the city limits. Thus the procession has to make its way beyond the city walls. As the funeral party could not wander too far through the countryside, most people were buried alongside the major roads out of the city.

A collection of Roman tomb artefacts. Roman bodies would be buried or entombed with artefacts for use in the next life.

Cremation and inhumation

Roman funeral practices changed throughout the long span of Ancient Rome. During the Republic, most bodies were buried. At the burial site the body would be inhumed, sometimes simply wrapped in a shroud, but wealthier people could afford a coffin made from wood, lead or stone. The deceased would be buried with objects for the afterlife; these could be marks of offices held during life, or personal items such as mirrors, jewellery or jars of food, drink or perfumes.

During the Empire period, for reasons of health and space, cremation became the norm. The objects for the deceased present at an inhumation were also part of the cremation ceremony and would be burned with the body. The ashes were placed in a container fashioned from a range of materials, some of which were made specifically for this function, but some of which seem to have been made for other purposes. The vessel containing the ashes was then buried.

A Roman mummy portrait from the Fayyum, Egypt, shows a woman with dark wavy hair wearing gold earrings and necklace set with gems and a gold fillet.

Grave markers

Many graves were marked by some sort of tombstone. A few, made from stone have survived. There are some that are inscribed with names of the dead, others with bas-reliefs which may indicate aspects of the person's life.

Fayyum mummy portraits

A collection of interesting grave goods is the mummy portraits from Fayyum. These are a large number of paintings on wooden panels, each of which depicts the face of the deceased on whose mummy it is laid.

Produced in Egypt between the first and the third centuries AD, when Egypt was a Roman province, the naturalistic paintings show, in vivid detail, the fashions and styles of the time.

Christian burial

Burial once again became popular in the late Empire with the advent of Christianity and the belief that the body had to be preserved for the afterlife.

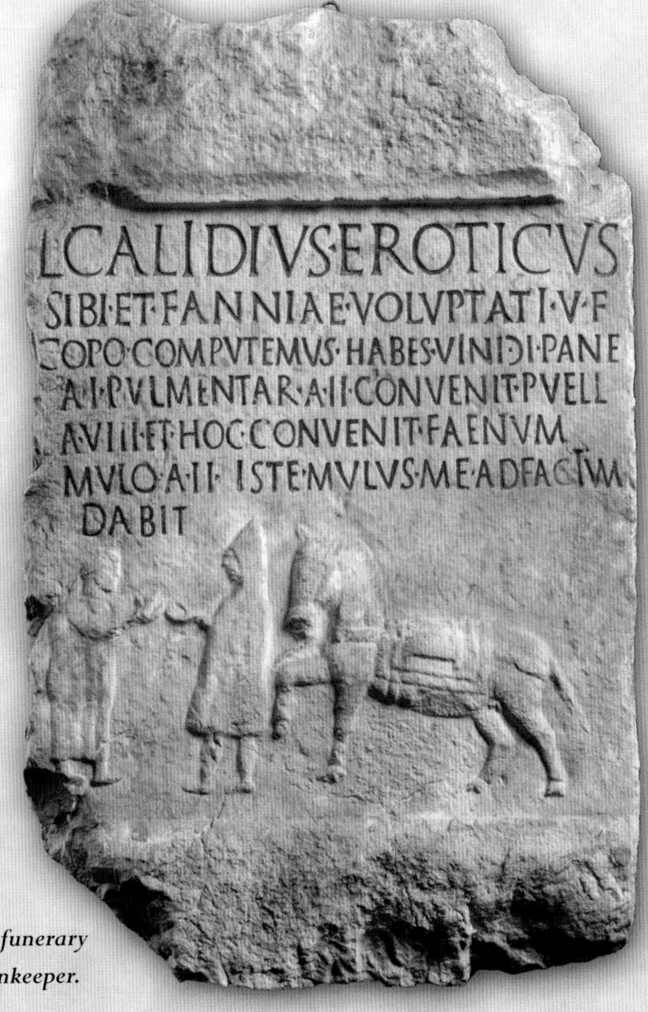

Found near Isernia, this funerary stele is a memorial to an innkeeper.

Claudius

Caligula's rule highlighted the inherent pitfalls of imperial rule; namely that too much depended upon the character of the Emperor himself. The system may have seemed to work under Augustus, but his successes resulted from his moderate nature and the system offered no safeguards against tyrannical rulers like Caligula.

Praetorian Guard maintain control

Such drawbacks were not overlooked by the Senate, who hoped that Caligula's assassination might result in the restoration of the Republic. However, this proved to be wishful thinking; the Praetorian Guard was unwilling to let this happen because its own power was tied to continuation of imperial control.

The Guard opted to replace Caligula with another Emperor, but one who they thought could be moulded as they saw fit. This next Emperor, Tiberius Claudius Drusus, was found quivering behind a curtain in the royal household when the Guard went about their purge of the royal family following Caligula's murder.

Related to Augustus

Claudius was well connected to the Emperors; he was Augustus' step-grandson, Caligula's uncle and the brother of Germanicus. The circumstances of his accession to the throne meant that he was never adopted into the Julian family and remained a member of the closely related Claudian family. During his reign, Claudius did try to shore up his links with the Julian family by pushing the idea that his father was the biological son, and not simply the stepson, of Augustus. He furthered this link during his reign by taking up Julius Caesar's unfinished business and successfully invading Britain.

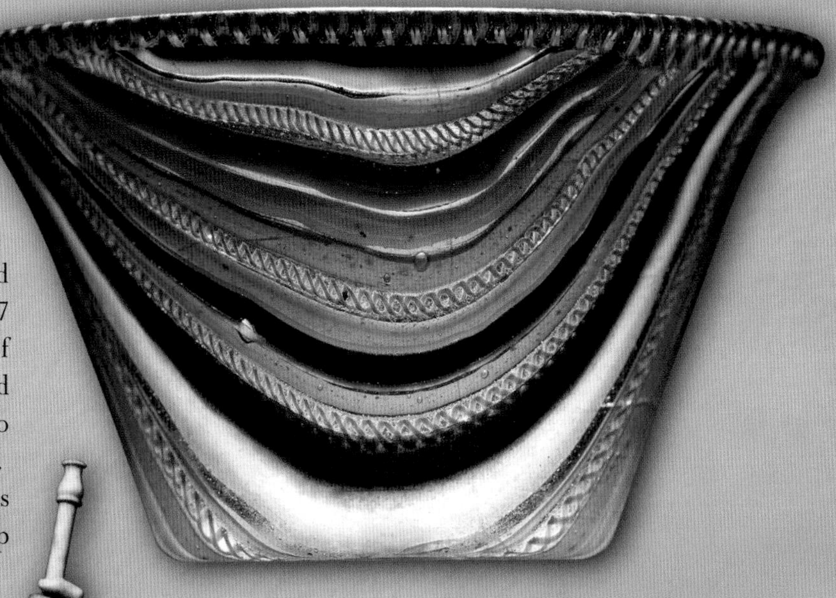

Claudius the historian

Claudius was always considered to be a peripheral member of the imperial family, who was not expected to amount to very much. Although he was clever and became a budding historian, the imperial family kept him out of public office and prohibited him from fulfilling his potential. Caligula had brought him to the fore by giving him a consulship in 37 AD, but this was simply because he was the brother of Germanicus and was no indication that Claudius had finally gained respect. On the contrary, Caligula loved to torment his uncle and make public jokes at his expense.

The imperial family's marginalization of Claudius was a key to his survival because he had managed to slip under the radar and escape not only Caligula's paranoia but the subsequent purge against the imperial family.

Return of the rule of law

It thus came as a surprise to many Romans that Claudius became an efficient emperor. He oversaw a return of the rule of law and peace to Rome after Caligula's excesses and Tiberius' treason trials.

Two famines struck Rome during Claudius' rule, which encouraged him to construct a new harbour at Portus, near Ostia and to embark upon agrarian reform.

Domestically, Claudius is best known for his bureaucratic reforms; he reduced the burden of responsibility on the principate by establishing an imperial civil service. This was placed in the hands of Claudius' freedmen (emancipated slaves), especially Polybius, Narcissus, Calistus and Pallas, who each amassed a great deal of power and wealth for themselves. Claudius had been careful not to antagonize the Senate but they were shocked and appalled by the power wielded by these freed slaves. This led to several attempts on Claudius' life, none of which was successful.

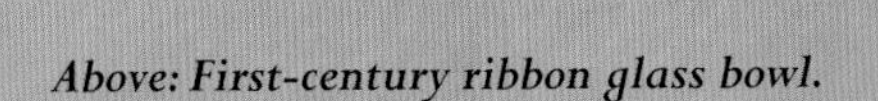

Above: First-century ribbon glass bowl.

Left: Sculpture of Claudius and Eagle.

Opposite: As a result of two famines during his reign, Claudius organized the construction of a new harbour at Portus, close to Ostia. The port of Ostia is well-preserved and the ruins are open to visitors.

Invasion of Britain

To the Romans, Britain was a mysterious, distant land; it was detached from the known landmass and sat in the great ocean that was believed to surround the world. Rome's first foray onto this remote island was in 55 BC under the leadership of Julius Caesar, but it was not until almost one century later that the Romans established a more permanent presence.

Caesar invades

During his mission to pacify Gaul, Julius Caesar led two preliminary expeditions to Britain, firstly in 55 and then in 54 BC. Ostensibly, the objective of the first raid was to remove a potential supply route from Britain to his Gallic enemies; however, it is highly likely that winning respect and esteem in Rome for being the first general to reach the far-off land would also have been at the forefront of Caesar's decision. The invasion was certainly well received in Rome, where the Senate announced a number of celebrations to mark the occasion.

Caesar invaded the island late in the campaign season and over-extended supply lines, combined with bad weather forced him to return to Gaul. During the first invasion he had met with resistance from the native tribes so he resolved to return the following year with a larger army to cow the Britons into submission.

Bronze statue of the Emperor Trajan which stands at the site of the London Wall.

Economic potential

During this second invasion he was able to weigh up the economic potential of the islands and scout out potential allies. He established a peace settlement with British tribes and took tributes, but was recalled to Gaul to deal with the uprising by Vercingetorix.

With difficult supply lines and the deepening crisis in Gaul, Caesar resolved to take all his soldiers back to the continent with him, leaving no one behind to consolidate Rome's gains; on this occasion, Britain was a step too far.

Collecting tribute

No Roman army returned to the British Isles for nearly a century. Nevertheless, Rome did maintain links with the islands, through trade and talks with its clients. Augustus had planned to return but had always been distracted by issues in other parts of the Empire, so it sufficed to collect tributes from Roman clients without the commitment that a full-scale invasion would warrant.

It is thought that a return was planned by Caligula, but he stopped short of this and simply ordered his men to pick seashells along the channel coast in order that he might win a war against Neptune, the god of the sea.

Close-up of a section of the Roman Wall constructed in the the second century AD around Londinium, London, which was by that period a strategically important port, offering trade with the rest of the Empire. The Wall was built from Kentish ragstone, shipped up the Thames from near Maidstone. Courses of red tiles were laid at regular intervals to increase its stability.

Full-scale conquest

It fell to Caligula's successor, Claudius, to pick up where Caesar had left off. Having come to power as a result of a coup led by the Praetorian Guard, and not being a member of the Julian family of the preceding Emperors, Claudius was in sore need of a military victory to shore up his tenuous authority. Britain seemed the perfect opportunity; not only would it be a prestigious asset to the Empire, but it also gave him a much-needed connection with Julius Caesar, who was the only Roman leader to have gone there before.

The first encounter

Claudius required a pretext to intervene on the island and this was provided when one of Rome's client kings, Verica of the Atrebates, arrived in Rome after fleeing from another British tribe, the Catuvellauni.

During the early 40s, the army of the Catuvellauni had been placed under the able command of its king's sons, Caractacus and Togodumnus. They succeeded in defeating the Atrebates, seizing their territory and consolidating control over southern England.

In 43 AD, Claudius responded to Verica's plight by dispatching four legions from Gesoriacum (Boulogne), in Gaul to Rutupiae (Richborough) in Kent, under the command of Aulus Plautius. The Catuvellauni presented a formidable challenge in Kent, but the Roman army pushed them back to the Thames, killing Togodumnus in the process.

Bastion at the Barbican, on the Roman Wall around London. There were around twenty such bastions on the wall and six fortified gateways which lead out onto Roman roads to other towns in Britain.

Claudius takes the credit

Once the Romans reached the Thames, they held position while Claudius caught up with them so he could join the final assault on the Catuvellauni capital at Camulodunum (Colchester). Claudius was not really there to lead the troops into battle, but rather to take credit for the victory, because by the time he caught up with his legions, (complete with his entourage of elephants), resistance from the Catuvellauni had largely been subdued.

Claudius and his legions marched unopposed into Camulodunum and established the city as their own capital. From there he received eleven tribes from the south and east of Britain, each of whom submitted to the Romans.

After spending more than two weeks in Camulodunum celebrating his victories, Claudius returned to Rome, leaving Plautius as governor in his stead.

The following year, in 44, the Romans pushed westward. A major thrust toward Isca Dumnoniorum (Exeter) in the south west of the island was led by Titus Flavius Vespasianus (Vespasian), who would later become Emperor. He was praised in Rome for winning a number of battles on his way and even captured Vectis (the Isle of Wight), off the south coast of England.

Castle Nick, a milecastle on Hadrian's Wall, built to defend the frontier. Milecastles were fortified gateways in the Wall which were built, as their name suggests, at Roman-mile intervals. They would have housed between twelve and thirty soldiers in what was quite basic accommodation.

Conquest of Wales

The push westward continued and the legions moved into Wales in 47, where they captured Caractacus, leader of the Catuvellauni, who had been proving a nuisance to them since his escape. Caractacus was treated extremely mercifully; he was exhibited in Rome for a time, before being allowed to retire into anonymity there.

By 60 AD the Romans had reached Mona (Anglesey), as the invasion of Wales continued into the reign of Nero. The Roman advance was only halted by rebellion among the Iceni tribes, which threatened the south-east and drew troops away from the west.

Iceni King's family treated with disrespect

Prasutagus, the king of the Iceni, a tribe from eastern Britain died in 60 AD. As a result of Prasutagus' submission to Claudius in 43, the Iceni had become allies of Rome.

Upon the death of King Prasutagus, the Romans took over the province and treated his family with the utmost disrespect: his daughters were raped, and his widow, Boudica, was flogged.

Boudica rises against Roman rule

While the governor at the time, Gaius Suetonius Paulinus was distracted in Anglesey, Boudica resolved to rise up against Roman rule and encouraged neighbouring tribes to follow her.

With the Roman army on the other side of the island, Boudica's forces marched on Camulodunum, followed by Londinium (London) and Verulamium (St Albans). All three cities were destroyed, and those who had not fled were brutally treated by the insurgents.

The rebels were such a menace that Nero even considered withdrawing the Romans from Britain altogether, but decided such a move would undermine the legacy of his adopted father, Claudius.

Romans regain control

Suetonius Paulinus marched his army back down Watling Street, the Roman road from Wales to Londinium, but decided he did not have sufficient forces to rescue Londinium or Verulamium from their fates. Instead, he regrouped his forces on Watling Street, somewhere in the Midlands, and lured the rebels onto the battlefield of his choice.

The numerically inferior Romans were protected to the rear by a forest and a gorge, which meant they could confront the rebels head-on, without fear of attack from behind. The result was that Rome won a decisive victory and completely wiped out men, women and children on the rebels' side.

Boudica decided to commit suicide to prevent being caught, and the Battle of Watling Street marked the last serious challenge against the Romans by the occupied tribes of the island.

A section of Hadrian's Wall.

Hadrian's Wall

Once the Iceni Revolt was crushed, the Romans conquered and occupied more and more of Britain in the following years.

Moving into Scotland

Under the governorship of Gnaeus Julius Agricola the Roman legions moved into Scotland. They took territory as far north as the Highlands, where they defeated the Caledonian tribes at the Battle of Mons Graupius in 83. However, the Romans were unable to consolidate their territorial gains and pulled back to forts further south. Agricola was recalled to Rome in 85 AD, leaving Britain to a series of weaker governors who gradually abandoned Scotland.

Antonine Wall

In 138, Antoninus Pius succeeded Hadrian as Emperor and endeavoured to penetrate beyond Hadrian's Wall. He moved into southern Scotland and erected his own 'Antonine Wall', 160 kilometres further north than Hadrian's Wall. The wall, stretching from the Firth of Forth to the Firth of Clyde, was started in 142 and only took two years to build.

However, the Romans had overextended themselves and the new frontier did not prove easy to defend. As a result, within just twenty years the Antonine Wall was abandoned, and the legions withdrew and the boundary of the Empire reverted to the safer frontier that Hadrian had established.

Hadrian visits

When Emperor Hadrian visited Britain in 122 AD he announced the construction of a 120-kilometre-long defensive wall between the Solway Firth on the west coast and the North Sea in the east. This was an attempt to consolidate the frontiers of the Empire and protect the northern most Roman province from attacks by the Scottish tribes. The construction of the wall took about ten years and was completed within Hadrian's lifetime.

Hadrian's Wall is still visible for much of its route across the rolling hills of northern England.

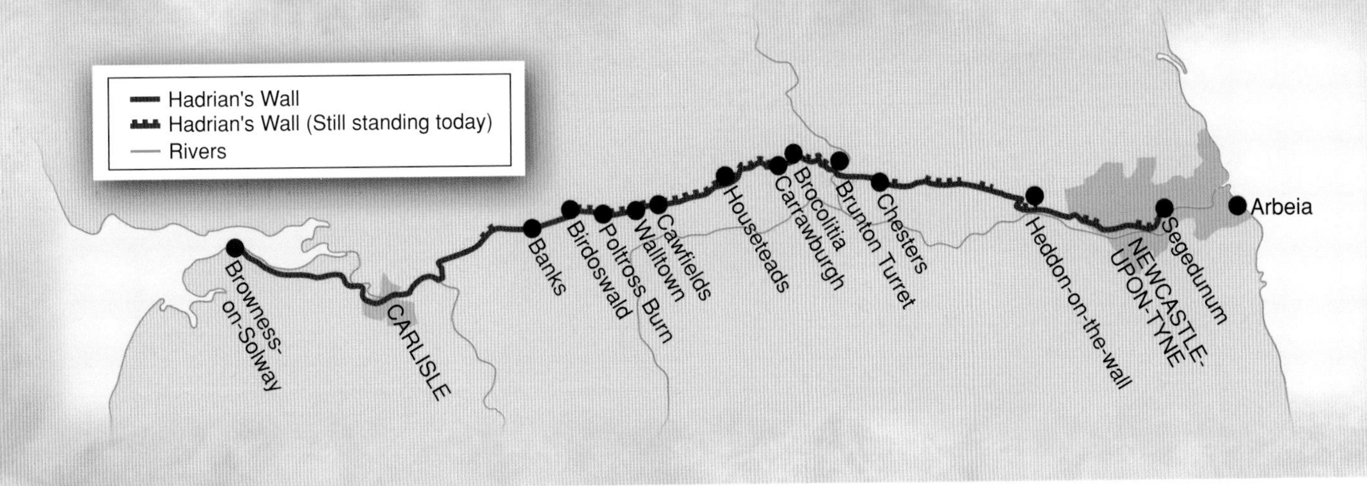

Roman Britain

The Romans left their mark on Britain in various ways; one was the development of several important urban centres, notably Londinium, which quickly overshadowed Camulodunum, and became the capital city of Britannia.

Londinium

The city is thought to have been favoured and first settled by the Romans because of its closeness to the Channel. This aided trade with the rest of the Empire.

In the third century AD, Roman Britain was divided into two separate administrative areas: Britannia Superior and Britannia Inferior. Londinium remained the capital of Britannia Superior, but it faced a rival in Eburacum (York) the capital of Britannia Inferior, which increasingly became the favourite British city of several Emperors.

This reproduction of a Roman fort at Vindolanda is constructed from images on artefacts found in the area.

Economic benefits to the Empire

Britain's main economic benefit to the Empire was in its mineral resources, including, tin, iron and even gold. It was also a ready source of hunting dogs and animal furs. Merchants from across the Empire are known to have come to Britain for the purposes of trade and commerce.

To further the economic development of the island and to move troops about with greater ease, the Romans constructed a network of roads. One of the most famous of these roads was Watling Street, which extended all the way from Durovernum (Canterbury) in Kent to Viroconium (Wroxeter) on the Welsh border, passing through the important towns of Londinium and Verulamium. Another road of importance was Ermine Street, which ran between the two capitals, Londinium and Eburacum.

A section of the remains of Vindolanda, which was one of the forts in the immediate hinterland of Hadrian's Wall. The fort at Vindolanda would have offered support troops and services for the frontier forts. A substantial civilian settlement, called a vicus, *grew up around the fort and, unusually, a lot of organic material from the fort and the* vicus *has been preserved.*

Christianity reaches Britain

Once Britain became part of the Empire, it was exposed to an assortment of new religions. People from across the Roman world brought these new faiths, and many of them acquired a degree of permanence.

Christianity must have come to Britain in a similar manner, but there is very little evidence of its existence until after Constantine legalized the religion in 313 AD. Within a year, a number of Christians had emerged, which suggests that Christianity had been on the island for some time, but that it was simply underground.

Latrine block at Housesteads, an auxiliary fort on Hadrian's Wall. The remains give an impression of what life was like here 1800 years ago. Seats would originally have run around the sides, with drains beneath. The sewage would probably have been used as a fertilizer.

First Christian martyr

The first account of a Christian martyr in Britain comes from the early fourth century, when Alban of Verulamium, in a gesture of kindness, hid a Christian priest from the authorities. During the priest's stay Alban was converted to the new faith; when the Romans arrived to arrest the priest, Alban took his place to allow the real priest to make an escape. Alban was executed by the Romans, but later canonized by the Christian church. His hometown, Verulamium, is now known as St Albans in his honour.

End of Roman rule

Towards the end of the fourth century, the Romans were finding it increasingly difficult to maintain control of Britain. 'Barbarians' were stretching Rome's resources by attacking frontiers throughout the Empire.

In 367, a blow was dealt to Roman rule by the 'barbarian conspiracy': the simultaneous attack on Roman Britain by Picts from Scotland, Scots from Ireland, and Saxons from Germany.

Over the following decades Roman rule was rapidly eroded and increasing numbers of troops were recalled to the continent. With their departure, economic links began to dry up.

In 410, the Emperor of the Western Empire, Honorius, instructed the Britons that they were responsible for their own defence and pulled out the last of his soldiers; Roman rule in Britain had ended.

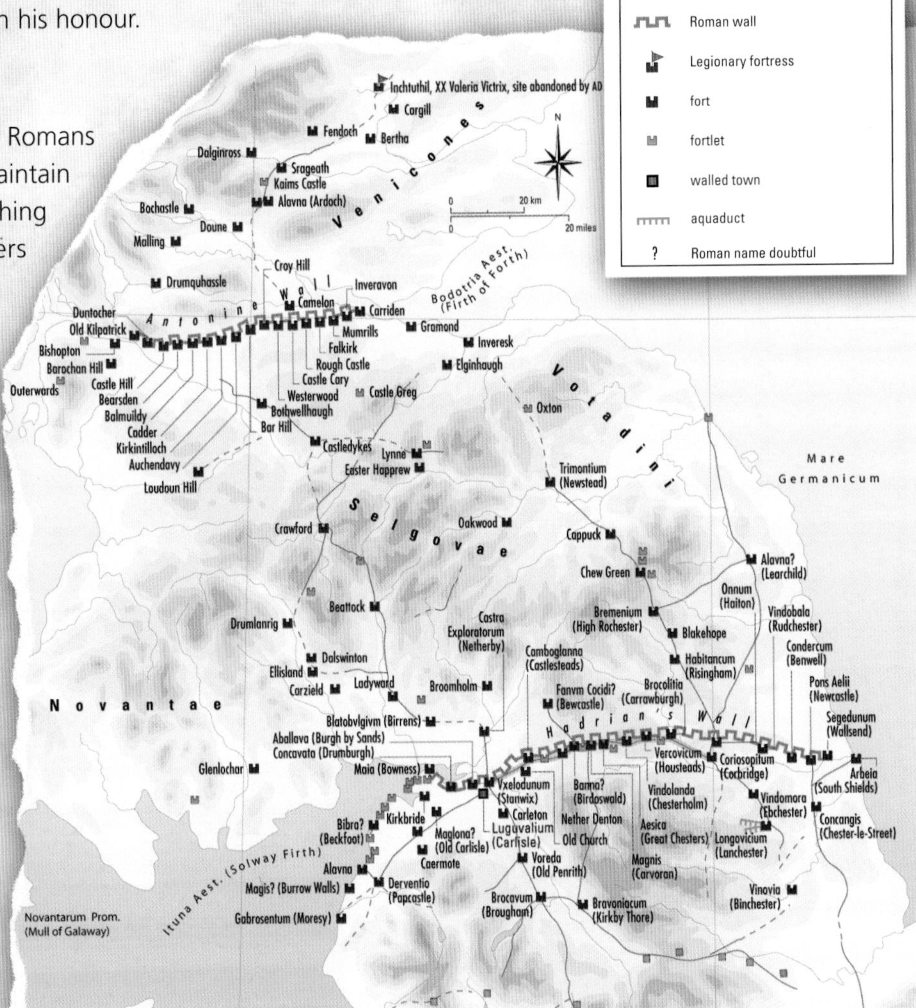

Nero

Claudius had intended that he be succeeded by his own son, Britannicus, but events conspired against him and Nero took the imperial crown.

Unlucky in marriage

Claudius married four times, but only two of his marriages coincided with his time as Emperor. His third wife, Messalina, was his first empress. She was a notorious woman – known to be unfaithful to Claudius on frequent occasions. In 48, a coup attempt, which she had orchestrated, was foiled by Claudius' freedmen and she was duly executed. However, Messalina had done Claudius one service; she had given him a direct male heir, Britannicus, who was born in 41 AD.

Agrippina the Younger

After Messalina's death, Claudius married his niece, Caligula's sister, Agrippina the Younger, who campaigned to have her own son, Lucius Domitius Ahenobarbus, named Emperor instead of Britannicus. Her machinations succeeded and Lucius was adopted by Claudius as his main heir and renamed Nero Claudius Caesar Drusus. Claudius thought this a prudent move in case he should die suddenly when Britannicus was too young to take power.

In 54, Britannicus neared the age of adulthood and Claudius was planning to replace Nero with Britannicus as heir, but he died before he could change his will. As a result, Nero became Emperor. It was widely speculated that Agrippina had arranged Claudius' murder in order to deny him the chance to change his will. This theory is not unreasonable; she certainly had the motive and the drive. With Nero as Emperor, she persistently meddled in imperial affairs and effectively made herself co-ruler with her son – her face even appeared alongside Nero's on coins at the time.

Right: Portrait bust of Nero.

Opposite above: Fresco showing a sleeping lunatic.

Opposite below: Cameo showing Claudius and his wife Agrippina, his brother Germanicus and his wife Agrippina the Elder.

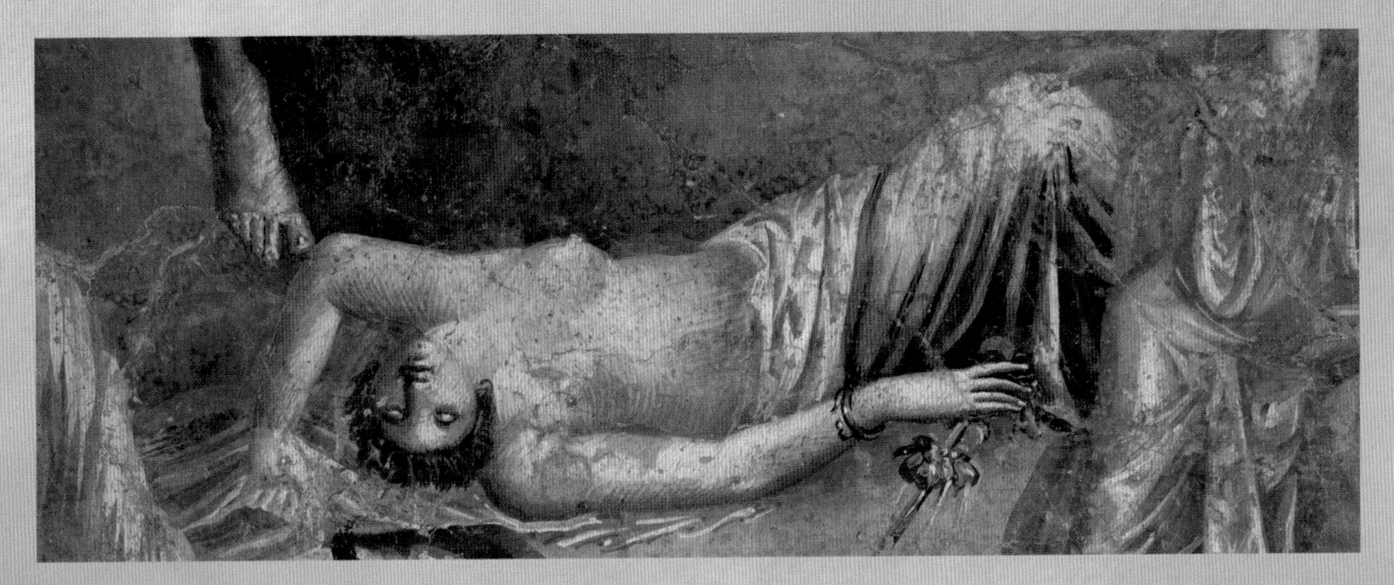

Nero and his overbearing mother

For the first five years Nero's reign was greatly influenced by others; besides his mother, his tutor, Seneca and the head of the Praetorian Guard, Burrus, had a good deal of influence. It is thought that it was these two men who encouraged Nero to dispose of his overbearing mother.

Initially Nero attempted to marginalize Agrippina, but this did not work and he realized he would have to kill her instead. He first determined a discreet method – he set her aboard a boat he knew not to be seaworthy in the hope she would drown. However, Agrippina did not prove to be such an easy target and she managed to swim to safety after the boat sank, leaving Nero with little choice but to deal with his mother directly.

Nero gains control

In 59 AD he ordered her murder and she was duly beaten to death. Seneca and Burrus thought they stood to gain from the removal of the domineering Agrippina, but the real winner was Nero, who no longer wished to share his power.

His opportunity for exclusive control came in 62, when Burrus died. As Praetorian Prefect, he posed the greatest threat to Nero's position and with him out of the picture, Nero moved against Seneca and reigned supreme from 62. Although Burrus' death might have been a stroke of luck for Nero, it was thought at the time that he might have poisoned the Praetorian Prefect.

Seneca was allowed to return to his writings but an increasingly paranoid Nero believed that Seneca was plotting to kill him. Without giving him a trial, Nero ordered Seneca to commit suicide in 65.

Nero the performer

It was Nero's love for entertainment that really defined his rule; he liked to stage great public events and even shocked Roman opinion by performing in many of them himself. He was an avid sportsman and participated in chariot races at a time when charioteers were slaves. He even entered numerous competitions and always won, but his victory was largely due to bribes and intimidation of the other competitors rather than his own sporting prowess.

His love of sports encouraged him to stage his own version of the Olympics, called the Neronia Games and to construct an artificial, salt-water lake in order to re-enact famous naval battles.

Nero also loved to act and often took to the stage for lengthy periods of time, forbidding any member of his audience to leave the room. The Roman historian Suetonius wrote that people used to pretend they were dead so they could be carried out before he had finished.

Violence and intimidation

Nero's childlike love for entertainment did not preclude him from acts of sheer cruelty. As his reign progressed he became increasingly poorer and resorted to violence and intimidation to replenish his treasury. He brought back the treason trials of Tiberius and, like Caligula, he found ways to get his hands on the inheritances of the rich.

He became deeply unpopular, not only because of his despicable treatment of his mother, but also his disregard for his wife, Octavia. Nero wished to marry another woman, named Poppaea, so connived to divorce his wife and banished her from Rome.

Octavia was the daughter of Claudius and was popular with the people of Rome, who were outraged at her exile. So great were the protests that Nero, at Poppaea's request, agreed to have his wife murdered.

One of the greatest criticisms of Nero was the Golden House he ordered be built; not only did it seem frivolous and greedy, but its construction was seen to profit from the land cleared by the Great Fire of Rome.

Revolts outside Rome

As people turned against Nero within Rome, the final blow was dealt from without. The Roman governor of Gaul, Gaius Julius Vindix, rose up in revolt against Nero's rule.

Nero was relatively unperturbed by the challenge, which he thought would be easy to overcome. However, he was not so confident when Servius Sulpicius Galba, his governor of Spain also rose up, allying himself with Vindix against Nero. Galba's insurrection encouraged more defection; two high-profile legates in control of the armies in North Africa and Lusitania joined him.

Nero loses support

As the list of his enemies grew, ever more of his allies in Rome began deserting Nero. The Senate even allied itself with Galba's forces and declared Nero an enemy of the people. Ordinary Romans began declaring support for the rebellion against him, largely because the grain supply to the city had began to dry up.

Forces loyal to Nero did manage to crush Vindix's rebellion in Gaul, but the death blow had already been dealt. Even the Praetorian Guard abandoned Nero, who could no longer hold on to power, even through the use of force.

With no allies left, Nero fled from the palace and had little option but to commit suicide. With his death, the great Julio-Claudian dynasty came to an end.

Above: Decorative fresco depicting an acrobatic entertainer.

Great Fire of Rome

In 64 AD a fire broke out near the Circus Maximus in Rome. It spread quickly because most Romans lived in tightly packed, flammable tenement buildings called *insulae*.

The fire raged for nine days and destroyed a large portion of the city. Although the exact proportion is unknown – estimates range from one tenth to as much as two thirds of the city – a large part of Rome was devastated by the fire. These figures do not indicate how many people lost their homes or livelihoods because the tenements were so densely populated.

The fire sparked rioting in the city from angry residents, many of whom blamed Nero for having ordered the fire for his own amusement. Others believed that if he had not started it, then he certainly relished it; 'Nero fiddled as Rome burned' became a popular saying. However, Nero was not in the city at the time so he could not have started the fire himself and he did not seem to delight in the fire and resolved, rather, to help the victims. Nero took it upon himself to rebuild Rome and ensure that the new buildings adhered to fire-safety regulations.

Nevertheless, the charges against Nero were not entirely untrue, because he was known to have seen a silver lining in all the destruction; the fire had cleared a space in central Rome for him to build a vast, ostentatious palace – the 'Golden House'. Regardless of the accuracy of the charges, the fact that Romans were so quick to blame Nero gives a good indication of how the public felt about their Emperor.

Nero was not sheltered from these criticisms and quickly found someone else to blame for the fire: the Christians. The Christians were a young sect that had originated in Judea during the reign of the Emperor Tiberius. They were peripheral in Rome at the time, but they were widely disliked by Romans and thus proved a useful scapegoat for the Emperor. Nero's punishment was state-sponsored persecution of all Christians, who were killed in an assortment of barbaric ways. However, he may have shifted the blame for the fire, but he still failed to endear himself with the Roman population.

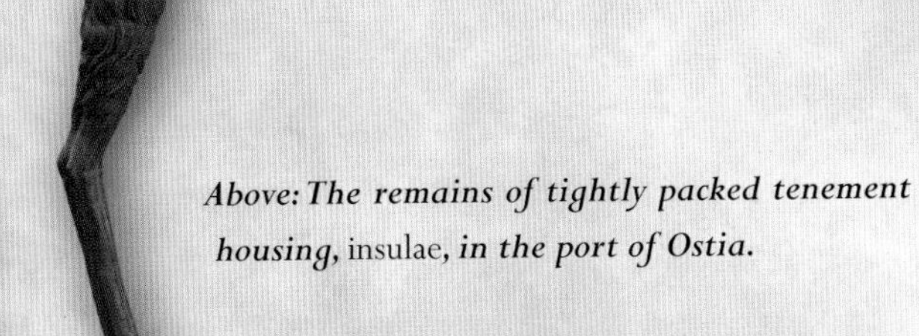

Above: The remains of tightly packed tenement housing, insulae, *in the port of Ostia.*

Left: Tripod for burning coal. While wealthy homeowners would have underfloor heating through a hypocaust, poorer Romans used open braziers which were a frequent source of house fires.

The Baths

As very few Roman houses had facilities for bathing, most cities, towns, settlements and even forts were equipped with a communal bathhouse. They served a dual purpose; the baths, or *thermae*, were not only a place to get clean but also a place to talk business or politics, to gossip and socialise, and also to relax.

Time to visit

For much of the Republic period, there was an entrance charge for attending the baths – later it became free. However, even when charged for it was relatively cheap. Children were admitted free and although women had to pay more than men, it was still within the reach of most citizens. Paying everybody's entry to the baths for a day was a way in which wealthy politicians would try to persuade people to vote for them.

Men and women did not bathe together, but visited at separate times, although some places had separate facilities. Women visited the baths in the morning and often took their children with them. Most Roman men only worked until the early afternoon. After work they would visit the baths, sometimes staying there until the close at sunset.

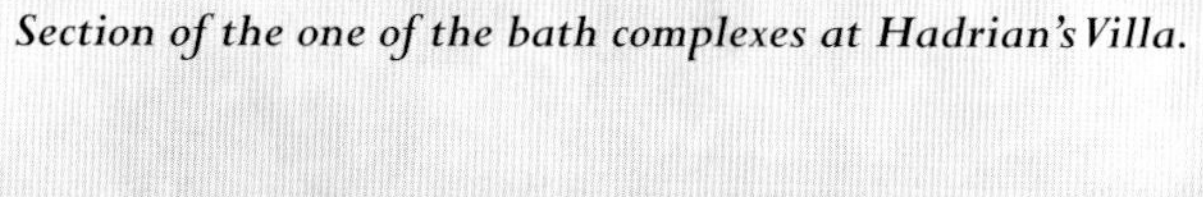

Section of the one of the bath complexes at Hadrian's Villa.

Working up a sweat

Although some people would go straight to the bathing pools, it was usual to take part in some form of exercise before bathing. There were spaces set aside for this – *palaestrae*. Men would wrestle, lift weights, engage in fencing and ballgames. Women would exercise with light weights and balls, or might play a game called *trochus* which used a hooked stick to roll along a metal hoop.

Bathing procedure

When ready for the baths the bather would go first into the *tepidarium*. This, as the name suggests, was a lukewarm room designed for relaxation. The bather would then progress to the *caldarium*, a hotter room, where oils were applied to the body. The oils were used as a cleansing agent – the Romans did not have soap. A metal tool called a strigil was then used to scrape off the oil and dirt; this was not an easy process and slaves were often employed to perform this procedure.

After the oil treatment, the bather would then dip in a hot pool in the *caldarium*, before proceeding to the cooler *frigidarium* for a plunge into a very cold pool.

Mosaic depicting a woman exercising with a ball. Women were able to attend the baths. They would usually visit at separate times from the men, although some complexes had separate areas for men and women. Both sexes would engage in some form of exercise before bathing.

Bas-relief of a gorgon's head.

After completing the bathing process the bather could finish off with a massage or, in some of the more luxurious bathhouses, a beauty treatment.

A growing pastime

During the Republic, bathhouses were relatively small, but during the Empire, a number of vast complexes were built at the expense of the Emperor or a wealthy citizen. General Marcus Vipsanius Agrippa, a friend and ally of the Emperor Augustus, built the first of these large public baths in 25 BC.

Baths of Caracalla

Other emperors followed suit, most notably Caracalla, whose baths, built between 212 and 219 AD could hold 1,600 people at a time. The Baths of Diocletian were even larger. Opened in 306, these baths are thought to have accommodated up to 3,000 bathers. Large parts of both these emperors' baths are either well-preserved or have been subsumed into later structures.

Throughout the Empire, huge bathing complexes were built throughout the Roman world. In the early second century Emperor Hadrian built an extravagant complex in the North African city of Leptis Magna which became, like many of these developments, the social hub of the city.

***Above:** Vestibule of the public baths at Herculaneum.*

Extensive facilities

The large bathing complexes that developed during the Empire period, were about more than just bathing, they provided a host of leisure facilities. They had gymnasiums where a visitor could take exercise, libraries for reading and writing, and food stalls to sit around and eat.

There were usually extensive and lavish gardens to walk around, and sometimes a theatre; the baths of Caracalla were so extensive that they even had a stadium.

As women could attend the baths for only a few hours each morning, it tended to be the men who enjoyed the luxuries of these complexes. After bathing, men often stayed into the evening. Here they would spend the time using the wide range of facilities on offer – maybe listening to a concert, playing board games with friends, reading or eating and drinking, perhaps discussing business.

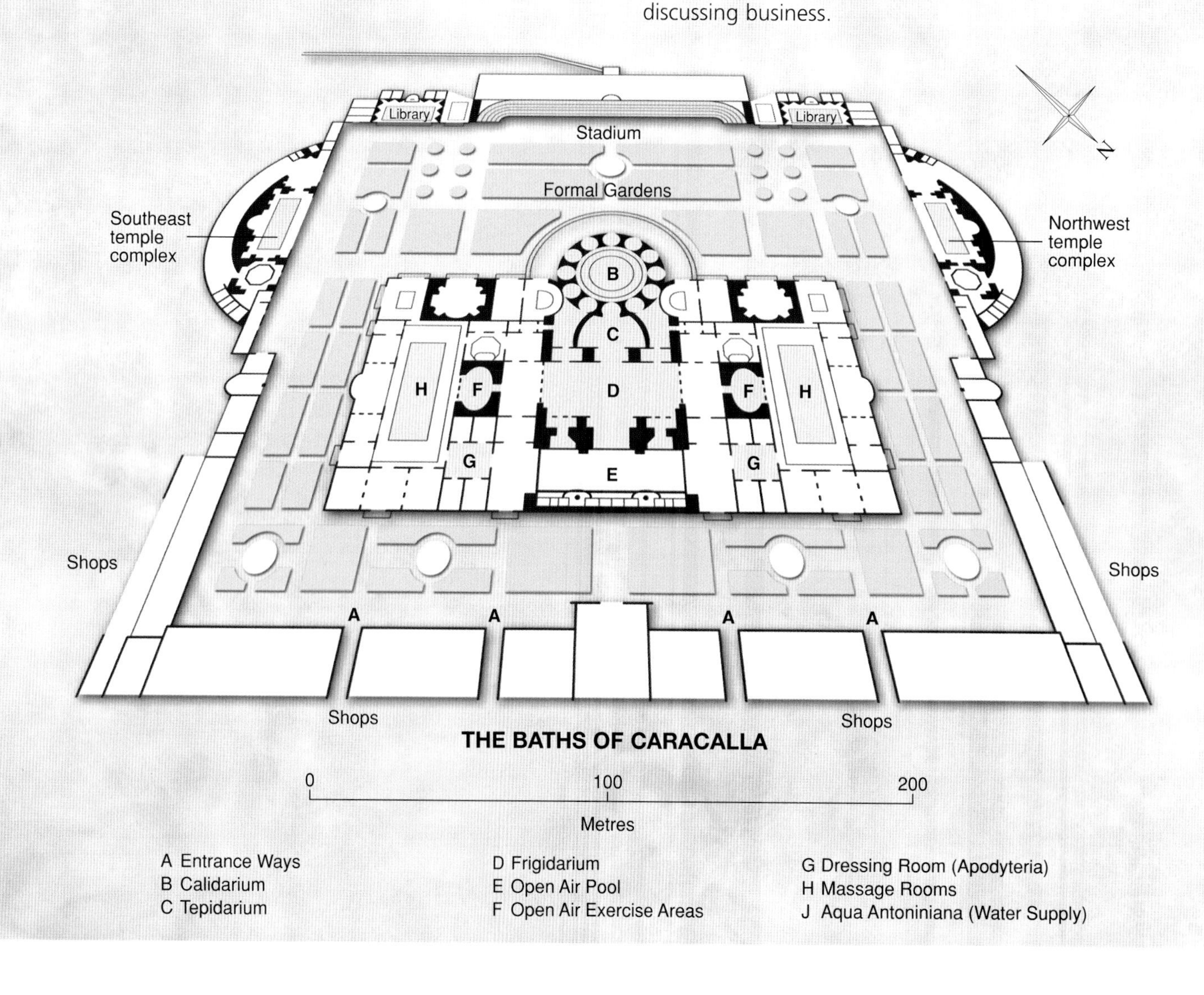

Ceiling fresco in the caldarium of the Oplonti Villa depicting a nude woman riding a scorpion-tailed bull.

Free baths

Before Agrippa built his baths, the citizens of Rome were served by a number of smaller bathhouses, which charged a small entrance fee. This meant that the rich could go every day, but the poorer Romans could visit less frequently.

Agrippa was the first to stop charging customers an entrance fee to visit his baths and all the large bathing complexes built subsequently followed his example and waived the admission fee.

However, the smaller bathhouses continued to charge entrance fees and were still patronised by the rich.

Heating the baths

The grandiose public baths needed a vast amount of water to function. Specially diverted or extended aqueducts were usually needed for the purpose.

Once the water had reached the baths, it was necessary to get each room to the right temperature. Using the unique Roman heating system of the *hypocaust*, it was possible to heat these vast areas, with their numerous different chambers.

Beneath the building an underground furnace called a *praefurnium* was kept alight by slaves, who worked under unbearably hot conditions. The floor of baths was raised on pillars, allowing the hot air created by the furnace to circulate underneath and heat the floor. Sometimes the floor got so hot that bathers were provided with wooden-soled shoes.

The *praefurnium* would also be used to heat the water for the bath in the *caldarium*. A similar system was used to heat Roman villas, albeit with a much smaller fire.

The frigidarium *in the Roman Baths in Bath, England. This bath complex is one of the best preserved buildings of its kind anywhere in the world.*

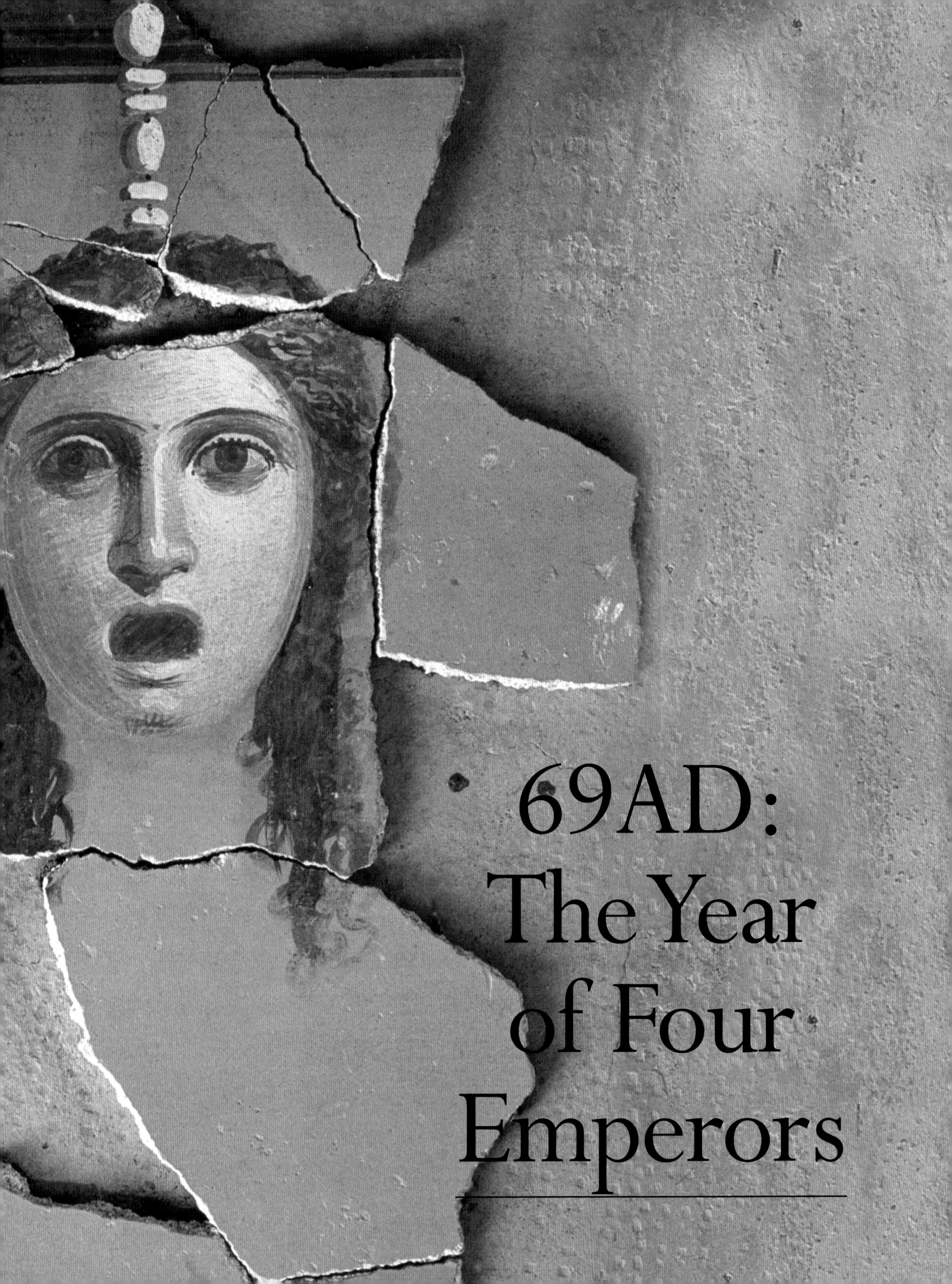
69AD:
The Year
of Four
Emperors

A return to turmoil

With Nero's death, power now lay with the Praetorian Guard and the Roman legions; whomsoever they favoured for the position of Emperor was likely to be given the role. This led to considerable uncertainty as a number of would-be Emperors tried the job out for size, so much so that, in the year 69 AD four different men served as Emperor.

Death of Nero

For all the drawbacks of the Julio-Claudian Emperors, they had provided Rome with a sense of stability that had been absent during the last century of the Roman Republic. The death of Nero may have been considered a blessing at the time, but it heralded the return to turmoil.

Nero had committed suicide, without leaving an obvious heir to the throne. The Praetorian Guard, the Senate and ordinary Romans were desperate to find a replacement so that the Empire did not revert to civil war.

Galba emerges as obvious candidate

With Servius Sulpicius Galba, the governor of Spain whose insurrection had heralded Nero's end, already marching on Rome to challenge the Emperor, he was considered the most obvious candidate. In June 68, when he heard that he was supported in

***Right:** Head of Mercury.*

***Main:** Detail of a fresco from the magnificent Oplonti Villa which belonged to Nero's wife Poppaea Sabina. Poppaea's second husband was Marcus Salvius Otho, but Poppaea left him to become Nero's mistress and then his wife. She died in 65 AD and when Nero committed suicide three years later, Otho was one of four men who, in quick and violent succession, took the imperial title.*

Rome, Galba changed his title from Governor to Caesar.

Although Galba was the most obvious candidate, he was not the only one and there were others in Rome who coveted the principate, including the head of the Praetorian Guard and Lucius Clodius Macer, a legate from North Africa who had originally risen up against Nero with Galba.

An insecure position

As the knowledge of rival contenders vying for his position combined with the fact that he was appointed in Spain and not in Rome, Galba felt his position was far from secure. This led him to instigate a new series of purges, which did little to endear him to the Romans, who had disliked Nero for exactly the same reason.

Galba's biggest mistakes were to anger the key players in Roman politics: the Army and the Praetorian Guard. As he marched on Rome, he had secured his authority by announcing bonuses for the armed forces, but he reneged on this promise once he was in Rome. Across the Roman world, the Army was incensed, but nowhere more so than the legions in Germany who demanded rewards for successfully crushing Vindix's uprising in France.

Rival Emperors declared

In early January 69, the embittered legions in Germany, led by the commanders Caecina and Valens, declared the governor of Rome's German provinces, Aulus Vitellius Germanicus as Emperor. At the same time, the Praetorian Guard began to turn against Galba as his purges began to affect their own ranks. The Praetorian Guard saw another candidate in Marcus Salvius Otho.

The Roman Forum

All Roman towns had a central meeting area, or Forum, where business was conducted, justice meted out and general gossip exchanged. Rome, as the imperial centre, had several bestowed by successive Emperors, with the oldest and most significant being the *Forum Romanum* around which the rest of the city grew and developed. Originally a piece of marshland next to the Capitoline Hill, the square began to take shape around 600 BC and was drained with the help of the Cloaca Maxima – the city's sewer system.

Over the course of a thousand years a succession of temples, government buildings and monuments were erected, destroyed, added to or built over. By the early medieval period much of the Forum had either been buried by sediment from the surrounding hills or had been built upon. Excavation of the ancient site began in the early nineteenth century, but was not fully uncovered until the twentieth century.

A place of triumph and religion

The Forum is bisected by the *Via Sacra* (Sacred Way) which runs from the Colosseum to the Capitoline Hill and the Temple of Jupiter. It was along this route that triumphal marches and religious festivals took place.

For example, during the December Saturnalia celebrations sacrifices would have been made in the Temple of Saturn. The foundations of this building are the oldest in the Forum and even today its eight standing pillars are one of the square's most dramatic sights.

The Arch of Septimius Severus stands close by and at right angles to the temple. Built at the foot of the Capitoline Hill in 203/4 AD it celebrated Severus' victories in the Parthian campaigns. A staircase still remains in one of the piers of the arch, leading to the top where statues of Severus and his sons, Caracalla and Geta were erected in their honour.

Castor and Pollux

As the patron gods of Rome, Castor and Pollux had a Forum temple built in their honour around 495 BC. It is said to have been constructed on the spot where the gods appeared declaring victory in the Battle at Lake Regillus, an early, perhaps legendary, battle.

Although only three columns of the Temple now remain, it was an important building during the Republic; it was the primary meeting place for the Senate, and speakers would use the podium for oratory.

View of the Forum from the Palatine Hill.

Inscribed tablet from the Forum.

Influence of Julius Caesar on the Forum

On the eastern side of the main square can be seen the round altar which is the only part remaining of the Temple of Caesar which was built by Augustus after the deification of Julius Caesar in 42 BC. It was supposedly erected on the site of Caesar's cremation.

The *Curia Hostilia* and the *Rostra* were both projects of Julius Caesar. Used by the Senate for meeting, the *Curia* lies next to the *Rostra*, or platform, from which orators would speak to the public of Rome. Both monuments were completed by Augustus after Caesar's death. Some sources say that Mark Antony used the *Rostra* for his funeral speech to the assassinated leader.

Remains of the inscribed marble cladding on a brick wall in the Forum.

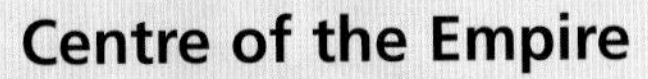

Centre of the Empire

Overlooked by the *Rostra* is the *Umbilicus Urbi*, a marble-covered structure, from which distances to all parts of the Empire were measured.

One of the oldest buildings in the Forum is the *Regia*, which was used by the kings of Rome as a residence, and then later by the *pontifex maximus* (high priest) in the Republican era. Completely destroyed by fire in 64 BC, it was rebuilt in 36 BC. Today, it is slightly cut off from the main square of the Forum by the Temple of Caesar.

Within the Forum complex stands the Temple of Vesta, which was partially reconstructed during the 1930s. Dedicated to the goddess of the hearth, the original building is thought to have been made of wood and straw and probably perished in the fire of Rome in 64 AD, subsequently being rebuilt.

A circular building with the entrance facing east, the Temple had a vented roof to allow smoke from the Sacred Hearth, tended by the Vestal Virgins, to escape. It was closed in 394 AD on the orders of Theodosius, who established Christianity as the official religion of Rome. Subsequently, several of the pagan temples in the Forum were recommissioned as Christian churches.

View of the eastern end of the Forum, looking towards the Arch of Titus and the Colosseum.

Galba hacked to death

Otho was the legate of Lusitania and had accompanied Galba on his march into Rome. He had hoped to be rewarded by being adopted as Galba's son and heir, but the elderly Galba instead adopted Lucius Calpurnius Piso, a young man of no particular note. Otho conspired with the Praetorian Guard to overthrow Galba and succeeded. On 15 January 69 AD, Servius Sulpicius Galba was hacked to death in the Forum by a group of soldiers. Piso was killed shortly afterwards, and Galba's head was put on a stick and paraded about for others to mock.

Detail from the frescoes at the Oplonti Villa which shows a bird eating figs.

Otho and Vitellius battle for the title

Otho set about trying to rule Rome, but by early spring of 69, it was clear even to Otho that Rome had two Emperors, one proclaimed in Rome and one proclaimed in Germany. Otho tried to negotiate with Vitellius, offering the hand of his daughter, to little avail; Vitellius had already begun his march on Rome.

Otho had fewer men at his disposal but had little option than to meet the challenge. He marched his troops north, where they encountered Vitellius' men on 14 April in the Battle of Bedriacum. Vitellius, trailing the legions from Germay, had military superiority and won the day, leaving Otho with little option but to commit suicide.

With Otho defeated, and Vitellius marching on Rome, the Senate was presented with no choice but to accept the appointment of Vitellius as the third Emperor in just over three months.

Below: This nineteenth century drawing depicts the assassination of the Emperor Vitellius by army officers loyal to Vespasian. Vitellius was the last of the short-lived successors to the Emperor Nero, who ruled for just eight months.

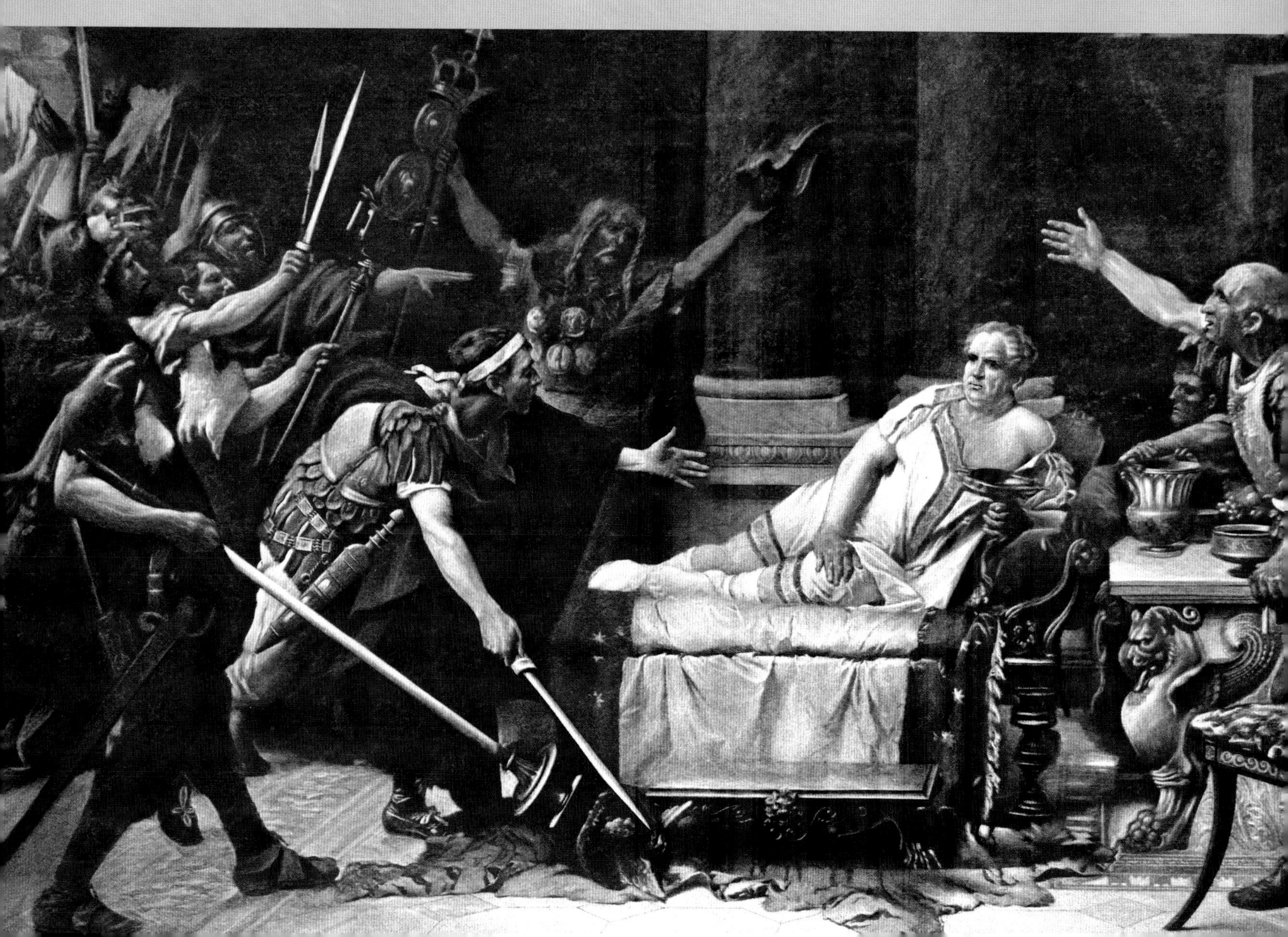

Vitellius as Emperor

Vitellius entered Rome and began the, by then, ritual purges to shore up his authority. The violence of the purges was reflected in the everyday brutality and licentiousness of the legions he had brought with him. He also replaced the existing Praetorian Guard with his own men.

As Emperor, he seemed to have met his own desires before he sought out the problems facing Rome. He is reputed to have been exceptionally gluttonous and was said to invite himself to several expensive banquets a day at different houses. And indeed, surviving images of him show him to be someone who ate to excess.

While the German legions at Vitellius' command had been sufficient in overcoming Otho, they were not adequate to control the entire Empire. Legions in the East had a distinct distaste for Vitellius and began declaring their support for a highly popular general, Titus Flavius Vespasianus (Vespasian).

A new challenger for the title

Vespasian had initially made his name as a general in Britain, where he had successfully invaded the south-west of the island. Towards the end of Nero's rule, he had become extremely popular with the military, and the Roman public, for successfully putting down a rebellion in Judea.

The war against the Jews had distracted Vespasian's army from the tumultuous politics of Rome, but at the beginning of July, his forces declared him Emperor. He was assisted by the governors of Syria and Egypt, as well as Roman legions in the provinces along the River Danube.

Vitellius' enemies presented an attack on two fronts: the Danubian legions attacked from the north, and those from the Middle East attacked from the south. The decisive blow was dealt against Vitellius in a second Battle of Bedriacum in September 69. Vespasian's forces were free to march on Rome, where they killed Vitellius in the Forum and then dumped his body in the Tiber.

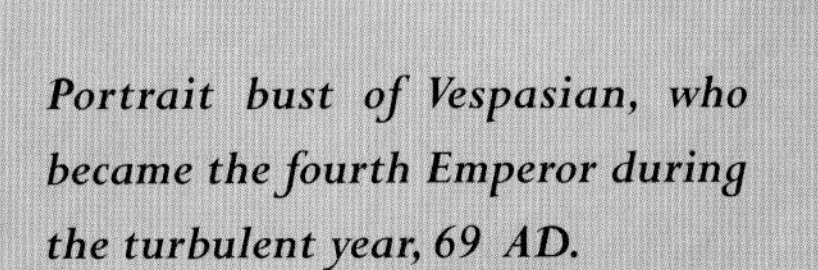

Portrait bust of Vespasian, who became the fourth Emperor during the turbulent year, 69 AD.

Chariot Races

A day at the chariot races was a favourite pastime of the Ancient Romans. Thousands of ordinary citizens could cram, free of charge, into one of the great circuses, where the races took place. The events would have been sensational – as many as twenty-four races occurred over the course of the day; violence and reckless driving were strongly encouraged.

A first century AD Roman trophy cup, with floral reliefs.

Supporting a team

Four different teams competed in the chariot races; they were called *factiones* and each was named after the colour of jersey the drivers would wear – white, red, green or blue. Fans of the sport usually developed a lifelong allegiance to one of the teams. The Emperor Domitian later added two extra teams, the purples and the golds, but these new *factiones* failed to gain a large enough fan base and petered out after Domitian's death.

Much as in professional sports today, the various teams fought for wealthy sponsors who would plough money into their chosen team to try and make it the best. Chariot racers came from the lowliest rungs of society – they were usually slaves, freed men or poor citizens. Drivers were not forced to stick to one team, they could be bought by the opponents in a way similar to that in which sportsmen are traded today.

Hooliganism

Fighting and hooliganism often broke out between the fanatically loyal supporters of the various *factiones*, sometimes leading to riots. One such occurence, the Nika riots, in Constantinople in 532 AD, resulted in at least twenty thousand deaths, and the destruction of much of the city.

Each team could enter three racers in an event, because a total of twelve chariots were allowed in the race. In addition to the ultimate goal of winning the race, chariot drivers desperately tried to drive their opponents off the road. This would not only remove the competition from the race, but it would make them incredibly popular with the spectators.

The various team members worked together to run their opponents off the road. Crashes often ocurred at the turning posts or *metae*, where drivers were forced to make a sharp u-turn, leaving them vulnerable to a challenge.

Below: Capable of seating 35,000 people, the amphitheatre of El Djem was built in the third century AD. Amphitheatres were used to stage spectacular public displays and games.

Opposite: Chariot races at the Circus Maximus in Rome. Chariot racing was an extremely popular spectator sport, the Circus Maximus could accommodate as many as 250,000 people.

Driving techniques

Roman chariot drivers tied the reins of their horses around their waists, which put them in a perilous position when they crashed. Each charioteer had a knife in his arsenal to cut himself loose, but when they did not manage to break free, they would be dragged to their deaths by the horses.

Life expectancy was relatively short for chariot racers, but if the driver could stay alive, the rewards must have seemed worth it; the winner was given money, was allowed to wear a crown and became an overnight celebrity. There was an added benefit for slaves who won several races; the prize money could have been used to buy their freedom.

At the circus

The venues for chariot races, called circuses, were vast stadiums, capable of seating thousands of people. The largest and most famous in Rome was called the Circus Maximus, which sat in the valley of the Palatine and Aventine Hills, near the imperial palace. It seated at least 250,000 people, and Trajan even increased its capacity during his reign.

For the Emperors it was the principal way in which they could be seen by the ordinary Roman citizens so they were keen to see the stadium as packed as possible. It also meant that the Emperor was obliged to attend the circus as often as possible on a race day, even if they did not enjoy the races. That was certainly not the case for Nero and Domitian; the former shocked opinion by participating in the sport himself, while the latter connected the imperial palace with the Circus Maximus for ease of access.

Circuses throughout Rome

Rome had four circuses in total. The earliest was the Circus Flaminius, which was built during the mid-Republic, near the Campus Martius, but it was abandoned during the early Empire in favour of the grander Circus Maximus.

After the Circus Maximus was built, Caligula and Nero built the Circus of Nero on the far side of the River Tiber. It was most famously used as an execution site for Nero's persecution of the Christians. It is thought that St. Peter was killed here and St Peter's Basilica in the Vatican City stands on the spot of the racetrack today.

A further racetrack was built as part of the burial site of the Emperor Maxentius during the late Empire.

Circuses were not exclusive to Rome and could be found across the Empire, from Arles in Gaul to Leptis Magna in North Africa – Constantine even took care to have one constructed in his new capital at Byzantium in the fourth century.

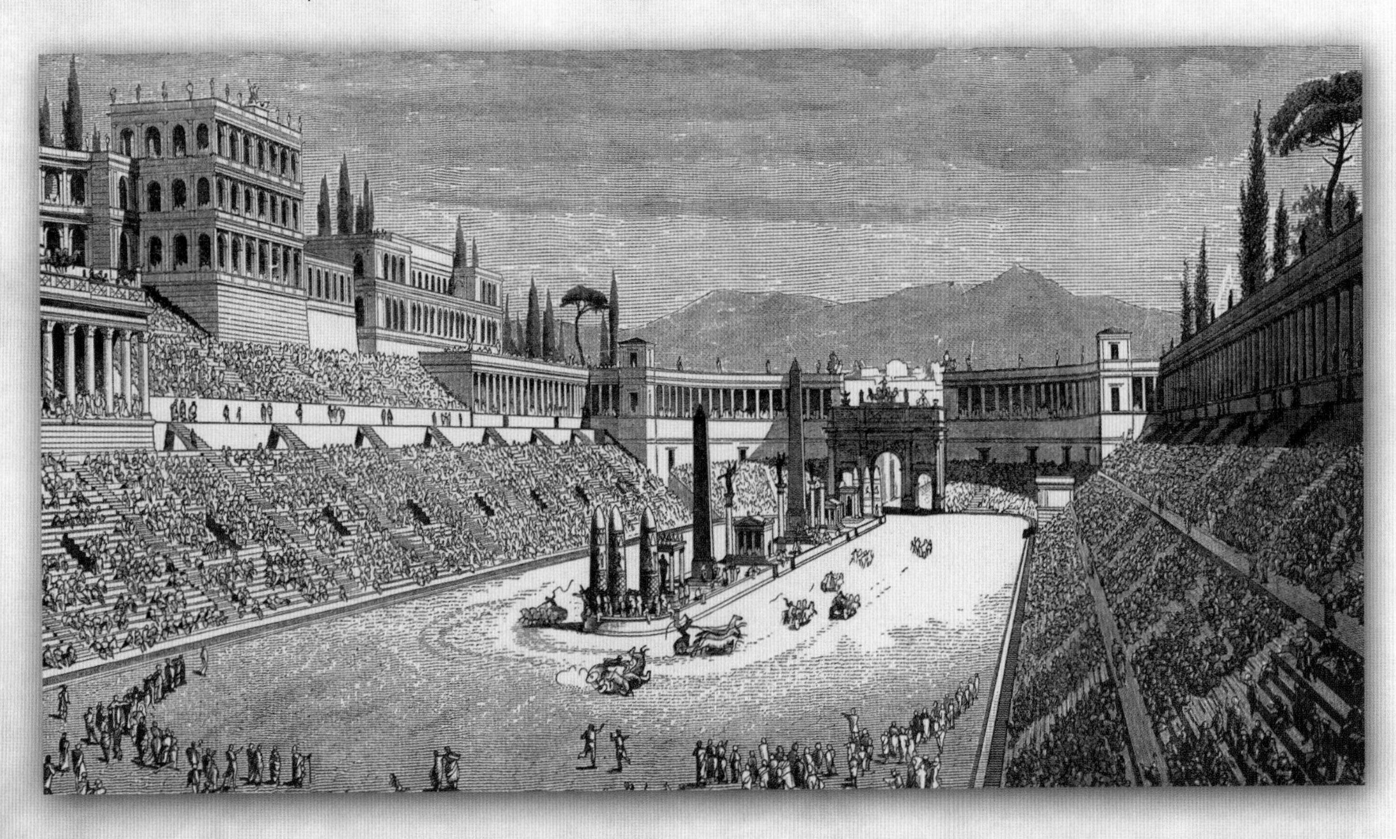

Judea

A dynastic dispute in the first century BC first brought Judea under Roman domination. Pompey was the first to intervene in the quarrel; he turned Judea into a Roman client, but failed to provide a lasting peace. After defeating Pompey in 47 BC, Caesar meddled in the politics of the kingdom; he allowed greater tolerance for the monotheistic Jewish religion and appointed a procurator, Antipater the Idumean, to look after Roman interests in the region. Antipater was assassinated and his son, Herod, emerged and was appointed king by the Roman Senate in 40 BC.

King Herod

Herod withstood the civil war between Octavian and Mark Antony and managed to rule Judea until 4 AD. Although Herod is remembered for his brutal policies and his ignorance of Jewish religious customs, his maintenance of peace and stability in Judea certainly pleased the Romans.

After Herod's death, order quickly began to break down when his sons proved to be ineffective rulers. Augustus had little option but to incorporate the province into the Empire and rule through a series of prefects. One of these prefects, Pontius Pilate, featured prominently in the story of the death of Jesus. These prefects were widely disliked and discontent smouldered beneath the surface.

Caligula added fuel to the fire when he ordered that a statue of him should be placed in every synagogue – an insult to Jewish monotheistic beliefs. Outright rebellion was perhaps only averted by Claudius' prudence. When he ascended to the imperial title, he appeased the population of Judea with the appointment of the highly popular Herod Agrippa as king in 41 AD. The unrest quickly calmed, but Judea was not to remain quiet for long; in 44 AD, Herod Agrippa died and the Romans sent their own procurators to rule the province.

A Jewish-Roman mosaic from the synagogue of Hammam-Lif in Tunisia, depicting a partridge.

Revolt in Judea

Two decades of seething unrest finally gave way to open revolt, the 'Great Jewish Revolt', in 66 AD. The rebellion was triggered by the Roman procurator, who requisitioned gold from a Jewish temple. There were Jewish protests at this act, which were met with Roman brutality; a number of the protesters were murdered, sparking insurrection across the rest of the province. Jerusalem was taken by the rebels and Roman soldiers and settlers were slaughtered.

Initially the Roman armies sent in to deal with the revolt were quickly repelled, so Nero sent Vespasian to crush the uprising. Jerusalem was too well defended by its network of walls for the Romans to cut the rebellion off at its source, so Vespasian set about terrorizing the rest of Judea. Much of the province fell to his brutal counterinsurgency, with only a few strongholds, including Jerusalem, holding out.

Vespasian recalled as Emperor

Vespasian became extremely popular and was forced to return to Rome as Emperor before Jerusalem was captured. He left the counterinsurgency in the hands of his son, Titus, who opted to besiege the city and starve the rebels into surrendering. The civilian population suffered terribly; anybody who was caught taking food into the city was crucified outside the walls as an example to other would-be traders.

A huge wall was constructed around the city to further isolate it, and after a long siege, the Romans finally managed to gain entry in 70 AD. They wiped out the insurgency, razed the city and plundered its riches.

Masada – the last stronghold

The last Jewish stronghold was Masada, a highly defendable fortress on an isolated cliff top in the south of Judea. In 73, the Romans moved to crush the last vestiges of resistance. After using a battering ram to breach the walls of the fort, Roman soldiers entered the citadel. Upon entering they discovered that all the inhabitants, approximately one thousand people, had killed one another to avoid capture by the Romans. With the storming of Masada, the Great Jewish Revolt came to a tragic end.

A second Jewish Revolt

In 132, after Emperor Hadrian outraged Jewish opinion on several counts, a second Jewish Revolt broke out. Hadrian had repressed Jewish customs and intended to rebuild the ruined Jerusalem as a centre of polytheist worship. Worst of all, he planned to build a temple to Jupiter upon the site of the principal Jewish temple.

When the Romans brought the revolt under control in 135 Hadrian decided to remove the Jews once and for all. Judea was thoroughly romanized, the Jews expelled and their religious practices were repressed.

Antoninus Pius practised greater tolerance after Hadrian's death, but the Jewish community had been scattered across the Empire. Judea remained under Roman control until the Arabs moved into the region in the seventh century.

MASADA

1 Small bathhouse
2 Herod's Place
3 Storerooms
4 Apartment building
5 Living quarters
6 Underground cistern
7 Southern bastion
8 Western palace
9 Throne room
10 West gate
11 Synagogue
12 Large bathhouse

N

Plan of Masada, the last Jewish stronghold during the 'Great Jewish Revolt, when the Romans entered the fortress, they discovered that the inhabitants had killed one another in order to avoid capture.

Mosaic of a Menorah with Lulav and Ethrog from the synagogue of Hammam-Lif in Tunisia.

Flavian Emperors

Vespasian

After the personal excesses of the Julio-Claudian Emperors and the civil wars of 69 AD, Vespasian and the Emperors that succeeded him were a breath of fresh air. Peace became a key feature for over a century, as three stable imperial dynasties ruled over a secure and relatively calm Empire.

Vespasian's early career

Vespasian was born in 9 AD, at the end of the Augustan period. He distinguished himself in military service in Britain, leading the conquest of the south-east of the island as well as the Isle of Vectis, present-day Isle of Wight, just off the south coast of Britain.

Despite his lauded background, when Nero ascended the throne, he fell out of favour with the imperial family, because Nero's mother and de facto co-ruler, Agrippina, had a distinct dislike for him. In order to survive he went into retirement.

Insulting Nero

This was a prudent move because Agrippina was soon disposed of and Vespasian was able to re-emerge on the political scene and was granted a governorship in North Africa in 63.

However, his rehabilitation was short-lived because he fell asleep during one of Nero's music recitals, which deeply insulted the Emperor and Vespasian once again found himself discharged. Given Nero's excesses, this was a relatively lenient punishment.

Proclaimed Emperor

Vespasian was not in the political wilderness for too long, because he was considered the perfect candidate to deal with the revolt against Roman rule in Judea. It was while fighting in the counterinsurgency against the Jews that Vespasian was pronounced Emperor by his men, and he returned to defeat Vitellius and take Rome.

Vespasian was more similar to Augustus than any of the Julio-Claudian Emperors had been: he was parsimonious; he commanded respect rather than fear; and he also sought to stabilize the Empire after years of conflict. In terms of dealing with old conflicts and wounds, he took a just approach. He sorted through backdated legal claims, paid and rewarded the soldiers and most importantly, he refused to reintroduce purges to settle scores against his old political enemies.

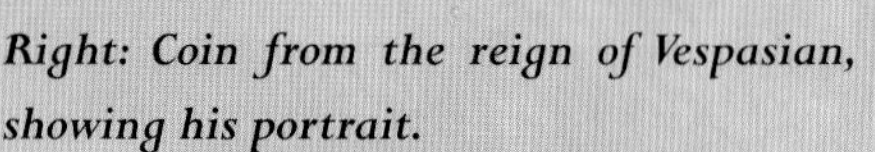

***Right:* Coin from the reign of Vespasian, showing his portrait.**

***Opposite above:* Detail from a fresco in the Oplonti Villa, depicting an insect hovering over some berries.**

The Emperor and the mule driver

It seems that Vespasian's only negative quality was a tendency towards miserliness. One famous account of this was when Vespasian's mule driver slowed down his carriage and the Emperor quickly realized this was part of an elaborate fraud. He knew that the mule driver would have been paid to slow down so that a citizen would have time to approach the Emperor for a favour. In spite of his wealth and position, Vespasian only agreed to the plan if the mule driver gave him a fifty percent cut of his fee.

His meanness prevented a return to the excesses of Caligula and Nero, but it did not preclude him from spending vast sums of money on construction. He continued the work of Nero in reconstructing Rome after the Great Fire, and personally inaugurated the rebuilding of the Capitol.

He also extended the *pomerium*, the sacred boundary of the city of Rome. This enlarged the city in order to reduce the problem of overcrowding. One of his grandest and most enduring constructions was the great Flavian Amphitheatre, or Colosseum, which still stands to this day.

Titus succeeds Vespasian

Upon Vespasian's death of a fever in 79 AD, he was succeeded by his biological son, Titus Flavius Vespasianus. His accession to the throne met with almost universal objection because Titus had a reputation for cruelty, greed, immorality and excessive behaviour.

When his father had returned to Rome from Judea in 69, Titus had carried on the counterinsurgency against the Jewish Revolt. Although he was thanked for his pacification of Jerusalem and Masada, he gained a reputation for ruthlessness. There was concern that Titus might undo his father's good work and plunge the Empire back into insecurity and chaos.

After his death, Vespasian was deified. In the right of the picture are the ruins of a temple dedicated to him in the Forum. The structure on the left is the remains of the Temple of Saturn.

Titus

With a reputation for cruelty and immorality,
it came as a surprise to many Romans to discover that they had misjudged Titus.
He was affable, generous and wholesome; he threw spectacular games for the citizens of Rome;
always heard every petition presented to him, and emphasized public morality and respect.
Titus' reign was quickly marred by natural disaster.

The eruption of Vesuvius

In the first year of his reign, Mount Vesuvius erupted, completely destroying the towns of Pompeii and Herculaneum. Titus acted quickly to help the victims; he established a committee of former consuls to arrange the relief effort.

While Titus was away visiting the region and assessing the devastation caused, a fire broke out in Rome, destroying several important buildings, most notably the original Pantheon, which had been built by Augustus' general, Agrippa. The newly rebuilt Capitol was also burned down, as well as a number of houses.

Titus' generosity

Titus excelled in bringing relief to the city in a way that Nero had never done when rebuilding after the Great Fire of Rome. Generously, he stripped his private holdings to refurnish public buildings in Rome, put a great deal of his own money into the relief effort, and re-housed the homeless in properties owned by families who had perished in the Vesuvian eruption. When a further disaster struck in the shape of an outbreak of plague, he dealt with that in a similar manner: using all means at his disposal to cure people and prevent its spread to others.

An early death

In 81 AD, just over two years into his reign, Titus fell ill and, at the premature age of forty-one, he died. Although he died from fever, Titus' appointed heir, his brother Domitian, was blamed for having murdered the Emperor.

This idea of a conspiracy against Titus was not entirely far-fetched; Domitian had very publicly plotted against his brother while he was alive: for example, by inciting the Army to revolt. Although he was aware of his brother's scheming, Titus forgave him and continued to treat him with dignity and respect.

With such a short reign, Titus' time as Emperor was very much defined by the three catastrophes that struck. However, they failed to overshadow his rule because he proved so adept at coping with them, such that he is remembered as one of Rome's greatest Emperors; the same cannot be said for his brother Domitian.

***Above:** Mount Vesuvius overshadows the ruins of Pompeii.*

***Left:** Under the shadow of Vesuvius, a concrete cast at Pompeii captures the moment of death of a Pompeian caught in the mountain's violent pyroclastic flow in 79 AD. The bodies of those who died in the hot flow of ash and mud left hollows, and poignant casts like these were made as the positions of the bodies were discovered by archaeologists.*

Pompeii and Herculaneum

On 24 August 79 AD, Mount Vesuvius erupted catastrophically, burying the towns of Pompeii and Herculaneum under piles of ash. Both towns were preserved under layers of ash, mud and rock for years, before they were both rediscovered in the eighteenth century.

Pompeii's early years

The settlement at Pompeii was founded just to the south of Mount Vesuvius by the Oscan civilization in the eighth century BC. The Greeks occupied the settlement during the sixth century, before it was taken over by the Samnites in the fifth. It is even thought that the Etruscan peoples might have controlled the town at one stage.

In 290 BC, after Rome's victory in the Samnite Wars, the town became an ally of Rome, but rose up in protest against Roman rule during the Social War of 91 BC. The war was short-lived; Lucius Cornelius Sulla's forces quickly conquered much of the Campania region and Pompeii had little choice but to capitulate. The town was turned into a Roman colony and renamed Cornelius Veneria Pompeianorum in honour of Sulla and Venus, the goddess he admired.

Villas of the powerful

The supporters of Sulla, the *Optimates*, were deeply involved in the politics of the town during the later Republic, and at this time many large villas were built by them in and around Pompeii. A number of army veterans were also awarded land close to the town. Amenities associated with Roman town life, such as bathhouses, and amphitheatre, temples and an odeon were built at this time.

As part of romanizing Pompeii, the state religion was established in the town. The principal Samnite shrine was turned into a temple to the deities of the Capitoline Triad, Jupiter, Juno and Minerva.

Changes in the Empire period

The onset of the Empire subjected the town to several changes as the ruling elites, who had been linked to Sulla, were replaced with allies of the imperial family. The imperial cult was added to list of Roman deities worshipped in the town and a temple to the Emperor Vespasian was built in the forum shortly before the town's destruction. A number of other honours were paid to the Emperors, including a statue of Augustus in the forum and an arch to commemorate Nero's reign.

Right: Portrait of Aulus Gabinius from Herculaneum.

Early warnings

In 62 AD, Pompeii received an early warning about its fate, when it was struck by a violent earthquake which caused extensive damage to the town. As a relatively wealthy settlement, Pompeii could afford to rebuild reasonably quickly. Excavations of the ruins suggest that a number of villas and buildings had been rebuilt, renovated and extended after this first earthquake In fact, investigations of the site suggest that the building work was still ongoing seventeen years later.

Eruption strikes

The earthquake was merely an appetizer for what was to come. On the morning of 24 August 79 AD, Pliny the Younger records seeing a cloud rise from Vesuvius in the shape of a pine tree as the eruption began. This must have been a surprise to the people living in the shadow of Vesuvius because the volcano had lain dormant for so long that no one knew the mountain's true nature.

A hail of pumice stones followed the cloud, accompanied by poisonous gas and a blanket of ash. The town was buried within just a few hours, but the gases had already killed many residents. Although people attempted to flee the city, the debris from Vesuvius settled over a seventy-kilometre radius, making escape difficult. Those who tried to make an exit by sea faced tidal waves and earthquakes, and indeed an eyewitness, Pliny's uncle, Pliny the Elder, was killed on a boat at sea, probably as a result of inhalation of poisonous gases.

Above: Fresco of water pot and fruit in a Pompeian kitchen.

Right: Gold ring in the form of twin snakes' heads, unearthed from Pompeii.

Dealing with the aftermath

As a result of the eruption, Pompeii was completely buried under more than four metres of ash and pumice stone. Emperor Titus immediately dispatched a committee of senators and ex-consuls to the region to assess the damage. Their report requested that the town be recovered and rebuilt at state expense. However, after visiting the area himself in 80 AD, Titus rejected this proposal because he believed the town was not salvageable. State funds and Titus' own wealth were, instead, invested in re-housing the survivors.

In the years following, there were sporadic attempts to dig up some of the town's treasures and re-use its marble, but the town remained buried and largely forgotten for more than fifteen hundred years.

Pompeii rediscovered

At the end of the sixteenth century, the town was discovered by an architect during excavations for a construction project. The discovery caused little interest; Pompeii was forgotten again for a century and a half.

It was not until 1748 that archaeologists began to excavate the site, although they were unaware that the town was Pompeii until they uncovered an inscription on one of the buildings in 1763.

Pompeii's bodies

Excavations continued over the following century, but it was not until 1860 that a systematic and professional dig began. Giuseppe Fiorelli, who oversaw this dig, developed an innovative technique which encapsulated the last moments of the residents of Pompeii.

Fiorelli noticed that there were hollows left in the layers of ash where human remains had decomposed. By filling the hollows with liquid plaster, a cast of the missing body could be created. The bodies recreated using this technique offer an eerie window into the past, revealing how these panicked people dealt with their impending doom.

Above: Porticoed entrances in a street in Pompeii.

Ruins offer a window on the past

The ruins at Pompeii are not quite the best preserved in the Roman world, but the uninterrupted extent of the site, together with the circumstances of its ruin, make them the most compelling. While most Roman buildings underwent changes over the centuries, Pompeii offers an unchanged view of what Roman life was like during the early Empire, and even more specifically, what life was like between 62 and 79 AD, when the city was extensively rebuilt after the earthquake.

The town had two forums, the main one of which was lined with statues and littered with temples, as well as political and municipal buildings. The town also had several bathing complexes and an amphitheatre near the outskirts, which could seat up to twenty thousand people. There were also food stalls, brothels, townhouses and a number of shops where wine was an important commodity.

A vast network of streets has been uncovered, which comprise large slabs of lava-based rock from Mount Vesuvius with raised pavements on either side of the road, as well as raised crossing points so pedestrians would not get their feet dirty in the gutters.

Grand frescoes

Frescoes were found in most of the townhouses. Those painted during the Republic are relatively austere in style, aimed simply at giving the walls the appearance of marble. During the late Republic and early Empire, however, tastes became more ostentatious. Grander frescoes adorned the walls for decorative purposes, with columns, landscape scenery and Greek or Egyptian features.

Risqué images

In wealthier households, the frescoes were less abstract; the paintings would involve images of people, animals or still life. Many of these frescoes have been noted for their graphic and erotic elements, many of which were considered so distasteful at the time of the early excavations, that they were removed or covered up and have only recently been put back on display.

The graffiti on the walls throughout the town was often equally risqué. Graffiti had a wide variety of purposes: it was used for slander, satire and gossip; it was also used by brothels to list their prices; and was used by politicians who were campaigning for election. It grants the modern reader a rare opportunity to understand the attitudes of ordinary Romans.

POMPEII
Vesuvius Gate
Capua Gate
Herculaneum Gate
Nola Gate
Sarno Gate
Nucerian Gate
Stabian Gate
Marina Gate
Buildings
Unexcavated Areas

Herculaneum

While Pompeii developed to the south of Mount Vesuvius, the region on the coast to the west of the volcano was first settled by the Greeks. They named it Herculaneum after their god, Hercules, whom they believed to have founded the town.

Herculaneum passed into the hands of the Samnites who pushed the Greeks out of the Bay of Naples area. Like Pompeii, Herculaneum became an ally of Rome after the Samnite Wars had ended, but challenged that alliance by joining the Social War against Rome in 91 BC during which time, Sulla's men stormed the town and turned it into a Roman colony and Roman settlers moved in.

Pyroclastic flow

Herculaneum had a different experience to that of Pompeii when Vesuvius erupted. The winds carried the pumice, ash and gas spewing from the volcano towards Pompeii, leaving Herculaneum relatively unscathed. Thus, while Pompeii was buried in just a few hours, residents of Herculaneum were given a chance to get away.

However, during the evening, the winds changed and a pyroclastic flow raced down Vesuvius and engulfed the city. This was a flow of gas, ash and rock at extremely high temperatures which is lethal to anything in its path.

Initially, it was believed that most people had escaped from the city, and avoided the fate of the residents of Pompeii. However, excavations have uncovered a large number of human remains huddled together at the port, suggesting that many residents tried but failed to get away.

Better preserved

The buildings at Herculaneum are better preserved than the ones found at Pompeii because that town bore the brunt of the eruption – pumice stones bombarded the city, destroying most of the roofs and damaging buildings. Herculaneum was largely spared the onslaught of the stones and was buried in a mudslide that did much less damage to the buildings and meant that many roofs did not collapse. However, the town was buried more deeply than Pompeii; in places as much as sixteen metres of mud and debris covered the town.

Herculaneum was rediscovered in the early eighteenth century and excavations began in 1738, ten years before those at Pompeii. Unlike at Pompeii, the skeletal remains at Herculaneum had not decomposed and these remains gave scientists extraordinary insights into the lifestyles of the people of Herculaneum, such as what the locals ate, how tall they were and what diseases were common.

Right: Interior of building in Pompeii, showing niche for statue and the remnants of vivid frescoes.

Opposite right: Roman amphora of blue cameo glass with cupids, discovered at Herculaneum.

Opposite left: Plan of Pompeii, showing the extent of excavations to date.

Villa of the Mysteries

A suburban villa lying a few hundred metres outside the city walls of Pompeii, the Villa of the Mysteries, is today renowned for the frescoes in its *triclinium*, or Hall of Mysteries.

The images in the wall paintings depict life-sized characters. Although the significance and interpretation of the frescoes have been hotly debated, the most widely accepted theory is that they portray the initiation of a young woman into the Dionysian mysteries.

A wealthy family villa

The residential, and main part, of the villa was built during the second or third century BC, and would have been occupied by Roman nobility, or a wealthy family, from the beginning of the first century AD, as they began to move out from the commercial and political hustle and bustle of Pompeii. Farm buildings and rooms for processing olive oil, wine, and produce from the surrounding orchards and agricultural land were added around this time.

Silver vessel from Pompeii.

Buried under a mountain of ash

The eruption of Vesuvius in 79 AD left the house buried under a mountain of ash; it was not until 1909 that it was uncovered, exposing its remarkable treasures for the first time in over eighteen centuries. Surprisingly, it had sustained little damage, with most of its rooms and frescoes remaining intact.

The Hall of the Mysteries, or *triclinium*, was probably once used as a dining room, where members of the household and their guests would recline on couches as they ate. The paintings that cover the four walls of the room date from about the first century BC, and were applied directly to wet plaster. They cover the four walls of the room and run for a length of seventeen metres. The entire painting, with decorative borders, is three metres high and the 29 figures that make up the frieze are shown life-size.

The triclinium, *or Hall of Mysteries, within the Villa of Mysteries at Pompeii. The villa was buried under the ash from the eruption of Vesuvius in 79 AD and remained covered for hundreds of years until it was discovered in 1909.*

Cult of Dionysus

The Dionysian cult originated in Greece and translated into the cult of Bacchus in ancient Rome. It was associated with wine, music and dance leading to the 'liberation' of the individual and the casting off of inhibitions and social constraints. Despite being banned by the Roman Senate in 186 BC for its excesses, it continued to attract followers and initiates. It is not beyond the realms of possibility that the villa was a meeting place for cult members, nor that the room itself may have been the scene of initiation rites similar to those portrayed on its walls.

Narrative sequence

The frescoes appear to depict a narrative sequence which runs around the the room from the entrance. In the first of the sequence the female initiate is seen on the left of the painting and seems to be entering the sequence looked upon by a priestess and a naked boy.

Although some of the frescoes are so badly damaged it is difficult to interpret the scene, much of the painting in the room remains in good condition and conveys the narrative in vivid detail. Figures from mythology, including a satyr and an ageing Silenus, are depicted, as is Dionysus himself who lies sprawled in the arms of his mother Semele. The ten frames of the frescoes end with the god Eros, god of Love.

Right A theatrical mask overlooks the proceedings in one frame.

Below: Figures from the frescoes, thought to be priestesses, perform a ritual while an ageing Silenus plays a lyre.

Domitian

Titus Flavius Domitianus' reign got off to a reasonable start; he inaugurated public works, gave generously to the citizens of Rome and presided over social and legal reforms.

Establishing popularity

Like Nero, Domitian loved public games and in 86 AD established his own version of the Olympics, the Capitoline Games, a no-expense-spared event, which made good use of the new Colosseum, built on the orders of his father, Vespasian.

Unlike his father and brother, he did not ascend to the imperial title with an already distinguished career, so he sought to compensate with a successful campaign in Germany. He was so pleased with his triumph in the north that he gave himself the name 'Germanicus', but his glory was short-lived.

Agricola removed from Britain

Another general, Agricola, began to steal the limelight. Agricola, the governor of Britain, was becoming popular as a result of his victories against the exotic Caledonians in the north of Britain, so Domitian jealously recalled him from service. Upon Agricola's return to Rome, the Scottish Highlands were abandoned and he was forced into anonymity, while Domitian continued to try to make a name for himself as a general.

He campaigned against the Dacians, a Danubian tribe, from what today is Romania, and against a Germanic tribe called the Chatti, with some degree of success, but these were never the victories that he proclaimed to great fanfares in Rome.

The Colosseum where Domitian held his lavish version of the Olympic Games, the Capitoline Games.

Greed and cruelty come to the fore

As Domitian's reign progressed he became increasingly cruel and avaricious. His own domestic entertainments and his foreign enterprises had taken their toll on his personal treasury, so Domitian resolved to recoup his monetary losses through confiscations. Thus he revived the reign of terror of his predecessors and proscribed senators and wealthy Romans so that he could get his hands on their fortunes. He also took more money from the Jews by tightening Vespasian's tax against Jews to include anyone even vaguely connected with the Jewish race.

His cruelty was not simply driven by the need for money, he seems to have had a sadistic side to his character; on more than one occasion, he condemned a man to death, then insisted on spending a pleasant day with him, before having the execution carried out in the evening.

His jealousy also seems to have been a factor in his cruelty; in addition to his petulant response to Agricola's victories, he also had the governor of Britannia, Sallustius Lucullus executed for naming a new type of lance after himself. Domitian's oppressive ways inevitably gained him powerful enemies among the senators and the wealthy of Rome. This led to several conspiracies but it was his own household staff who eventually killed him in 96 AD. With Domitian's death, the Flavian dynasty came to an end.

Above: The ruins of the excavated Roman Vindolanda Fort on the route of Hadrian's Wall in the rolling hills of Northumberland, England. A reconstruction of a stone wall with a turret and a timber milecastle have been added to the original found ruins.

Decorative stone cornice from the Forum in Rome.

The Colosseum

Although it is not the best-preserved building of Ancient Rome, the Colosseum is certainly the civilization's most iconic. Years of neglect, earthquakes, weathering and stone robbers have meant that the Colosseum has fallen into disrepair, but even in its ruined state, the structure manages to capture the imagination.

Flavian amphitheatre

Building began in 72 AD, during the reign of Vespasian and was completed eight years later in 80, when his son, Titus, had assumed the imperial title. Although we know the structure as the 'Colosseum', in Roman times, it was called the 'Flavian Amphitheatre', in honour of Vespasian's dynasty, the Flavians.

The Colosseum is situated on a site to the east of the Forum in the grounds of the *Domus Aurea* or 'Golden House'; a lavish private home with a lake, gardens and pavilions which Nero had built for himself. The population of Rome hated this residence as the land to build it had been cleared only when the Great Fire of Rome destroyed thousands of people's homes.

Vespasian's decision to site the amphitheatre in such a location was clearly a populist gesture, designed to highlight that the new Flavian dynasty would not emulate the excesses of Nero.

Arcades on the inner wall of the Colosseum

Built from the plunder of Jerusalem

The Colosseum was partly paid for by using the revenue from the plunder brought back to Rome from Jerusalem. Following the Great Jewish Revolt, the city and all its riches had fallen to the Romans, under the leadership of Vespasian and then Titus, in 70 AD.

Built from travertine stone, the outer walls of the Colosseum were nearly 50 metres in height – most of the present day façade is actually the inner wall. From what remains of the original façade it can be seen that it was composed of three rows of arcades,topped by an attic. The whole facade was decorated with columns framing the arcades, and pillasters on the attic. Many of the arches in the arcade would have held statues of deities.

The arena floor has not survived and the hypogeum, *the underground part of the Colosseum has been exposed, revealing the chambers which housed wild animals, weapons, slaves, prisoners, scenery and other props. When needed, the props and the animals were heaved to the surface by a system of weights and pulleys.*

Status in seating

Seating up to 50,000 spectators at a time, the Colosseum was the largest Amphitheatre in the world. Entrance to the games was free, but strict, class-based seating arrangements applied to the spectators, in line with regulation set by Augustus.

Senators would sit in the front row, on the Podium, closest to the arena, while the rest of the nobility would sit behind them in the *Maenianum primum*. The middle and upper tiers were reserved for the plebs. Wealthier plebs were allowed to sit in a separate tier, the *Maenianum secundum immum*, closer to the arena than the poorer plebs who sat in the *Maenianum secundum summum*.

Special sections were reserved for other groups, such as non-citizens and youths. The Emperor Domitian added a further seating level at the very top of the building, the *Maenianum summum in ligneis*, in which sat the poorest people, including slaves. When the Emperor attended the games, he sat in the imperial box.

Maenianum summum in ligneis

Maenianum secundum summum

Maenianum secundum immum

Maenianum primum

Senatorial

Arena or level

View of the Colosseum showing part of the remains of the outer wall to the left of the picture.

One hundred days of celebration

To celebrate the opening of the Colosseum in 80 AD, Titus lavished on the citizens of Rome one hundred days of grand events; besides the normal gladiator shows he flooded the amphitheatre and staged a mock sea battle, then drained it again in order to stage an extensive hunt for wild animals.

Roman historian Dio Cassius, writing in the following century, claimed that in the course of Titus' celebrations over 11,000 animals were killed. Once the inaugural festivities were concluded, the Colosseum mostly hosted gladiatorial contests and hunts.

A decorative capital displayed in the interior of the Colosseum.

Gladiators need to please the crowd

Gladiators were expected to exert themselves in the arena. If they failed to put on a good enough show, they faced execution. When a gladiator had been defeated, he was allowed to request mercy from the Emperor, or whoever was presiding over the games – their decision was often based upon what would be the most popular with the crowd.

Victorious gladiators were rewarded with fame and money. An additional reward was emancipation, especially enticing given that most gladiators were slaves or prisoners.

Hypogeum

The underground chambers or *hypogeum* were completed by Vespasian's younger son, the Emperor Domitian. Wild animals, weapons, slaves, prisoners, scenery and other props were kept under the ground. When needed, the props and the animals were heaved to the surface by a system of weights and pullies.

The present-day façade of the Colosseum is not what the Roman citizens who flocked to Emperor Titus' hundred days of celebrations for the inauguration of the Flavian Amphitheatre would have seen. This is the inner wall, less decorative than the outer wall which has largely disappeared and is extant in only a few places around the 550-metre perimeter.

Detail of a mosaic depicting a gladiator fight.

Animal hunts

The arena of the Colosseum was used for a number of displays and shows. Gladiatorial battles were popular, as were animal hunts, or *venatio*. A huge variety of wild beasts was used, mainly imported from Africa and stored in the *hypogeum*. Elephants, big cats, giraffes, crocodiles and hippopotamus are among some of the animals hunted in the arena.

Elaborate sets were constructed with moveable trees and buildings into which the animals would be introduced and the hunters would stalk their prey. For the urban-dwelling Romans this would all add to the exotic experience of the *venatio*.

Over five hundred years of use

The Colosseum remained in use for its original purpose for over five hundred years. Gladiatorial contests seem to have died out during the fifth century AD but wild animal hunts continued into the sixth century. Throughout that period it saw a number of repairs and restorations as the building suffered damage through fire, earthquake or deterioration over time.

Interior view of the walls of the Colosseum.

Hunting baths at Leptis Magna take their name from the frescoes that adorn their walls. It has been suggested that the frescoes indicate that the baths were owned by a guild of local hunters who supplied wild beasts to the Colosseum and other amphitheatres of the Roman Empire.

Five Good Emperors

Nerva

The three emperors of the Nervo-Trajanic Dynasty, together with the first two Antonine Emperors are called the 'Five Good Emperors'. In an era, already defined by relative peace and stability, these Emperors stand out as the best Rome ever had. One reason for this was because each heir was adopted, allowing the best man for the job to be chosen.

A hasty appointment

Domitian was murdered without an heir so Marcus Cocceius Nerva was hastily appointed to the imperial throne to avoid a political vacuum, which could have meant recourse to unrest and violence.

Despite the haste of his appointment, Nerva was deemed the most suitable candidate because he was a popular member of the Senate, but he was also a respected member of the Flavian courts. Domitian had marginalized Nerva in the last years of his campaign, but Flavian supporters were satisfied that his appointment would guarantee the safety of their person and their interests.

There is no doubt that Nerva was a 'stop-gap' Emperor; he was in his sixties, was known to be in ill-health and most importantly he had no male heir. He was simply a temporary arrangement to hold the Empire together while a suitable candidate could be found.

Nerva provides domestic stability

Nerva styled his rule on that of Augustus' – he quickly set to work expunging the legacy of Domitian; the Jewish tax was relaxed, political prisoners were freed and Domitian's laws were revoked. After Domitian had extorted money by every underhand means possible, Nerva reintroduced fiscal health through more legitimate channels; he tightened the public purse and sharply reduced the amount of public games and building works.

Nerva's reign provided domestic stability, which made him popular in Rome, but not necessarily with the troops. To appease the Army, Nerva appointed a successor with a military pedigree; however, it came as a surprise to many Romans that his chosen heir was not, strictly speaking, an Italian.

Main: Theatre at Merida in Spain. The town was originally named Emerita Augusta. Spain was the birthplace of Trajan, the first non-Italian emperor.

Above left: Amber ring, showing the head of a woman, produced during Trajan's reign.

Trajan

Marcus Ulpius Trajanus was born in Italica (Seville) in the Roman province of Hispania. Although his family were originally from Italy, they had settled in the Iberian Peninsula long before, making Trajan the first Emperor from outside of Italy. His family had an impressive military reputation, which endeared Trajan to both the Praetorian Guard and the Army.

Trajan's father had been governor of Syria and he himself had come to the fore by helping Domitian in his Dacian Wars. In 91 AD, Trajan was granted his first consulship and managed to avoid the reign of terror that Domitian unleashed back in Rome.

Co-ruler with Nerva

Nerva ensured a smooth transition of power by allowing Trajan to rule alongside him whilst he was still alive. However, when Nerva died in early 98 Trajan was preparing for another war against the Dacians. He did not return to Rome immediately, but continued his preparations for more than a year. When he did return, he made a great show by entering the city on foot, a very humble gesture, which gained him the support of ordinary Romans.

Trajan's military success

Trajan was a highly successful Emperor; he sought to expand the Empire and succeeded. Between 101 and 106 he picked up where Domitian had left off and mounted a campaign against the Dacians. Domitian had never achieved a decisive outcome, but Trajan certainly did – the Dacians were beaten and Dacia was turned into a province of the Empire.

The following year, the Empire underwent further expansion when the king of Rome's client state, Nabatea, died. Trajan opted to annex the region, creating a new Arabian province within the Empire.

In 107, with Dacia and Nabatea under his belt, Trajan returned to Rome to begin a seven-year stint as a 'civilian Emperor'. He set to work on a number of construction projects, especially a widespread road- and bridge-building programme.

Ruins in the Forum. Trajan established a large, new forum in Rome, the Trajan Forum, complete with a new shopping centre and a monument to celebrate his victories in Dacia – 'Trajan's Column'.

Roman Spain

The direct Roman presence in Hispania (the Iberian Peninsula) began in 218 BC during the Punic Wars, when troops moved in to dislodge the Carthaginians established there. By 206, the Romans had made important gains, moving into the peninsula as the Carthaginians moved out. The Roman conquest took almost two centuries, until Augustus decided to occupy the peninsula once and for all.

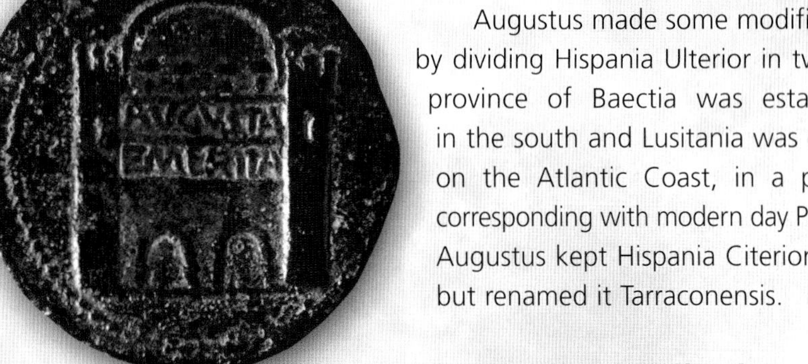

Bronze coin showing the gate to Augustus Emerita, the city of Merida in modern Spain.

Crushing opposition

In 29 BC, after defeating Antony and Cleopatra, Augustus sent his prized general, Marcus Vipsanius Agrippa to Spain to crush all tribes opposed to Roman rule. Chief among the dissident tribes were the Cantabri of northern Spain.

The Cantabri were skilled fighters and the Romans campaigned for ten years, bringing in a number of legions, as well as the Army. The campaign lasted so long that Augustus himself intervened on occasion to try to bring a swift victory, but to little effect. In 19, the Cantabri finally fell to the Romans and with them, the entire peninsula came under Roman control. Resistance did continue for a time, but it was limited because all the Cantabri males were wiped out; they were either killed by the Romans, or they killed themselves.

Occupation strategies

Even before the entire peninsula had been pacified, Hispania was divided into two provinces of the Empire, Hispania Ulterior in the south and west, and Hispania Citerior in the north and east.

Augustus made some modifications by dividing Hispania Ulterior in two; the province of Baectia was established in the south and Lusitania was created on the Atlantic Coast, in a position corresponding with modern day Portugal. Augustus kept Hispania Citerior intact, but renamed it Tarraconensis.

Economic contributions

Hispania's economy was predominantly based on agriculture and mining. Initially, Rome relied on Hispania as a ready source of oil for cooking, cleaning and lighting. However, North Africa began to replace the Spanish provinces as a source of oil during the Empire.

Farmers on the peninsula continued to produce fish sauce and wine, although Italy was still a major source of these two sought-after commodities, and it was rather Hispania's metal wealth that kept the Romans interested. Tin, silver, iron, lead, copper and even gold were mined on the peninsula.

Magnificent Roman aqueduct near Nerja, Andalusia, Spain.

Political contributions

In addition to its metals, Hispania proved to be a rich source of good Emperors – two of Rome's most famous, Trajan and Hadrian, were born on the peninsula. In addition Galba, Emperor for a brief time in 69 AD, began his rebellion against Nero from his post in Hispania.

Galba's revolt was not a new departure for the province. The peninsula had already developed a reputation for insurrection in 83 BC, when Quintus Sertorius broke with Rome and ruled Hispania for over a decade. Sertorius, a supporter of Marius and the *Populares*, stood opposed to the government of Sulla and his *Optimates* in Rome. He allied with the local tribes, especially the Lusitanians, and took control of Hispania Ulterior and much of Hispania Citerior.

Battleground for Pompey and Caesar

The *Optimates* sent Pompey to deal with the rebellion, but he was unable to bring Hispania back under the control of Rome. In 72 BC, the uprising collapsed because Sertorius' forces had been worn down by years of war, and his native allies had proved unreliable.

The peninsula was brought back under the control of Rome, but Pompey had many forces deployed there, with the consequence that Hispania was later to become a battleground between the forces of Julius Caesar and Pompey. Caesar's last war against Pompey loyalists took place in Hispania, at Munda in 45 BC.

Developing Spanish cities

Most of the cities in Hispania pre-dated the Romans, Gades (Cadiz), for example, had been Hannibal's operational base before the Romans had invaded and the name of Carthago Nova (Cartagena) reveals its Punic origins.

Rome developed its own cities on the peninsula, most notably Tarraco, the provincial capital of Tarraconensis, which sat at the mouth of the River Ebro. Although the settlement certainly pre-dated the Romans, it was not significantly developed until their arrival. The Romans gave the city an amphitheatre, and aqueduct an even a large circus for chariot racing.

Establishing new settlements

While Tarraco was simply developed by the Romans, Italica, near Hispalis (Seville), was actually founded by them. The town was established by Scipio Africanus in 206 BC to settle soldiers who had fought for him on the peninsula during the Punic Wars.

For much of its history, the town was largely eclipsed by Hispalis until its two most famous sons, the Emperors Trajan and Hadrian, invested considerably in its regeneration. Of the two, Hadrian took the greatest interest, which meant that much of it was built in his favoured Hellenic style. One of his greatest gifts to the town was an amphitheatre capable of seating 25,000 people – just half the capacity of the Colosseum; an incredible gift for a city with a population a fraction of the size of Rome's.

Arches of the aqueduct that runs through the city of Caceres in Spain.

Silhouette of the colonnades of the Roman theatre in Merida, Spain.

Trajan's Forum

Trajan established a large, new forum in Rome, the Trajan Forum, complete with a new shopping centre and the famous 'Trajan's Column' – a one-hundred-feet-high pillar designed to commemorate his victories in Dacia.

He also inaugurated the construction of a new aqueduct and a new public baths in Rome, as well as a new harbour at Ostia to increase the grain supply to Rome. His administration was particularly successful because he was courteous towards the Senate, employed first-rate administrators and allowed women an important role in public life.

Ruined building in the preserved remains of the port of Ostia. Trajan instigated the building of a new harbour at the Roman port to increase the grain supply to Rome.

A return to army life

After seven years of civilian life, Trajan was itching to return to the army. His opportunity came in 113 AD, when a dynastic dispute in Armenia provided him with the pretext to invade Parthia, Rome's long-time rival in the East. Trajan was highly successful; his troops easily overran the Parthians, quickly occupied their capital, Ctesiphon, and declared Mesopotamia as a Roman province.

The addition of Mesopotamia saw the Empire reach its greatest-ever extent, stretching all the way from the Atlantic Ocean to the Persian Gulf.

Trajan relished his time with the army, and it was said that, had he not been so old, he would have pressed on through Persia, in the footsteps of Alexander the Great.

Popular with the people

Trajan was one of Rome's greatest Emperors and was exceptionally popular in his own time because he had managed to strike a perfect balance of providing glorious victories without impinging upon the lives of ordinary Romans.

Detail from the carvings on Trajan's Column.

Hadrian

In 117 AD, Trajan died, and Publius Aelius Hadrianus (Hadrian) was declared Emperor in his place. Officially, it was stated that Trajan had adopted Hadrian on his deathbed, but a number of people cried foul play.

Arguments in the Senate

It was believed that Trajan's wife, Plotina, had tampered with the adoption after Trajan's death so that Hadrian, her favoured candidate, could take power. There were heated arguments in the Senate, but Hadrian's supporters won out; Hadrian became Emperor and several of the dissenters, namely four ex-consuls, were executed.

In spite of the questionable circumstances of the adoption, Trajan had certainly groomed Hadrian as a potential successor by advancing his political career and establishing a close relationship with him.

Coin depicting the head of Emperor Hadrian.

Reducing the frontiers

Hadrian's imperial policy was dramatically different to his predecessor's; Trajan emphasized expansionism, while Hadrian focused upon defence and consolidation. Hadrian believed the Empire to be overstretched so some of Trajan's territorial gains were quickly reversed under Hadrian. Troops were recalled from the East, Mesopotamia was put in the hands of client kings and expansion was halted in Britain, Germany and North Africa. The aim was to reduce the Empire to a more manageable size, and to revert to naturally defendable frontiers.

Hadrian seeks support

These seemingly inglorious policies did little to endear Hadrian to the Army. He was already suffering a lack of popularity in the Senate, where it was believed that the execution of four popular ex-consuls was too high a price to pay for Hadrian's succession.

Hadrian was forced to seek support among ordinary Romans; he cancelled all debts, which was an extremely popular gesture and certainly helped to win him the hearts and minds of his subjects. He further pleased the public by placing a strong emphasis on culture and entertainment as well as initiating a large number of civic building projects right across the Empire.

A section of the ruins of Hadrian's Villa, a country retreat built by the Emperor at a site near Tivoli, a day's march from Rome.

Hadrian's travels

During his reign, Hadrian travelled to almost every corner of his Empire, where he micromanaged the affairs of each province, and sometimes even each fort.

His first trip, which began in 121 AD and lasted four years, encompassed visits to Britannia, Hispania and Mauretania in the West, as well as Galatia, Asia and Syria in the East. While he was in Britannia in 122, the Emperor commissioned the construction of the famous 120-kilometre-long defensive wall which bears his name.

Hadrian's second trip took him to North Africa in 128, and the third and final trip from 128 to 132 took him exclusively to the East of the Empire, where much of his time was spent in Greece. Hadrian was an admirer of Hellenic culture; he took to following Greek fashions and spent a considerable amount of money on improvements and gifts for Athens.

Lover drowned

Hadrian's lover, Antinous, usually escorted the Emperor on his travels, but in 130, disaster struck when they were in Egypt. Antinous drowned whilst swimming in the Nile. Hadrian was devastated; Antinous was deified and statues of him were built across the Empire, and even a city, Antinopolis, was founded in his honour.

The Second Jewish Revolt

In 130, before reaching Egypt, Hadrian's travels took him to the province of Judea where his decisions and actions were to have long-reaching effects.

Initially, Hadrian had been relatively tolerant of the Jews, and boasted of plans to rebuild Jerusalem after it had been largely destroyed by the Roman Army in 70 BC, after an uprising against Roman rule. However, outrage spread among the Jewish population when it emerged that the city would be renamed Aelia Capitolina and a temple dedicated to Jupiter would be constructed on the site of the main Jewish temple.

The population rallied under the leadership of Simon Bar Kokhba and a revolt broke out in 132. The rebels were highly successful at first, but eventually capitulated to the Roman counterinsurgency, and by 135 the revolt had collapsed. The rebellion led Hadrian to believe that Judaism was inherently troublesome, so he sought to stamp it out; those lucky enough not to have been killed were forced out of the region as slaves or exiles. Judea was romanized, leaving the Jews without a homeland for more than eighteen hundred years.

Below: Archway entrance into the complex of Hadrian's Villa, just outside Tivoli, 30 kilometres north-east of Rome.

Right: Head of Antinous, the lover of Emperor Hadrian, who drowned while swimming in the Nile. After his death, Antinous was deified and statues of him erected throughout the Empire.

Hadrian's Villa

In 118 AD, work was begun on a villa for Hadrian's personal use. He disliked the imperial palace on the Palatine Hill and wished to build a retreat outside the city. His villa, *Villa Adriana* in Italian, was located just outside Tibur (Tivoli), a town thirty kilometres from Rome.

As his reign progressed, more and more time was spent there, until eventually he governed the Empire from the Villa. As a result there was a large court in permanent residence, with a postal service directly linked to Rome.

Caryatids *line one of the sides of the water of the* Canopus, *an artificial pool, named after the canal at Alexandria.*

The villa was so extensive that it would have appeared more like a small town, complete with theatres, libraries, bathhouses, swimming pools and an infirmary.

A carefully chosen site

The site was carefully chosen; it was on a hillside surrounded by two tributaries of the Aniene that flowed into the Tiber, providing an easy means of transport between the Villa and Rome. There was also a plentiful supply of water from the aqueducts serving Rome – essential to fill the number of baths in the Villa. Quarries were also available nearby for the building materials required, including travertine, lime, pozzolana and tufa.

Construction took place between 118 and 138 AD, probably in two distinct and separate phases, with the buildings laid out to follow five alignments. Unusually the planners did not use the usual rigid Roman town planning patterns but instead mapped the structures along the natural terrain.

Looking towards the Euripus, *the semi-circle of arches with statues at one end of the* Canopus.

Inspired by Hadrian's travels

Covering an area of at least 100 hectares, and containing over thirty separate buildings, there is evidence of many different types of architecture, all inspired by Hadrian's travels. He was widely acknowledged to be a gifted architect in his own right and was no doubt responsible for many of the stunning ideas, and often emulated a particular place or building he had seen with a building or garden design.

Although inspired by various types of architecture, the methods used were very much Roman, with buildings constructed in *opus mixtum*, a technique invented by Roman builders that combined cement, tufa blocks and bricks. The bricks were often stamped with the names of the Roman consuls in the year of production, giving archaeologists a perfect dating tool for each individual wall and structure.

Mosaic from Hadrian's Villa depicting a theatre mask.

The imperial palace was built on top of an older villa dating back to the first century BC. This was the nucleus of the residence, and the *cryptoporticus* can still be seen with its intricate mosaic decorations.

Significant features

Close by is the Maritime Theatre, named after the patterns used, based on marine themes. There is a circular island in the centre with a small Roman house, complete with baths and an atrium. It is surrounded by a lake and was probably used as a retreat for the Emperor – dating shows that it was one of the first structures to be built.

The *Pecile* is a huge courtyard surrounded by four porticoes, measuring approximately 230 by 100 metres with a 100 by 25 metre pool inside. The north side would have acted as a *porticus miliaria*, planned to a specific length that measured the distance advised by doctors for a healthy walk (*ambulatio*) at the time.

One of the best-preserved features is the *Canopus*, a long pool surrounded by a colonnade, based on the canal stretching from Alexandria to *Canopus*.

There were three sets of baths in the residence with the Small Baths being one of the most luxurious spaces inside the villa. These were beautifully decorated in marble, with intricate architecture, and no doubt used by the Emperor.

The Maritime Theatre was actually a small villa surrounded by a moat. During Hadrian's day the moat was crossable only by a portable wooden bridge, giving the appearance of an unapproachable island home and offering a peaceful retreat.

Other occupants

The villa is served by a warren of underground tunnels, used to transport servants and goods around, while the higher-ranking residents used the roads above.

After Hadrian died in 138, Antoninus, his adopted successor, continued to use the residence, as did Marcus Aurelius. Wall paintings found from the third century also show that it was occupied under the Severans.

However, Constantine I did not use it and had many valuable objects removed to Constantinople. It fell into ruins and was then an easy source of marble and other building materials needed for new constructions.

Reconstruction of Doric colums in a corridor area.

Discovery and decimation

Pietro Ligorio and other humanists began to excavate the villa in the sixteenth century, a time when it was officially identified as Hadrian's residence. An eminent architect, he discovered the fountains and *nymphaeums* with all the statues and decorative work.

Ironically his discovery led directly to the decimation of the villa. In the seventeenth and eighteenth centuries the land was divided, with the owners removing any remaining valuable objects, such as statues or mosaics, which were dispersed through Europe; many ended up in papal collections that can now be viewed in museums.

Excavation finally began in the late nineteenth century after Italy was unified. The site became protected and Pietro Rosa began a systematic and scientific exploration. This work was then continued by Lanciani, Aurigemma and Vighi, along with many foreign academies centred in Rome.

Hadrian's Villa is now a UNESCO World Heritage Site and widely regarded as one of the most stunning Roman excavations, giving a privileged insight into the interests and lifestyle of the Emperor.

View down the Canopus *to the* Serapeum, *a hemispherical dome, the interior of which was decorated with paste glass mosaics.*

The Arts

Much of early Roman art was influenced by the Etruscans and then the Greeks. When Syracuse in Sicily fell to the Romans in 210 BC, many Greek works of art, particularly sculptures, were plundered and brought back to Rome. Collecting Greek sculptures became a major occupation, and later, as Greek artists moved nearer to the centre of the Republic, works were commissioned in the Greek style.

Roman realism

The style of Greek classicism gradually gave way to Roman realism and many of the sculptures which survive today are un-idealized portraits of real Roman people. Busts or portrait sculptures were often made to display in the home. Larger pieces, made to signify importance or power – often of gods and goddesses, emperors or heroic soldiers – were erected in prominent places around Rome, and other towns and cities throughout the Republic, and later the Empire.

This bust of Emperor Caracalla shows the realism which was a feature of Roman sculpture.

Bas-relief sculptures – shallow carvings – were used to decorate arches, columns and temples; a magnificent example of this is Trajan's Column which stands in Trajan's Forum in Rome.

Most Roman sculpture was made in marble or bronze, although there is some evidence that more common and less expensive materials, such as terracotta, were used and painted over.

Fresco painting

Very few paintings from Roman times have survived to date. Most of the images rendered in two dimensions during the period were wall frescoes, where paint is applied to the walls of houses and other buildings. As most of these structures have been destroyed or buried, so the paintings have perished.

Much of our knowledge comes from the well-preserved houses of Pompeii and Herculaneum, buried under metres of ash after the eruption of Vesuvius in 79 AD. One of the most stunning examples of mural work can be seen in the Villa of the Mysteries just outside Pompeii. Here, the fresco runs for seventeen metres around the four walls of a room, depicting life-sized figures in a Dionysian initiation rite.

The Romans' interest in nature and daily life is evident in the paintings of landscapes and in portraiture. The artists of the time had mastered the technique of perspective, and by painting onto the walls were able to create the illusion of windows looking out onto gardens. Paint was applied to wet plaster and it is thought that this has helped preserve the colours and detail of many of the murals that have been uncovered.

Sculpture of a reclining figure from the port of Ostia.

Mosaics endure

Unlike painting, mosaics were more easily preserved and numerous examples of this art form can be found throughout the countries of the old Empire, although the quality of preservation varies.

An invention of the Greeks, mosaics were first worked in black and white, with colour making an appearance in the Western Empire and Africa at a later date. Traditionally, mosaics were laid on the floor, using tesserae, small tiles of coloured stone and glass, laid on mortar. The excavations of Pompeii and Herculaneum have revealed that wall mosaics were also popular.

Melodies without harmonies

Very little is known about the music of Ancient Rome, although it was probably influenced by the Greeks and likely to have been played as simple melodies with no harmonies. Music was played on many occasions: at private and public functions, funerals, religious ceremonies and at gladiatorial games.

The Romans possessed stringed instruments such as the lyre, lute and kithara; wind instruments were also played, using a reed. A double-reed instrument, known as an *aulos*, sounded rather like a clarinet, and a form of bagpipe, called an *ascaules*, was played. There were also drums, cymbals and castanets.

Roman writers

Throughout the Roman Republic and Empire periods, writers produced numerous works of literature in the form of poems, plays, history and comedies. Many have survived today and the Latin language itself continued for many centuries as the written medium around much of Western Europe.

Wall fresco which depicts a horned theatre mask.

Early Latin literature, up until the first century BC, can be exemplified by the comedies of Plautus and Terence. From about 100 BC to the beginning of the first century AD, The Golden Age produced poets such as Virgil and Ovid, the prose of Julius Caesar and historical works by Livy. This was succeeded by The Silver Age, when Pliny the Elder and the Younger were writing, along with Petronius and Juvenal.

Theatre at Ostia. Most plays were staged in a semi-circular theatre, rather than the circular or oval amphitheatres which were used for gladiatorial contests, animal hunts and other grand public displays.

Antoninus

The first Antonine Emperors upheld the good governance of the Nervo-Trajanic rulers and perfected it. Although the dynasty was sullied by Commodus, who reverted to the capricious megalomaniacal ways of the Julio-Claudians and set the Empire on a path to its eventual downfall, the first of the Antonines, Antoninus the Pius was a 'good Emperor'.

Death of Hadrian

Hadrian had firsthand experience of the problems that arose when an Emperor did not appoint a clear successor. He wished to avoid making the same mistake as Trajan and in 137 AD, he adopted Titus Aurelius Fulvus Boionius Antoninus, a man just ten years his junior.

Antoninus was a prudent choice because he came from a family of consuls and was sure to be an acceptable candidate to all parties, which meant he could maintain peace and stability in the Empire. In 138, Hadrian died at his Villa in Tivoli, and Antoninus became Emperor in his stead.

The Senate was not disposed to deify Hadrian, but Antoninus insisted on this and presided over the funeral of his adopted father. Respectfully honouring Hadrian in this way earned Antoninus the name 'Pius', a name he lived up to as Emperor. Hadrian was entombed in a grand mausoleum that still stands today, called the Castel Sant'Angelo.

Stability a priority

Antoninus was in advanced years when he became Emperor and although he was not expected to live long, he ruled Rome for twenty-three years.

Unlike his predecessors, he did not impose his personality on the Empire, but ruled modestly and frugally. This made him a rather uncontroversial character who made few enemies during his reign.

His chief policy was to maintain stability, which was achieved by keeping Rome's finances in check. Antoninus opted for austere economic measures and cut back luxury public spending, reducing the amount of civic construction.

In his foreign policy, Antoninus was less conservative. He is most famous for extending north of Hadrian's Wall in Britannia. He added an extra one hundred miles to the Empire when he ordered the construction of a second defensive wall, the 'Antonine Wall', which stretched from the Firth of Forth to the Firth of Clyde.

Above: Inscribed stone tablet probably from the reign of Antoninus. Found in the ruins of Sabrath, one of the three cities which made up ancient Tripoli (Three Cities). The text makes reference to Nerva, Trajan and Hadrian, Antoninus' three predecessors.

Bust of Antoninus Pius, the first of the Antonine Emperors and one of the 'five good Emperors'.

Marcus Aurelius

Hadrian had first noticed the promise in a young Marcus Aurelius and had encouraged Antoninus to adopt him. Antoninus, already having a familial link to Aurelius as his uncle by marriage, happily complied.

Dual rulers

Following Aurelius' adoption, he effectively ruled alongside the ageing Antoninus and was ready to assume control upon the Emperor's death in 161 AD. However, he was not to rule alone. Hadrian had convinced Antoninus to adopt a second heir, Lucius Ceionius Commodus Verus (Lucius Verus).

Worried that Verus was similar in character to the errant Julio-Claudian Emperors, the Senate tried to overrule his appointment after Antoninus' death. However, Aurelius held firm to Antoninus' and Hadrian's wishes and convinced the Senate that Verus should rule alongside him. To strengthen the relationship between the two Emperors, Aurelius married his daughter to Verus, a gesture which confirmed Aurelius as the senior partner.

War with Parthia

The first concern facing the co-rulers was a new war with Parthia in the East. Since Hadrian had pulled out of the region following Trajan's successes, the Parthians had once again begun meddling in the affairs of Armenia. Neither Emperor had military experience, but Lucius Verus was sent to lead the campaign.

Although Verus frittered away much of his time behind the frontline, the Romans defeated the Parthians and the Emperors were able to take credit for their first military victory.

Celebrations were short-lived because plague spread across the Empire and killed scores of people. One of its victims was Verus himself, who died in 169 at just thirty-nine years old. Aurelius became the sole Emperor and moved to pacify the Germanic tribes for much of the following decade. In 177, he decided to revert to diarchic rule and appointed his son, Lucius Aelius Aurelius Commodus as a co-ruler.

Meditations

Marcus Aurelius is best remembered for his book, *Meditations*. The work offers an important contribution to Stoic philosophy, which had a profound impact over Aurelius' life. It also acts as an insightful autobiographical account of his life. Aurelius had a favourable reputation at the time, which has largely endured, but is somewhat tarnished by his occasional persecution of Christians.

The column of Marcus Aurelius. Modelled on Trajan's Column Marcus Aurelius' celebrates his triumph over the Germanic tribes.

Commodus

When Marcus Aurelius died in Vindobona (Vienna) in 180 AD, his biological son and successor, Commodus, had already had three years experience of ruling alongside his father as co-Emperor.

Unfitted to the role

However, such experience seems to have counted for very little and Commodus proved himself to be a poor emperor. With his accession to the imperial role, the line of 'Good Emperors' came to an end.

Aurelius is often blamed for reverting to a dynastic succession, rather than appointing the best person for the job. It is worth noting that each of the five 'Good Emperors' was adopted, not the biological son of the previous Emperor.

Pleasure of the imperial position

Although his father, Marcus Aurelius, had invested the last years of his life in pacifying the Rhine and the Danube borders Commodus had little interest in these wars. He quickly concluded a treaty with his father's enemies so that he could return to Rome and enjoy the pleasures that the imperial position opened to him.

It is reputed that he was debauched, avaricious and cruel. He was so convinced of his physical prowess that he believed that he was a reincarnation of Hercules – a number of statues show him masquerading as Hercules in a lion skin and carrying a club.

He further outraged Roman opinion by participating in gladiator fights – a sport usually undertaken by slaves. He has often been likened to Caligula because he and Aurelius were another example of a popular father and megalomaniacal son pairing.

Commodus' wayward behaviour eventually resulted in his murder in 192. His rule had signalled the end of the Pax Romana, a two-hundred-year period of relative peace and prosperity, and pushed Rome headlong into a period of crisis.

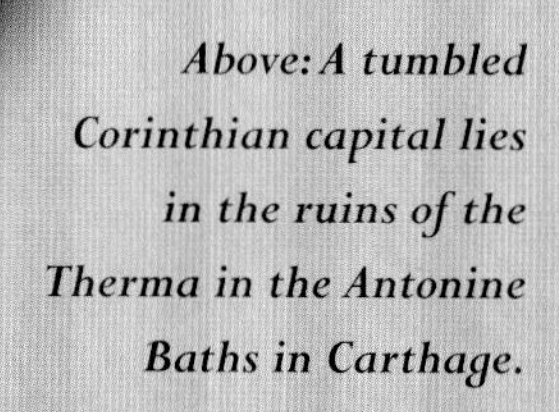

Above: A tumbled Corinthian capital lies in the ruins of the Therma in the Antonine Baths in Carthage.

Portrait bust of Commodus

Education and Thought

During the early Republic most children were educated at home by their parents. Mothers would teach their children until the age of seven, at which time a son's development would be transferred to his father's charge, while the mother would continue to teach her daughter.

Fathers taught their sons all they would need to know for everyday life in Roman society; a son would even receive clients with his father as practice for when he himself would become a patron. While boys learned a whole range of disciplines, girls were usually only instructed in the domestic tasks expected of them once they were married.

Greek schools

After the conquest of Greece, many Roman children received a Hellenized education, which meant sending children out to school for their academic development. Between the ages of seven and twelve, Roman children went to elementary school, called a *ludus*, where a Greek teacher, who was often a slave, taught them.

Ancient Rome had a relatively high literacy rate, which indicates that a significant proportion of the population would have received elementary schooling, despite having to pay fees. Class sizes would have been very large to keep the costs sufficiently low for ordinary Romans to have been able to afford them.

Rich and poor

The poorest Roman children would not have been able to go to school because families could not afford either the cost of sending them in the first place or the cost of the child not working.

Richer families often preferred not to send their children to school, but rather to bring a tutor, called a *paedagogus*, into their home. Like an elementary school teacher, tutors were usually Greek slaves. However, they would be exclusively attached to one family and would become a member of the household staff like the other slaves.

Roman mosaic depicting the academy of Plato. Greek thinkers like Plato had a huge influence on Roman thought.

Further education

At the age of twelve, ordinary Roman children, lucky enough to have gone to school, would go out into the workplace. For the boys of richer families there would be an opportunity to go on to further education at a *grammaticus*. At these secondary schools, lessons were given in both Latin and Greek; pupils were expected to study and recite various works of classical literature, ranging from Homer to Virgil. After completing secondary school, a handful of the wealthiest boys were sent for further education where they were taught rhetoric, in practice for a career in politics or law.

Girls from richer families were not allowed to receive a secondary education but were instead expected to get married.

Literature

As with education, Roman literature drew greatly on the influences of the Ancient Greeks. At the end of the third century BC, Plautus began adapting Greek comedies into Latin, and Ennius, who is widely regarded as the father of Latin poetry, began styling his own works on those of the Ancient Greeks.

The end of the Republic and the beginning of the Empire is considered to be the Golden Age, when Latin literature came into its own, (albeit still intensely influenced by Homer). The seminal work of this time was Virgil's nationalist epic, the *Aeneid*, which developed the legend that the Romans were the descendants of the people of Troy.

Virgil and Horace

The poem took Virgil ten years to write and had only just been completed at the time of his death in 19 BC, which meant he had no time to revise the piece. The *Aeneid* was popular with Augustus because it chimed well with the traditional values he was trying to reintroduce. Augustus wanted more of the same and encouraged Virgil's patron, Gaius Cilnius Maecenas, to find more of these aspiring Latin poets. Virgil introduced him to Horace, who was to become another celebrated 'Augustan Poet' and coined the famous nationalist phrase '*Dulce et decorum est pro patria mori*' – 'It is sweet and proper to die for one's country'.

Fresco painting from Pompeii of a young woman holding a stylus. It is suggested that the picture portrays Sappho, the famous Greek poet who was born on the island of Lesbos in the late seventh century BC.

Ovid banished

The support of Maecenas and Augustus certainly helped make the Golden Age, but not all of the great poets of the era met with the Emperor's approval; Ovid was banished by Augustus to a life of exile on the Black Sea. The reasons for this are not clear, but it is believed that the liberal nature of some of Ovid's love poems did not sit easily alongside the Emperor's drive for family values.

Livy's History

The Romans were accomplished historians, a trait which has allowed modern readers unprecedented insights into the civilization. The most famous was Titus Livius (Livy), an Augustan historian who wrote a grand historical survey of Rome from its foundations to the rule of Augustus.

Livy's history was written over one hundred and forty-two books, but unfortunately only thirty-five survive. Tacitus and Suetonius picked up where Livy left off and wrote about the lives of the early Emperors in their books *Annals* and *The Twelve Caesars*, respectively.

Emperor's accounts

Dio Cassius' *Roman History* spanned an even longer period; he began his study at the time of Aeneas and ended it in 229 AD during the reign of Alexander Severus. Although it covers a significant time period, the earlier sections in *Roman History* are less detailed than Livy's work and the book is most useful for its accounts of the later Emperors.

Many Romans enjoyed writing histories; Caesar's *Gallic Wars* and *Civil War* provide his perspective on the histories of the war in Gaul and the war against Pompey. Even the Emperor Claudius took to writing history in his youth, but his works have, unfortunately, been lost.

Fresco depicting a meditating Philistine.

The Neumagen School Relief. This bas-relief, depicting students and their teacher is housed in the Roman Archaeological Museum (Landesmuseum) in Trier, Germany.

Economy

Roman trade and industry was largely an internal affair; little was needed from outside and most trade and industry occurred within the Empire. Rome owed this self-sufficiency to an abundance of natural resources, a complex network of roads across the Empire and above all, the exploitative use of slave labour.

Moving materials round the Empire

The roads allowed cargo to be transported from one part of the Empire to the other; they connected merchants in Britannia with those in Egypt, although much of the trade was destined exclusively for Rome. Transporting goods across land was slow but steady because horses, camels, donkeys or people were required to haul the cargo over the long distances. Towns along the trade routes felt the economic benefit of these traders and couriers passing through, and grew in importance as a result.

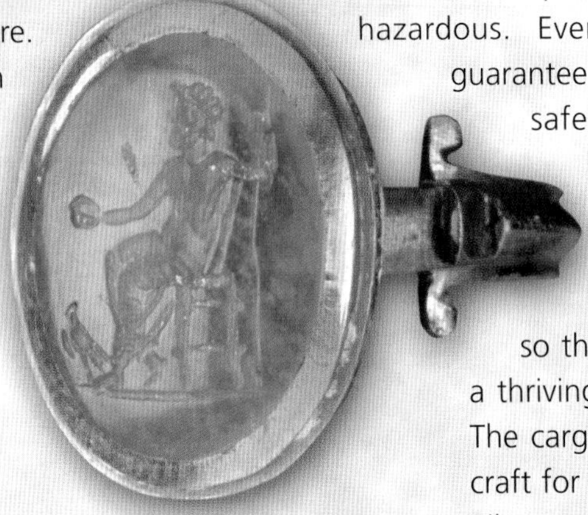

Gold ring set with translucent, engraved gemstone.

When there was a need to transport heavier cargo, there was little option but to do so by sea. This was hazardous. Even if the Roman Navy could guarantee safety from pirates, it could not safeguard against bad weather, which could easily wreck merchant vessels. Cargo ships were unable to reach Rome along the narrower River Tiber, so their cargo was offloaded at Ostia, a thriving port town at the river's mouth. The cargo was then loaded on to smaller craft for the last leg of the journey up the Tiber to the city.

Materials, foodstuffs and manufactured products were traded within the Empire and the Romans rarely resorted to importing from without. One of Rome's few notable exceptions was silk from China. Romans did not have the resources to manufacture silk, which made it an exotic and luxurious commodity, enjoyed only by the richest citizens. Silk initially reached Rome through the Parthian Empire, but after Trajan extended Roman territory to the Persian Gulf, the Romans were able to develop direct links with China.

Street in the remains of Ostia, Rome's port. Cargo ships were unable to reach Rome along the narrower River Tiber, so the cargo was offloaded at Ostia. It was then loaded on to smaller craft for the last leg of the journey up the Tiber to the city.

An economy built on slave labour

Slavery was vital to the Roman economy; by using people as mere commodities, the Romans were able to drastically reduce the cost of production of all they grew, made, mined and transported. Although slaves provided free labour in theory, many owners chose to provide some form of payment to give slaves an incentive to work hard. Even limited funds would have been sufficient incentive because when slaves earned enough money they were able to buy their freedom.

During the late Republic and early Empire, the Roman economy thrived because fresh sources of slaves were made available by successful Roman conquests. Rome had a particularly bountiful supply in 146 BC, when the cities of Carthage and Corinth were both destroyed and all the surviving inhabitants were sold into slavery. The crucial role played by slaves was revealed when the Roman economy went into decline in the third century AD, once Rome had stopped expanding and the supply of slaves had dried up.

Keeping the country fed

Agriculture was the mainstay of the Roman economy. Grapes and olives were staple crops, but grain was by far the most important. Around the Empire, most grain was grown and used at a subsistence, or local level, but Rome's demand outstripped the supply capabilities of its hinterlands and it was forced to import grain on a large scale from North Africa, which earned the name 'the Granary of the Empire'.

This grain supply to Rome was of vital importance because a considerable proportion of the city relied on a free corn-dole to survive. Even after Caesar and Augustus reduced the number of people receiving free grain, it remained important to keep supply ahead of demand, to keep the prices low for ordinary Romans.

Mining conditions

Mining was an important industry, as a number of different metals were required to make a whole range of everyday items including coins, weapons, jewellery, piping, ornaments and paint. Mining was among the worst jobs available in Ancient Rome, so slaves were used for the task. With such an abundant supply, merchants did not need to worry about the terrible working conditions.

Slaves were forced to endure long hours of backbreaking work in cold, cramped, dark underground mines, which were prone to flooding and collapse. During the later Empire, when slaves became less plentiful, better working conditions were introduced to help extend life expectancy so that fewer slaves could work more years to compensate for the shortfall.

The Romans mined a variety of metals right across the Empire, especially in Hispania, where lead, iron, tin, silver, copper and gold could be found. Rome's manufacturing industry was relatively low-key. Basic goods such as glass, pottery, weapons, jewellery and textiles were manufactured on a small scale, although a large glassworks has been discovered at Colonia Agrippina (Cologne) in Germany.

Ruins of Las Medulas mine in Spain. It was the most important gold mine in the Roman Empire. Mining techniques, requiring vast amounts of water to eat away the hillside, led to the construction of a 100-kilometre-long system of channels to import water to the area, which is now a World Heritage site.

Taxing the population

In the early days of the Republic, Roman citizens were very lightly taxed on their land and possessions, even during times of war. Following a number of successful conquests, Roman citizens were no longer taxed at all; instead the occupied peoples of the Empire were forced to shoulder the tax burden.

During the period that Roman citizens had paid tax, they were counted by a census; however, the Romans were unable to conduct accurate censuses of their provinces. Instead they had to rely on a system of tax farming, which essentially privatized the collection of taxes – allowing tax farmers called *publicani* to impose additional fees on top of the taxes so they could take their cut.

At the start of the first century BC, Rome's Italian allies became so angered by having to pay tax, while the neighbouring Romans did not, that they declared a breakaway Republic. A short war followed during which Rome annexed large parts of the peninsula and agreed that most Italians could stop paying tax.

The rest of the Empire was not afforded the same luxury, although Emperor Augustus did scrap the abusive system of tax-farming. By compiling better census data, Augustus introduced direct taxation; on the one hand this meant that individuals could no longer be exploited by the *publicani*, but on the other, it allowed him to introduce a regressive head tax where everybody paid the same amount, irrespective of their personal wealth or income.

Roman money from the reign of Nero.

Chamber in the remains of the Forum in Rome. Most towns had at least one forum which was a political and economic meeting place for the citizens.

Early currency

In the early days of the Roman Republic, the Roman economy relied upon a direct exchange of goods or services, with one of the key units of payment being livestock. As Rome expanded, this system proved less practical and a new one, based upon payments in lieu, was developed.

The early Romans would exchange lumps of bronze, called *Aes rude*, for the goods and services they needed. Although this system was more efficient than the previous one, it still had its own impracticalities; the worth of the lump was in its weight, which required a weigh-in each time anyone carried out a transaction. Moreover, the system was open to easy forgery.

Coinage systems

At the start of the third century BC, war brought Rome into contact with the Greeks in the south of Italy and their system of using coins as currency. Rome began to adopt these Greek practices and established mints in its own territory.

Although bronze initially continued to underlie Roman currency, it was quickly replaced by silver coins, called *denarii*. The *denarii* was the foundation of the Roman economy for centuries, although it was significantly devalued over time.

Gold coins (*aureii*) were less readily available, especially during the Republic. The Emperors later took to minting gold coins to pay for costly foreign wars, but Augustus stipulated that they could only be made in Rome.

Economic inflation

The *denarii* became progressively weaker over time and although in 215 AD, Caracalla tried to reform the silver coinage by creating a new unit, the *antoninianii*, Rome slid into decades of political and economic chaos.

During the crisis of the third century, a rapid succession of ambitious army generals tried to appoint themselves Emperor using troops to back them up. To buy the loyalty of troops, the would-be Emperors took to minting their own coins, which led to inflation and a decline in central control of the money supply.

Diocletian brought about political stability at the end of the third century and with it, he returned Rome to economic health. He increased the value of Roman coinage by insisting on a greater rate of metal purity in the coins and then imposed strict limits to stop the value of the currency from fluctuating in the future.

Cornices with inscriptions lie in the Severan Basilica of Leptis Magna. The birthplace of Severus, Leptis Magna in North Africa had a number of lavish building works constructed in it during his reign.

Severus and his legacy

Severus

Commodus' reign upset the momentum of the Empire; within months of his death, Rome had once again reverted to civil war. Respite was briefly offered by the stable, if ruthless, reign of Septimius Severus. But after his death, Rome slid into five decades of disorder.

Publius Helvius Pertinax was appointed Emperor upon the death of Commodus. Like Nerva, he was in advanced years, making him very much a 'stop-gap' arrangement. Pertinax tried to restore the Empire to economic health and saw the need to reduce the bonuses and rewards paid to the Army. This was an unwise move; the Army believed the cuts were politically motivated and the Emperor was murdered just a few months into his reign.

Buying control

Without an obvious heir to Pertinax, the Praetorian Guard saw the perfect opportunity to sell the principate to the highest bidder. Didius Julianus' offer of 25,000 *sestertii* won the auction and the Senate was forced to recognize his authority.

However, this appointment was not widely accepted and three other men were emerging as contenders for the throne: Pescennius Niger, governor of Syria; Clodius Albinus, governor of Britannia; and Septimius Severus, who had command of the troops in Pannonia.

Pannonia was the closest of the three provinces to Rome, so it was Severus who posed the most immediate threat to Julianus. After marching on Rome, Severus gained the crucial support of the Praetorian Guard and the Senate. He brought Julianus' two-month reign to a conclusion by ordering his execution, and then set himself against his rival contenders, Niger and Albinus.

Bust of Emperor Septimius Severus.

Civil war ensues

Severus first concluded an expedient peace with Albinus to secure the West while he went to war with Niger in the East. By giving Albinus the conciliatory title 'Caesar', Severus hinted that he would appoint Albinus as his heir. This placated Albinus who agreed not to declare his own imperial ambitions, giving Severus a free hand to deal with Niger in the East.

Niger was quickly defeated and killed at the Battle of Issus in 194 AD – on the same field where Alexander the Great had scored an historic victory against the Persians in 333 BC.

Many of Niger's forces fled into neighbouring Parthia to escape Severan punishment. However, Parthia was too weak to act as a safe haven and in 195, Severus chased Niger's troops into the region and mercilessly hunted them down.

With the last vestiges of Niger's support removed, his province, Syria, was broken up, and the East was pacified.

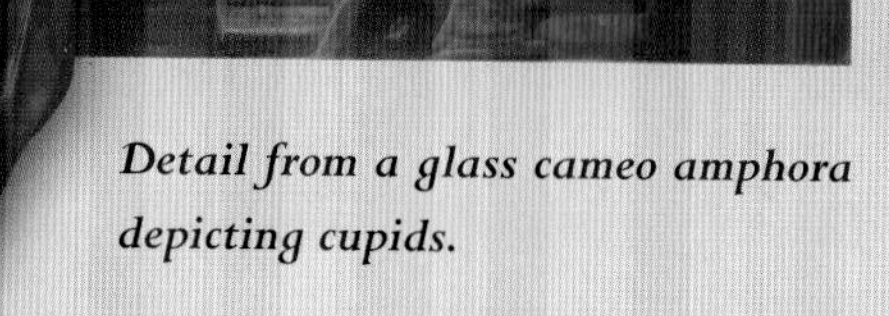

Detail from a glass cameo amphora depicting cupids.

In 196 AD, confident of his power in the East, Severus then turned his attentions to the West, when he reneged on his unwritten understanding with Albinus by appointing his own son as his heir. This was a veiled challenge, which Albinus took up. He declared himself Emperor while in Britannia and crossed with his troops into Gaul to begin the march on Rome.

Albinus advanced only as far as Lugdunum (Lyon), where Severus had come out to meet him. The resulting battle was closely fought, but Albinus was murdered, leaving Severus as the unchallenged ruler of the Roman world.

A popular but ruthless leader

Severus accrued a reputation for ruthlessness during the civil war, which he continued to live up to. Soon after Albinus was defeated, Severus invaded Parthia and captured the capital, Ctesiphon. Here, the male population was butchered, the women and children were sold into slavery and Upper Mesopotamia was reincorporated into the Empire.

Despite such ruthlessness, Severus became popular in Rome because he reintroduced stability. He shored up his authority by disbanding the Praetorian Guard and replacing them with a personal bodyguard comprising his loyal army officers.

Lavish construction work

Severus was the first Roman Emperor from Africa. He had been born to a romanized family in Leptis Magna, a city that had come to prominence under the Carthaginians. He lavished a great deal of attention on the city and helped regenerate it to become a leading metropolis in the Empire.

Nor did he overlook his adopted home of Rome. Severus is remembered for contributing a number of new buildings, most notably the Arch of Septimius Severus, built at the entrance to the Forum to commemorate his victories over the Parthians.

Frigidarium of the Hadrianic Baths in Leptis Magna, Libya. Leptis Magna was the birthplace of Septimius Severus, who lavished a huge construction programme on the city during his reign.

Caracalla

Before being succeeded by his sons, Caracalla and Geta, Severus spent the last years of his reign campaigning against the 'barbarian' tribes in the north of Britain, where he died in 211 AD.

The Antonine Wall had been abandoned but the Romans had not retreated to the safety of Hadrian's Wall. Although Severus scored several victories, he realized that advances offered little solution to the Caledonian menace. He resolved to revert to Hadrian's line of defence, and had the wall repaired and brought back into action. Severus never returned to Rome; he died in Eburacum (York).

Warring heirs

Severus' rule provided temporary stability for the Empire, but the appointment of both his sons, Septimus Bassianus Caracalla and Lucius Septimus Geta as his heirs, seems to have lacked forethought.

Severus knew that his sons did not get on and must have expected some sort of trouble in the future.The initial plan was to divide the Empire between them, but Caracalla prevented this by murdering his brother and reigning supreme.

Caracalla did not stop at fratricide; during his reign, thousands were killed during his terror campaign. He spent much of his time away from Rome, fighting wars, and much of the legislation he passed was designed to benefit the military.

Of his more populist acts, Caracalla granted Roman citizenship to all freeborn men of the Empire. He also commissioned the construction of an extensive bathing complex in Rome, which housed 1,600 bathers at a time. Extensive remains of the complex are still visible today.

Bust of the Emperor Caracalla. After his father Severus' death, he succeeded to the imperial position with his brother Geta, becoming supreme ruler when he murdered Geta.

Ruins of the Severan Basilica in Leptis Magna, Libya.

Caracalla's death

Caracalla was murdered in 217. For all his shortcomings, he had provided a relative degree of stability for the Empire.

His Praetorian Prefect, Marcus Opellius Macrinus, was widely believed responsible, but he proclaimed himself Emperor and managed to find a scapegoat for Caracalla's murder. Macrinus was not well liked. He did not ever visit Rome and his military campaigns were rather lacklustre.

The Severan women

The females of the marginalized Severan family used Macrinus' unpopularity to their advantage – they plotted a coup to return a Severan to the throne. In 218 AD they claimed that Caracalla's cousin, Elagabalus, was in fact his illegitimate son and proclaimed him Emperor.

The unpopular Macrinus was executed by his troops and the seventeen-year-old Elagabalus became Emperor. Much of his power was vested in his mother, Julia Soaemias, and his grandmother, Julia Maesa; Elagabalus is remembered for little other than his decadence and his promiscuity.

Julia Maesa in control

It became clear that power really lay with Julia Maesa. In 222, when the family was divided by a dispute, Julia Maesa had Elagabalus, her grandson, and Julia Soaemias, her daughter, killed and promoted another grandson, Alexander Severus, to the position of Emperor.

When he assumed the imperial title, Alexander was even younger than his cousin, Elagabalus, had been. This allowed the overbearing Julia Maesa to continue ruling the Empire. Her authority was shared with her other daughter, Alexander's mother, Julia Mamaea.

End of the Severan dynasty

Unlike her unfortunate sister, Julia Mamaea outlived her mother, who died in 226, and continued to dominate imperial politics until the end of Alexander's reign.

Alexander never proved much of a tactician and his troops murdered him in Germany in 235, after several mediocre campaigns. His mother, who usually accompanied him to the front, suffered the same fate.

With Alexander's death, the Severan dynasty was brought to an inglorious and bloody conclusion.

Women's Lives

The rights of Roman women seem very limited when they are judged by modern standards, but Roman women did enjoy greater freedoms than their counterparts in contemporary civilizations. By any standards, Rome was a highly patriarchal society where a woman's chief function was to have children and maintain the home. Men were supported by the law in this regard – if a woman could not, or would not, have children, her husband was free to divorce her.

Nevertheless, women in Ancient Rome were not simply considered instruments of reproduction, they played important roles in raising children and supporting their husband. Over time, some of the patriarchal barriers that Roman society threw in their way were overcome, and a handful of women even enjoyed especially prominent positions in society.

Wife and mother

Roman women spent their lives under the complete control of their fathers until they were married, when authority was transferred directly to their husbands. Women were married between the ages of twelve and fifteen to men who were usually several years older; after the wedding, they were expected to reproduce. As infant mortality was high and many children died before reaching adulthood, a woman would spend a large portion of her life having as many children as possible. The frequency and number of pregnancies and births endured by Roman women meant that it was relatively common for women to die in the process.

Household roles

In the Roman family, it was the woman who was responsible for the formative years of the children; she would usually give them a basic education before they went to elementary school at the age of seven. This differed from Ancient Greece, where the men were in charge of education.

Most women did not work and were charged with keeping the house instead; in richer households this meant managing the slaves; in poorer ones, it meant doing the work themselves. Some poorer women had little choice but to seek paid work as midwives, hairdressers or dressmakers. It is likely that many women would have also assisted their husbands in a family shop or workshop. Although wealthier women did not work, the wives of politicians did assist their husbands through providing support and sometimes offering opinions.

Fresco showing a woman pouring perfume into a vial.

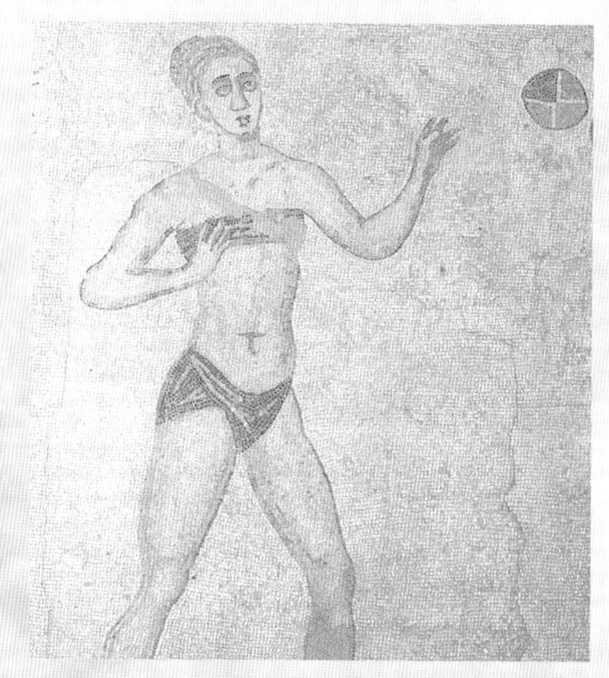

Detail from a mosaic in the Villa Romana del Casale in the Piazza Armerina, Sicily, Italy, depicting a young woman exercising.

Limited lives

Women's lives were confined by a variety of restrictions. They were also not allowed to vote, run for political office, or own property. They were often not free to make purchases without the agreement of their husband or father, and drinking wine was punishable by death. Perhaps most restrictive of all was that women were inferior before the law, especially during the early Republic.

There were some exceptions, notably the Vestal Virgins, who were fortunate enough to be outside these restrictions because they were free of the control of their paterfamilias (father of the family). Some women were also able to channel their political ambitions through their husbands or sons.

Personal freedoms

Although they were stifled publicly, Roman women enjoyed a relatively high degree of personal freedom. They were allowed to leave the house without their husbands, and could visit the baths – albeit for a limited time in the morning – as well as the theatre and even the games.

During the late Republic, these freedoms became more commonplace, as Rome underwent a social transformation and the stuffier constraints of the early Republic were lifted. Women enjoyed greater independence and better treatment before the law. Moreover, with the death of almost a generation of landowning Romans in the Second Punic War, many Roman women found themselves taking over the roles traditionally played by their husbands.

Constraints re-imposed

These newfound freedoms for women led to a sharp decline in the birth rate. This led the Emperor Augustus to curb many of the freedoms women had enjoyed. They were expected to stay at home more, so constraints were imposed on their attendance at the games and the theatre, and tougher laws were re-imposed on adultery. These were expedient measures to restore the birthrate, because as soon as a woman had more than three surviving children, she was allowed to resume her relatively independent lifestyle.

An intricately adorned gold necklace.

Powerful women

Although men dominate the history of Rome, a few women were able to make a name for themselves, especially during the Empire, when the mothers, wives and even grandmothers of Emperors involved themselves in affairs of state.

Perhaps the most prominent woman in Ancient Rome was Livia Drusilla, the wife of Augustus. It is believed that she had considerable influence over her husband's decisions and enjoyed a good deal of independence from him – she even had clients of her own. Livia publicly supported her husband's attempts to re-impose family values and portrayed herself as an image of frugality and traditional womanhood. However, she is also remembered for being privately ambitious; she is thought to have tampered with Augustus' succession and removed all competition to her son, Tiberius. Livia became the first woman to join the Imperial Cult when Claudius deified her in 42 AD.

Agrippina and Poppaea

Nero's mother, Agrippina the Younger, had less discreet ambitions – it is thought that she murdered her husband Claudius, so that her son, Nero would inherit the throne. Agrippina then proceeded to rule alongside her son – going so far as to have coins minted with her head on. She became such a nuisance to Nero that in the end he resolved to kill his own mother to get her out of the way.

Nero continued to be influenced by women, when his second wife, Poppaea, stepped up to fill Agrippina's shoes. She is thought to have had a good deal of power – even encouraging Nero to murder his popular ex-wife. However, Poppaea faced the same fate as his mother; she died when an angry Nero kicked her in the stomach while she was pregnant.

Women of the Severan Family

In the third century, the women of the Severan Dynasty managed to maintain a lengthy grip on power. Julia Donna, the wife of Septimius Severus exerted considerable influence over her husband, which was then transferred on to her son, Caracalla, after Severus' death. She accompanied both Emperors on campaigns which took her from Britain in the West to Parthia in the East.

When Caracalla was overthrown, Julia Donna killed herself, but her sister Julia Maesa kept the ambition of the Severan women alight. She overthrew the incumbent ruler, Macrinus, and together with her equally determined daughter, Julia Soaemias, placed her grandson, Elagabalus on the throne. After Elagabalus proved to be a weak ruler and a liability, Julia Maesa conspired with her other daughter Julia Mamaea to kill Elagabalus and Julia Soaemias, and place another grandson on the throne.

Fresco Painting of Female Saint with a Mirror

Virtuous women

Although most famous women of Ancient Rome are remembered for their political roles, a small number are remembered for either their virtue or their vice. Cornelia Scipionus Africana, the mother of the Gracchi brothers, was considered so honourable that a statue was erected in her memory in Rome in the first century BC.

At a time when social norms were breaking down and many women were seeking greater freedom, Cornelia lived the life of a traditional Roman woman; she was pious and frugal as well as being a devoted wife and mother – she even bore her husband twelve children, although only three survived to adulthood.

During the Roman Monarchy, the son of King Tarquinius Superbus raped a Roman noblewoman called Lucretia. She reported the crime to her family, having them swear to punish the prince; she then committed suicide out of respect for her own virtue and her husband's honour.

Both Lucretia and Cornelia became role models for Roman women, but there were also women who became infamous and served as a lesson for how women should not behave.

Treachery and inconstancy

Tarpeia was the original wayward woman; right at the dawn of Rome, it is believed that she opened the gates of a well-defended Roman fortress for the Sabine enemy to enter, provided they gave her their jewellery in exchange. Her behaviour was considered so treacherous that even the Sabine soldiers, who stood to gain from her treason, were repulsed; each took a turn at striking her with a shield until she was killed.

The only child of Augustus, Julia the Elder, is also remembered for her vice; at a time when Augustus was emphasizing family values, she was scandalizing public opinion with stories of drinking alcohol and extramarital affairs (she was married to the future Emperor Tiberius at the time). Julia was fortunate not to have been executed by Augustus, her paterfamilias; instead, she was exiled to an inhospitable island. Her story reveals something of the double standards men held towards women, because Augustus was notorious for scandalous behaviour himself.

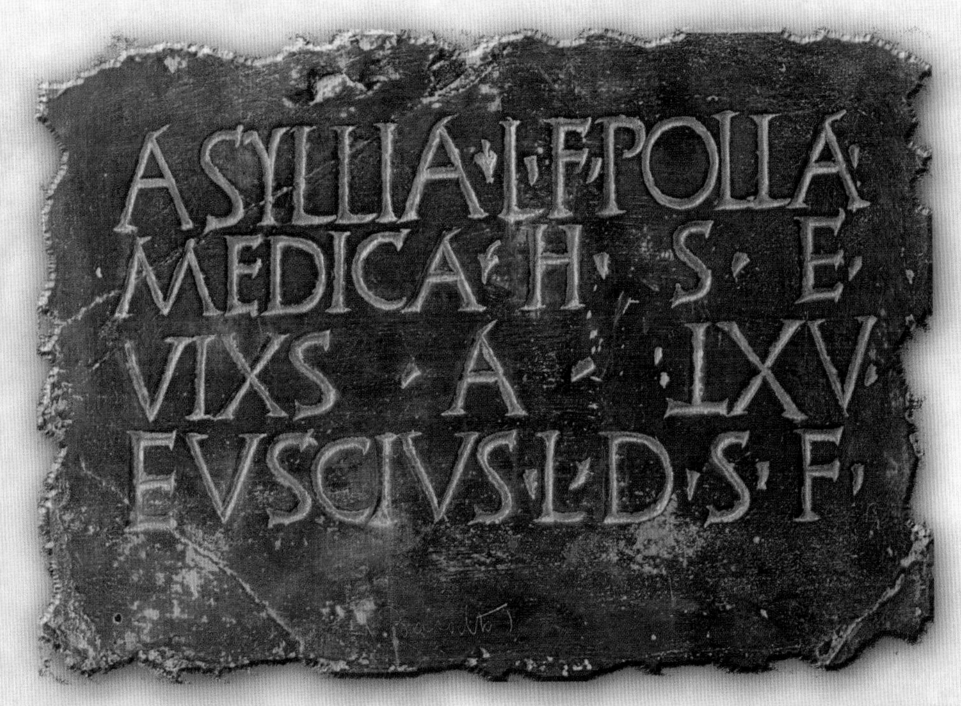

Above: Faustina the Younger, wife of Marcus Aurelius often featured on coins symbolizing various virtues. Here she is depicted holding a globe and cornucopia, symbolizing constancy.

Right: Roman funerary inscription for a female medic, Asyllia Polla.

'Soldier Emperors'

After the death of the last Severan Emperor in 235 AD, the Empire was plunged into five decades of chaos as a number of ambitious men vied for the top job.

Anarchy

Signs of an impending crisis had been evident for some time: the previous five Emperors had been assassinated; plague was devastating population numbers; and the Roman economy was pounded as trade began to break down across the Empire.

With the legions, the Senate and the Praetorian Guard providing opposing support bases for a range of contenders, the result was a rapid series of imperial successions. During this period, a number of so-called 'Soldier Emperors' struggled for power, but none proved able to lift Rome out of its malaise.

Maximinus Thrax

The first of the soldier Emperors was Maximinus Thrax. He was elevated to the imperial position by the Praetorian Guard. However, he was despised by the Senate; not only was he from a low socio-economic background, but he had never set foot in Rome. During his reign, a revolt in the province of Africa resulted in the ageing governor, Gordian, being proclaimed Emperor by the troops there.

Gordian, father and son

Gordian was of advanced age, so his son, Gordian II, was pronounced co-Emperor. The Senate leapt at the opportunity to support a challenge to Maximinus Thrax and backed the Army's insurrection. However, political support from the Senate did little to safeguard against the governor of the neighbouring province of Numidia, who was allied to Maximinus Thrax. He invaded Africa, defeated the Gordians' troops, killed Gordian II, and forced the elder Gordian to commit suicide.

Two new Emperors

Senators realized that their defiance of Maximinus would not go unpunished and swiftly appointed two new Emperors, Pupienus and Balbinus, to replace the Gordians. The co-Emperors abided by the interests of the Senate and defeated Maximinus Thrax, who was killed by his own men.

In spite of their victory, Pupienus' and Balbinus' positions were not safe; the plebs disliked the appointment of two patrician Emperors and called for their overthrow. The Praetorian Guard, who also disliked the men, obliged the people; Pupienus and Balbinus were murdered and were replaced with Gordian III.

Bas-relief cut into a rockface showing Shapur I receiving submissions from the defeated Emperors Philip and Valerian. This is a symbolic representation as Philip was one of the seven Emperors who reigned in the nine years following Gordian III's death. Valerian is the standing figure whose uplifted arms are being grasped by the victorious Shapur.

Valerian

Less than four years had elapsed between the murder of Alexander Severus in 235 AD and the accession of Gordian III, but in that time, Rome had six different Emperors.

This was a trend that was set to continue. In the decade following the death of Gordian III in 244, Rome had seven different Emperors. Such rapid turnover was only halted in 253, when Valerian acceded the throne as co-Emperor with his son, Gallienus.

A decaying Empire

Two decades of decay within the Empire had encouraged challenges from without. When Valerian came to power, a new Persian Empire, called the Sassanids, were pushing in from the East, while the Alamanni and the Franks, two Germanic tribes, were threatening in the West. To counter these menaces, Valerian took to the East, while Gallienus managed the West.

In 256, the Sassanids took the city of Antioch from Rome and also overran Armenia, a Roman client state. After Valerian dispatched himself to the region, the Romans scored a number of successes, including the recapture of Antioch.

Valerian humiliated

When Goths invaded Asia Minor in 258, Valerian became distracted and diverted his forces from the Persian front. The Sassanids, under the leadership of Shapur I, defeated a weakened Roman Army at the Battle of Edessa in 259 AD, and managed to capture Valerian in the fighting.

Rather than killing the prisoner straight away, the Persians humiliated the Emperor, who was forced to kneel as a footstool for the Persian king. Eventually, Valerian was murdered, but his body was skinned and stuffed, so that even in death he could be kept as a trophy to the might of the Sassanids.

After Valerian's death, Gallienus continued to rule Rome for a further eight years. Such durability was rare in the third century, but Gallienus faced his share of usurpers. Zenobia, the client Queen of Palmyra, formed her own breakaway 'Palmyrene Empire' in the east, while Postumus, one of Gallienus generals in Germania, proclaimed himself ruler of a breakaway 'Gallic Empire' in the west.

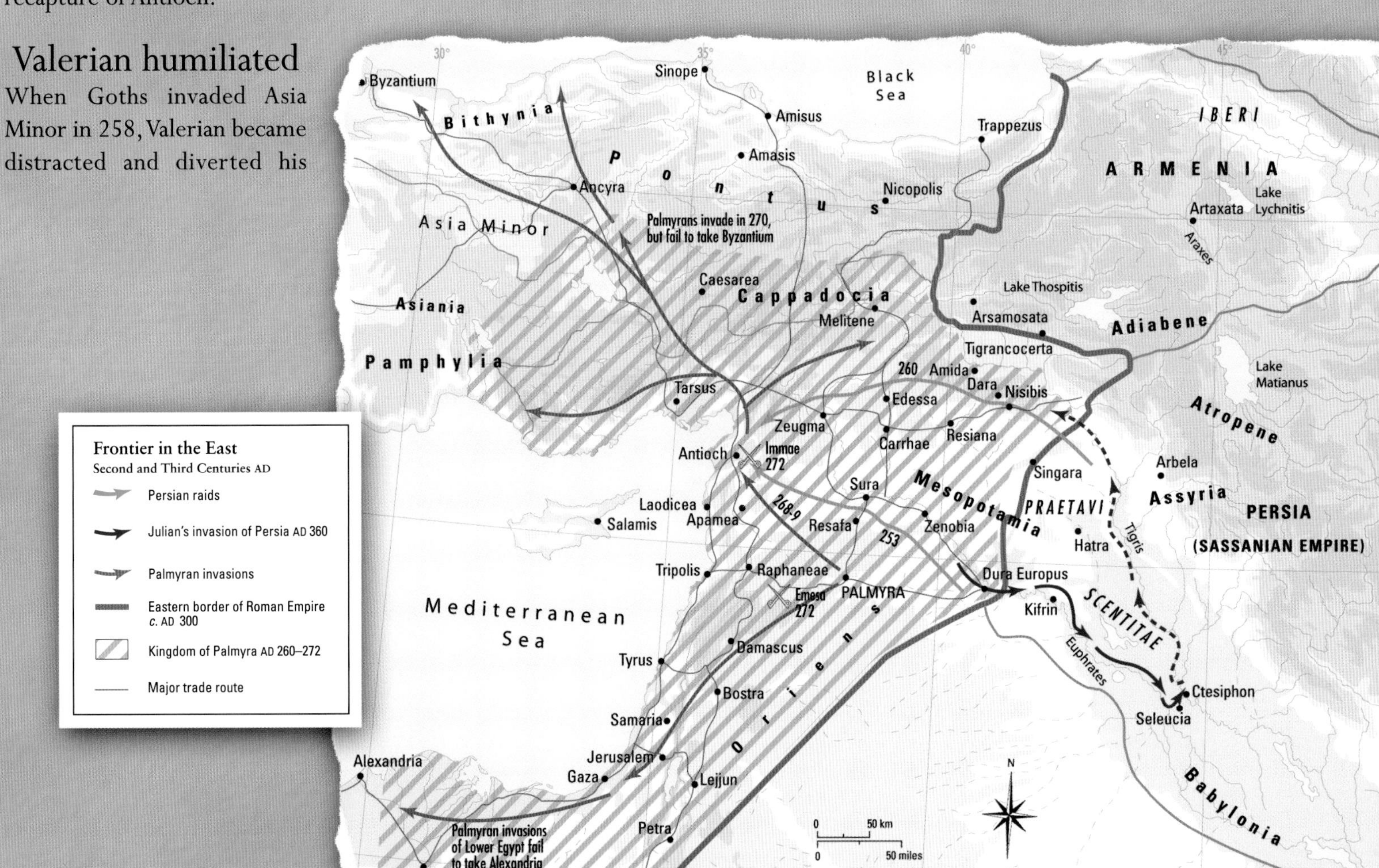

Aurelian

In 270 AD, Lucius Domitius Aurelianus (Aurelian) came to power. He ruled for a relatively long period of five years, during which time he restored the Empire by defeating, and re-incorporating, the Gallic and Palmyrene Empires back into the Roman Empire.

'Restorer of the world'

As well as his successes in re-establishing the Empire, he successfully dealt with the Alamanni. This Germanic tribe had been such a great threat to Rome that Aurelian had ordered the construction of new defensive walls around the city.

Having re-established some degree of security and stability to the Empire, the Senate proclaimed him *'Restituor Orbis'* – 'restorer of the world'.

Conspiracy against Aurelian

In 275, Aurelian prepared to move against the powerful Sassanid Empire, but fell prey to a conspiracy en-route. His secretary plotted against him and managed to convince the Praetorian Guard that Aurelian was going to order their executions. This encouraged the Guard to move pre-emptively against the Emperor and in Caenophrurium, Thrace, they murdered him.

The death of Aurelian was yet another disaster for the Empire; the crisis deepened as a further six Emperors followed over the next decade.

The Arch of Titus, constructed at the eastern end of the Forum in Rome.

Feats of Engineering

Driven by military need and imperial expansion, the Romans became skilled constructors, building many structures which are visible today, and engineering solutions to many of the problems they faced in their building programmes or everyday life.

Early roads

The Romans may not have been the first civilization to develop roads, but they were certainly unparalleled in terms of the extent of their network and the sophistication of their building techniques. Roman roads were not surpassed until the invention of Macadam in the nineteenth century, and many of the routes developed still form the basis for roads in use today.

It was from the Etruscans and the Greeks that the Romans learned the art of road building. In the early days, most of the roads they developed were on a small scale and in urban centres.

It was not until 312 BC that the first major Roman road was constructed between Rome and the city of Capua in the south. The road was named the *Via Appia* (the Appian Way), after the censor, Appius Claudius, who ordered its construction. In the short term, the road was designed to strengthen Rome's link with Capua, its ally in the second war against the Samnite tribe. In the longer term, the road paved the way for Roman hegemony, and expansion in Campania.

The Romans mastered the techniques for the construction of arches and domes. This dome is from the nymphaeum *at Hadrian's Villa.*

The Appian Way

After defeating the Samnites, the Romans began to dominate the region by establishing colonies, and forging alliances with the independent Campanian city-states. Once the Romans had penetrated further southward, the Appian Way was extended beyond Capua to nearby Beneventum, where a Roman colony was founded on the site of an ancient settlement.

At the start of the third century BC, the Romans pushed further south, threatening the Greek city-states along the coast. In this, the Appian Way proved to be a vital supply route for the Roman Army in the resulting 'Pyrrhic Wars' against the Greeks. After the Greeks were defeated in 275 BC, a further extension of the Appian Way to Brundisium, on the south-east coast, took place. From here sea crossings could be made to Greece.

Decorative cornice from Ostia.

Military origins

After the construction of the Appian Way, the Romans continued to build roads across their growing Empire. They were primarily constructed for military purposes, namely transporting men and supplies quickly to the frontlines, or to troublespots within Rome's occupied territories. As the roads were developed with marching soldiers in mind, they were built very wide, direct and straight.

Over time this developed into a major road network crisscrossing the Empire and linking cities as far and wide as Lugdunum (Lyon) in Gaul with Carthage in North Africa. Even Britannia, separated from the rest of the Empire by sea, was carved up by a system of Roman roads. Rome sat at the hub of this vast network, giving rise to the saying that 'all roads lead to Rome'.

Civilian use

Although the military were given primary use of the roads, a good deal of civilian traffic developed as well. Traders and travellers from across the Empire used the roads to get from one place to another. Most people preferred to travel by these overland routes than by sea, where passengers faced the very real threat of drowning in a storm.

With so many people using Roman roads in need of refreshments and places to stay, many towns and villages grew up along the roadside to catch passing trade.

To allow people to navigate the roads, milestones or *milliaria* were put up every one thousand paces to let people know how far, and in which direction, the nearest town or city was. Most of these milestones also made reference to the distance to or from Rome.

Road construction

The Roman government paid for the construction of roads, which were built by the legionaries, often assisted by slaves. Although Rome tried to standardize road building across the Empire, the roads usually depended upon the available time, material and space. Road construction at the frontiers was more improvised than for those closer to Rome.

To build a new road, surveyors would first plot the best possible course for the road, and plan its route in detail. Once this was calculated, the legionaries would dig down to the bedrock to establish a firm base for the road; they would be guided by rods planted along the route where the road was to be built. If it was available, a layer of sand was placed on top of the bedrock and then covered with a layer of stone and gravel mixed in cement. The surface of the road, comprising large stone slabs would sit in the cement mix. The road was built on a very slight gradient so that any rainwater would run off into drainage ditches at the side.

A street in Pompeii.

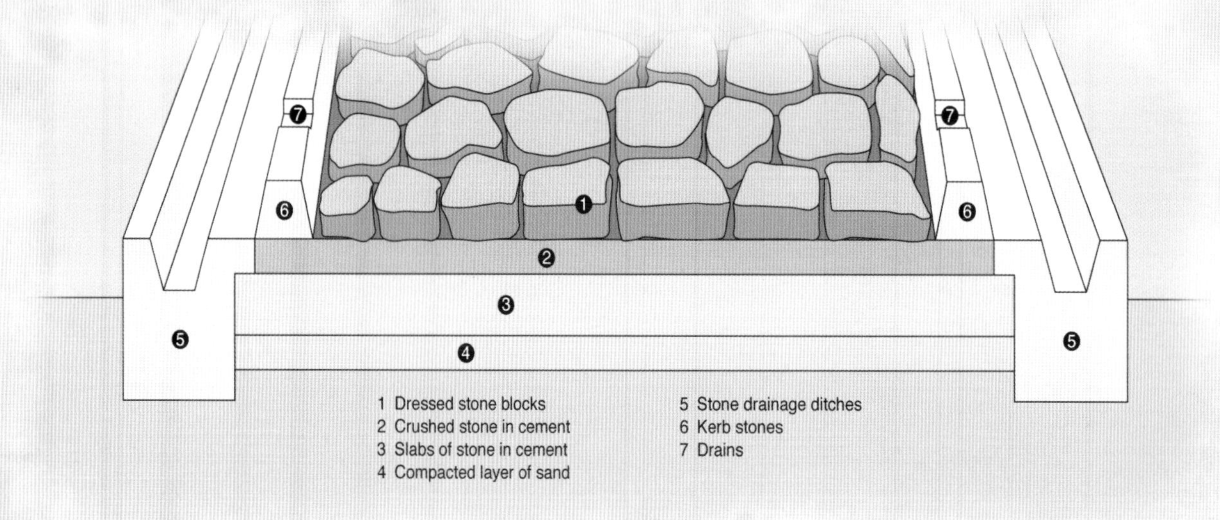

Postal Service

The road network was also used by couriers, established under Augustus, who acted as an early form of postal service. These couriers were allotted for official business only and were used to transport messages from Rome to the generals, governors and forts across the Empire. A network of relay stations was established so that as soon as one rider began to tire, another could take over. This meant that official correspondence was able to cover a vast distance in a short space of time.

The postal service made communications much quicker across the Empire, which allowed the Emperors' wishes to travel with greater ease and meant they did not necessarily have to rule from Rome. During Hadrian's rule, when he retired to his villa at Tibur outside Rome, the postal service provided him with a quick and easy connection to Rome.

Sanitation

Although the Romans' understanding of medicine was relatively primitive and many basic diseases were not properly treated, their understanding of hygiene was exceptionally advanced. Through relatively sophisticated sanitation systems, they were able to prevent many diseases, and maintain high levels of public health.

One of Rome's most exceptional engineering feats was the development of the aqueduct. The innovation of a system to bring fresh water to a city was first made in the East, but the Romans refined and developed the idea.

Bringing water

The first Roman aqueduct was built at the command of the censor, Appius Claudius, in 312 BC. Before that time, the population of the city had used water from the Tiber and nearby springs, but the river had become polluted and the springs did not meet the needs of the increasing numbers. Over the centuries, eleven aqueducts were built to serve the city of Rome alone, and others appeared across the Empire.

Aqueducts were principally a system of underground pipes, which brought water from its source in the mountains down to a city. The system simply relied on gravity taking its course and the pipes were set at a slight gradient to assist the flow. A benefit of the use of underground conduits was that it prevented the water from becoming contaminated by animals or dust, and also protected from heating by the sun.

Wall from a building in Ostia.

Spectacular structures

The spectacular, arched structures that are most readily associated with Roman aqueducts were only built when the aqueduct encountered a river valley or a low plain. Such features disrupted the gradual downward flow of the water and so the over ground section of the aqueduct was built to compensate.

Cisterns and pipes

Once the water reached the city, it was stored in a cistern called a *castella*, where it was distributed to the city through a network of pipes. The cisterns were usually located on the highest ground outside the city to allow the pipes to run water down into the city by gravity.

Pipes directly supplied the imperial residence, and some public amenities and richer Romans paid for the pleasure of having pipes bring water directly to their homes. Private Roman baths also paid for their own water pipes from the cisterns, but the larger public baths were usually served by their own aqueduct. These aqueducts did not usually come all the way from the source, but were spurred off a main aqueduct specifically for use at the baths. The poor did not enjoy such a luxury; they had to get their water from one of the public fountains that littered Roman cities.

Removing waste

Long before the first aqueduct was built, the Romans had developed a sewage system to take excess water, together with human waste, away from the city. Rome's first sewage system, the *Cloaca Maxima*, (Greatest Sewer) was built during the sixth century BC, at the time of the Roman Monarchy. The ruling monarchs at the time were Etruscan and it is believed that the *Cloaca Maxima* was influenced by Etruscan designs.

The sewers probably originated as a system which comprised an open channel of waste and water that flowed into the River Tiber. An open sewage system was not only highly unpleasant, but it also took up a lot of space; the solution was to cover up the sewers and build over them.

Left: The latrines of the Hadrianic Baths in Leptis Magna, Libya.

Below: The Pont du Gard – an aqueduct spanning the River Gardon in France.

A boost to public health

The underground sewage system provided an excellent boost to public health, but large openings were still necessary to allow surface water to run off into them. The stench near to these openings became unbearable when the sewage did not flow quickly enough into the river. This problem was overcome once the aqueducts were built and excess water stored in the cisterns could be used to flush out the sewers and move the waste away from the city quickly.

The considerable public health benefits offered by the sewer system in Rome was undermined by a shortage of drains. Bathhouses, public toilets and the houses of the rich were usually equipped with drains that took waste directly to the sewers. However, the majority of the population did not have immediate access to drains to the sewers. Their waste was left to run down the streets and into the openings in the sewage system designed for run-off water.

Although most Romans frequently used public toilets, it was not always practical and many people opted to use chamber pots, which they emptied onto the streets. These public latrines are a part of the Hadrianic bathing complex in Leptis Magna, North Africa.

Public toilets

Although there were public latrines, it was impractical for Romans to make several trips there each day, especially as, in the early period, there was an entrance fee. Thus, urine was often among the surface run-off. When a chamber pot was filled, it would be emptied in the street; often its contents were simply ejected through the window of one of the Roman tenements, onto the street below.

In spite of the popular use of chamber pots, Romans did make regular use of the public latrines. The toilets were communal, so customers would sit and catch up with friends, almost as if they were at the baths.

Urine was regularly used to stiffen clothes in the process of cleaning them, which meant that some people were actually employed to collect urine from the streets and from the public toilets. Although it was widely agreed that this was among the nastiest of jobs, the thrifty Emperor Vespasian saw it as an opportunity for extra revenue and introduced a tax on urine. In honour of his tax, French public urinals became known as *vespasiennes* in the twentieth century.

Rejuvenating the Empire

Diocletian

The long period of anarchy following the death of Aurelian finally came to a conclusion with the accession of Diocletian. He brought about much-needed reforms, which gave the Empire a new lease of life.

Humble origins

In 284 AD, Diocletian, an Illyrian of humble origins, was pronounced Emperor by his troops in Nicomedia. In early 285, he defeated the incumbent ruler, Carinus, and moved to unify the Empire.

Diocletian encouraged a more obvious form of despotism; he was to be known as '*dominus*' – meaning lord, instead of '*princeps*' meaning first-citizen. Augustus and his successors had been careful to maintain the pretence that Republican institutions were not contravened by their rule; Diocletian and his successors no longer adhered to such fiction.

The Tetrarchy

Diocletian's most famous political reform was his institutionalization of the system of co-Emperors. One Emperor was charged with the West, while the other controlled the East and each Emperor appointed a junior Emperor to assist him – the result was a rule of four men called a 'Tetrarchy'.

Not only did the Tetrarchy ensure easier and better management of the Empire, it also provided a clear system of succession because the junior Emperor could take over on the death of the senior one, removing any uncertainty over succession, and putting an end to the instability of the preceding decades.

Diocletian appointed Marcus Aurelius Valerius Maximianus, a fellow Illyrian, as his co-Augustus in 287 and gave him control of the western half of the Empire, while Diocletian looked after the affairs of the East. In 293, Galerius and Constantius were appointed as Caesars to Diocletian and Maximianus respectively.

The Tetrarchy allowed the rulers to deal with several problematic fronts simultaneously, helping to end the incursions by the Alamanni and the Sassanids, thwart revolts in Britannia, Mauretania and Egypt, and restore order within the Empire.

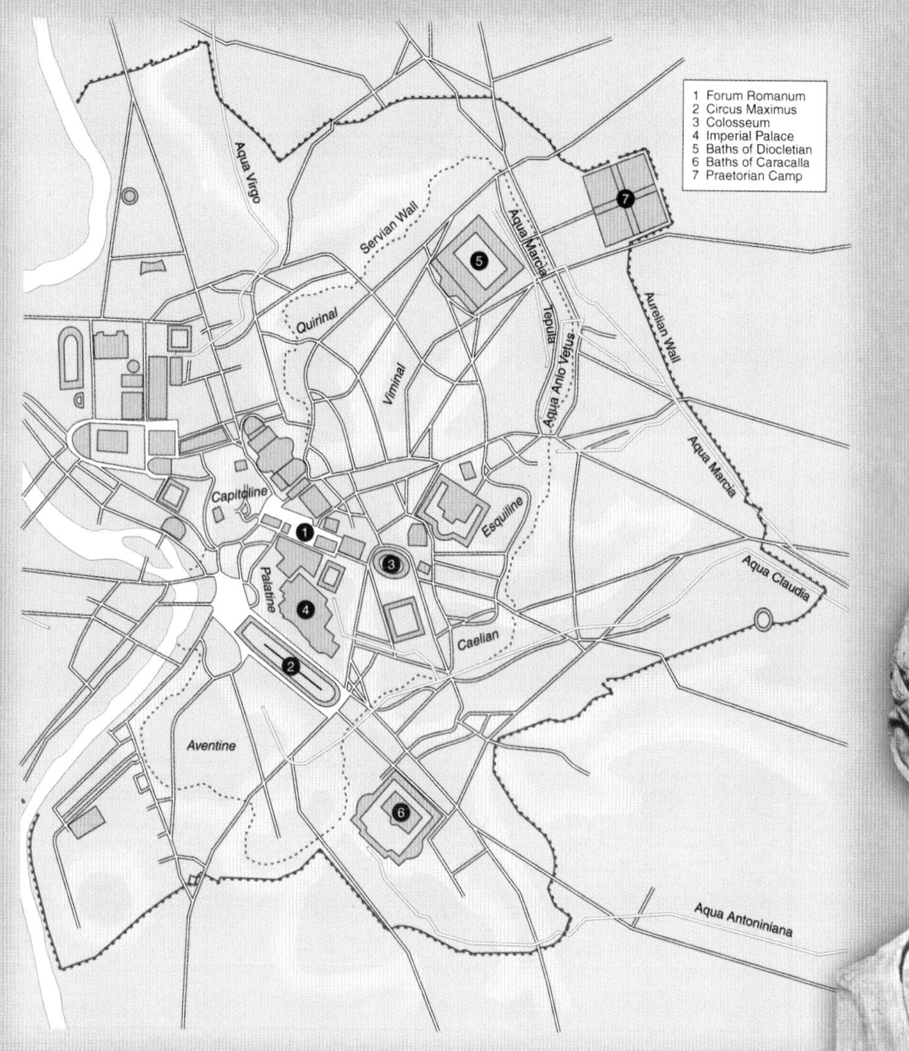

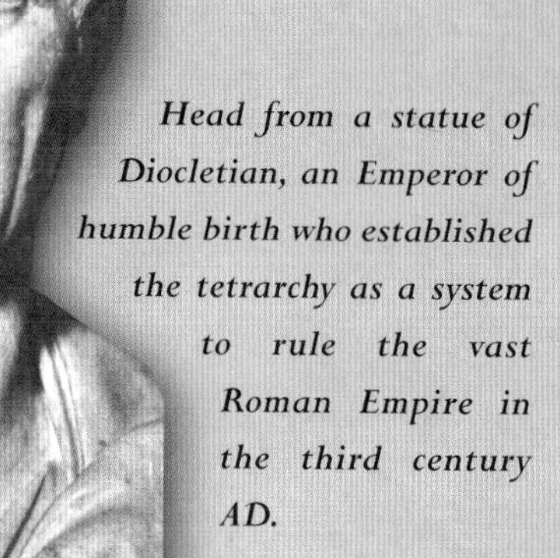

Head from a statue of Diocletian, an Emperor of humble birth who established the tetrarchy as a system to rule the vast Roman Empire in the third century AD.

Restoring order

Diocletian introduced bureaucratic reforms to bring the Army under control and decrease the number of challengers for the imperial title. He doubled the amount of provinces in order to reduce the number of men under the command of one general, although to maintain efficiency the smaller provinces were grouped into dioceses – a new administrative unit that was later adopted by the Christian Church. In addition to the Army, a civilian militia was established to increase defence in border regions.

One of the underlying problems of the decades of anarchy had been a growing economic crisis. Diocletian attempted to bring hyperinflation under control, firstly by strengthening the price of gold, and when that failed by introducing price-fixing using the Edict on Maximum Prices of 301. This edict insulated the poor from the harshness of the devastated economy in the short term. However, this strategy offered no long-term solution and encouraged the emergence of a vast and expensive black market.

Stone sculpture from the third century AD depicting two of the four Tetrarchs at the west entrance to the Basilica San Marco in Venice, Italy.

Persecution of the Christians

Diocletian was a strong believer in traditional, pagan Roman religion. He identified with Jupiter, while Maximianus found affinity with Hercules, and he expected to be treated somewhat like a god. Christian monotheism could not be reconciled with Diocletian's religious views and he resorted to persecuting the sect as a result. Christians were banned from the Army, terrorized, and often forced to worship Roman gods.

In 305, Diocletian abdicated in favour of his junior Emperor, and encouraged his co-Emperor to follow suit. He retired to the Illyrian town of Spalato (Split), and lived just long enough to see his political system unravel.

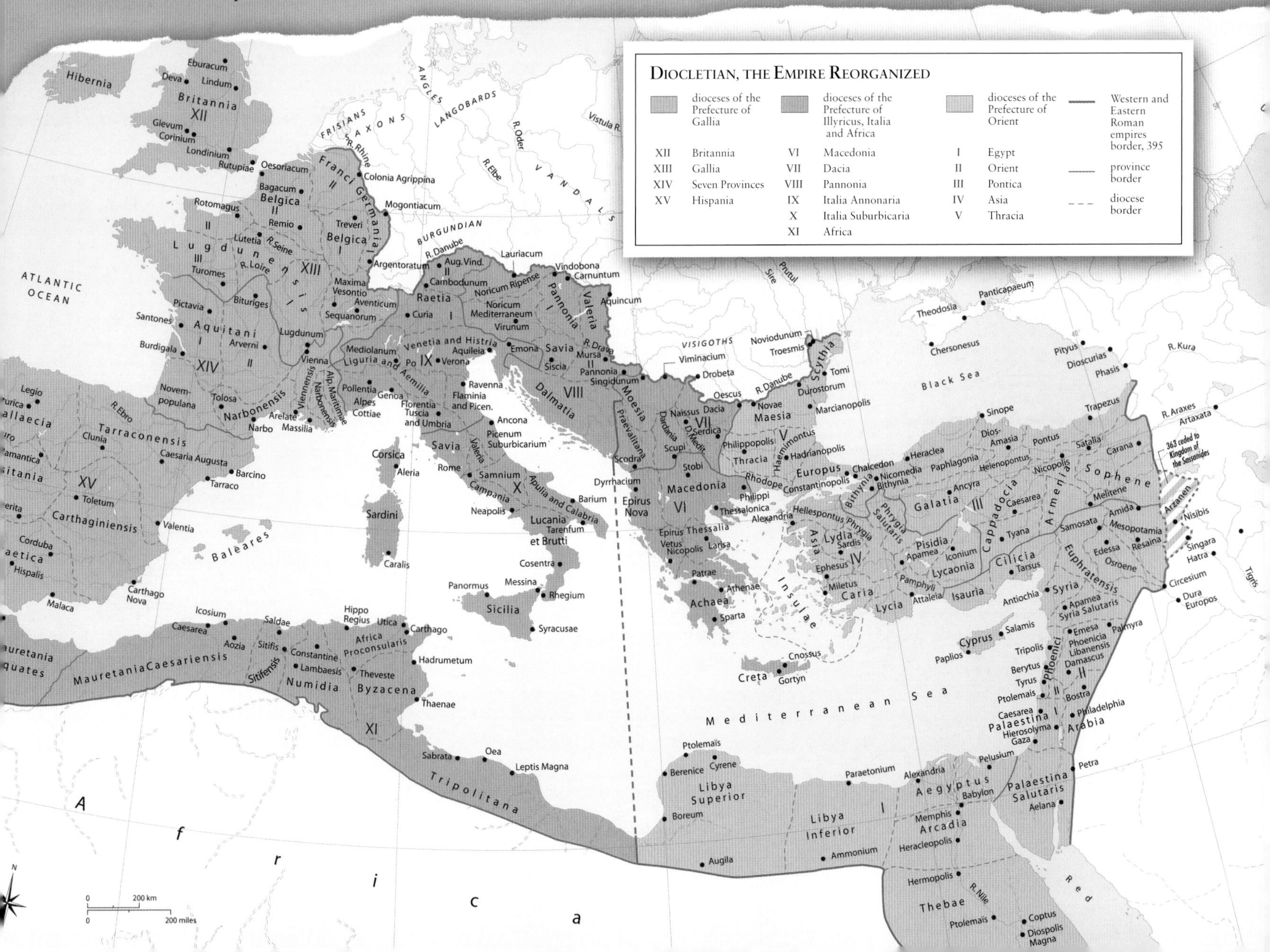

Urban Life

Across the Roman world, it is estimated that as many as one in every ten people lived in urban areas. In a culture which emphasized social interaction and activities, urban living provided a perfect platform for Roman values. Additionally, the city offered a more reliable and plentiful supply of jobs than in rural areas. This acted as a magnet, pulling people in to the cities.

Insulae – a space-saving solution

Most people in Rome lived in tenement buildings called insulae. At times in Rome's history, more than one million people needed housing near the city centre because they had no means of transport to live further out. This made land expensive and forced the Romans to build upwards, in order to provide affordable housing for ordinary people.

This problem of space was not exclusive to Rome and insulae were built in towns across the Empire, albeit to a lesser extent. Some of the best ruins of the tenements are to be found at Ostia, the bustling harbour that linked Rome with the sea.

A plaque on a wall in a Pompeii street depicts two porters bearing an amphora hung from a pole indicating that the use of porters is obligatory.

Overcrowding

These tenements were exceptionally overcrowded; often an entire family would be forced to live in just one room. They were also densely packed together and some were as high as seven storeys, which placed them in serious danger of collapse.

Fire was an additional hazard because the upper floors were made of wood, and there was a serious risk of it catching alight when people were cooking. This was probably the cause of the Great Fire of Rome in 64 AD, which burned for nine days through these tightly packed, wooden tenements.

To try to prevent such calamities, the Emperor Augustus introduced legal restrictions on the height of insulae; they could be no higher than twenty metres. He also introduced a night watch to keep a look out for fire. Both Nero and Trajan imposed even stricter height limitations.

Remains of tenements, or Insulae, in Ostia, the port of ancient Rome.

Living above the shop

The ground floors of insulae were usually used as shops and the living quarters were located on the upper floors. With the threat of fire and collapse, as well as a precarious staircase, the higher, wooden floors were the least desirable place to live in the building.

Most apartments had small, open windows, but some of these openings looked onto an internal courtyard, which would not have allowed in much light. It is even thought that some homes might have had no access to natural light at all.

Middle-class Romans also lived in insulae, but unlike the poorer citizens, they would have been able to afford better apartment blocks in which they would have occupied more than one room.

A model of how Roman insulae might have looked. Many would have been several stories higher than this. Additional floors were constructed with wood, which was a perennial fire hazard.

Domus

Wealthy Romans could afford to live away from the crowded tenements in their own single-storey houses, called a domus. Many of these were located on the Palatine Hill, away from the plebs and close to where the Emperor's palace stood.

The front door of these houses opened onto an atrium, where guests were received, and a shrine to the household and ancestral gods was located. The ceiling in the atrium was open to the elements to allow sunlight, and more importantly rainwater, to enter the house. Rainwater was also collected from the roofs of these houses which were slanted to channel water through the opening in the atrium ceiling. The water would be caught in a small basin on the floor below, and put to good use around the house.

The remains of Trajan's Market, a large shopping complex commissioned by Emperor Trajan, alongside the construction of his Forum.

Layout of a domus

All the main rooms in the domus were located off the central atrium, including the study or office at the back where the head of the family would conduct business. The atrium was flanked by the family's bedrooms, which were usually small and functioned only as a sleeping chamber.

This type of Roman home tended to be sparsely furnished,giving the illusion that the house was larger than it actually was. However, it would be elaborately decorated to convey an impression of grandeur.

Entertaining al fresco

To the rear of the house was a small walled garden, where much of the entertaining was done and many meals were enjoyed al fresco. Originally, the garden would have been relatively understated, but during the late Republic, many families preferred to model their gardens on the Hellenic style, complete with columns, expensive frescoes and exotic fauna. If it was too cold, or even too hot, to eat outside, then a domus had a separate dining room.

The house also had a simple kitchen with a stove, where the slaves would work. Some houses also rented out their frontages as shops.

Decorative oil lamp from Pompeii.

Employment in the city

Much of the backbreaking and menial work in Rome was done by slaves, which meant that ordinary Roman citizens had to seek employment elsewhere. Most men worked as traders, such as bakers, fishmongers and wine vendors. Others worked as craftsmen or carpenters, making clothes, trinkets, furniture or utensils.

Shops and workshops would usually be based on the ground floor of the insulae and the family and employees would normally live in the same building, often in cramped conditions behind the shop. These workers were often members of guilds, which served as social clubs, as well as looking after the communal interests of the industry.

Street and temple ruins in Ostia.

Working practices

Roman women, however poor, were not usually expected to work, but it is likely that many would have assisted their husbands. Sons would usually follow their fathers into the family business, although after the Army was opened up to ordinary Romans, many would follow a military career instead.

Ordinary Romans worked a strict six-hour day, which began at dawn and left the afternoon free for leisurely pursuits, especially a trip to the baths, the games or the races. Some traders opened their shops again in the early evening to catch a last bit of trade before Rome settled down for the evening.

High status jobs

Employment as a trader or craftsmen was considered beneath patrician Romans, whose job options were almost exclusively limited to the interconnected fields of politics, law and the Army. Their jobs were not strictly regimented, but like plebeian males, the afternoon was usually spent at the baths, where they would continue to talk politics.

With the rich limiting their employment options and the poor unsuitably skilled, slaves had to undertake highly skilled professions, such as teachers, doctors, surgeons and architects. Technically, any money the slaves made went directly to their masters, but they were mostly allowed to keep a percentage as an incentive to work hard. When they had earned enough money they could buy their freedom. Many continued to work in the same profession after their emancipation, meaning that highly skilled jobs became the preserve of these freedmen and their progeny.

Bakery in the ruins of the port of Ostia. The free-standing concrete structures are the remains of bread ovens.

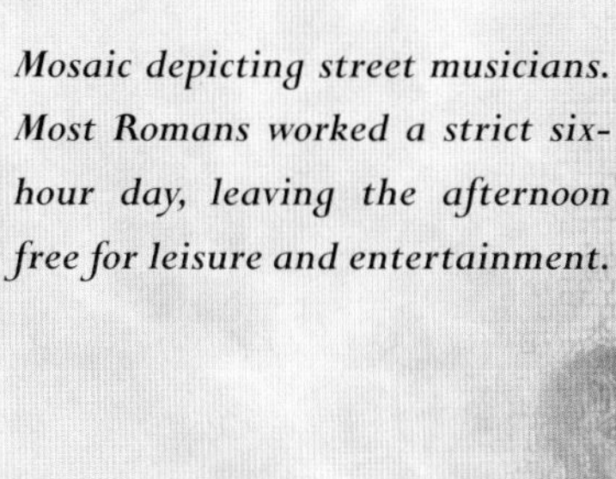

Mosaic depicting street musicians. Most Romans worked a strict six-hour day, leaving the afternoon free for leisure and entertainment.

Clothing and fashion

Roman clothing was relatively plain and straightforward, so most Romans tried to follow the latest fashion for haircuts, jewellery and cosmetics. Such accessories reflected a person's social status; rich Romans would bejewel themselves and adopt elaborate hairstyles, while poorer Romans tried to follow whatever trends they could afford.

The Toga

The toga was the standard Roman dress worn by all male citizens from the earliest days of the Republic. It consisted of a long woollen sash, which was wrapped carefully around the body. These garments were usually hot and uncomfortable, making them particularly impractical for soldiers or workers. As a result, the toga was usually saved for special occasions, and a less cumbersome cloak was worn. However, wealthy Romans would usually wear a toga in public to show that they did not have to work.

Different togas were worn at different stages in life; boys would wear a *toga praetexta*, with a purple hem, and would only be able to wear an adult's plain, white *toga virilis* at fourteen, when they had come of age. When men were in mourning, they were expected to wear a dark grey *toga pulla*. For a time, a general celebrating a great military victory was allowed to wear a purple toga, until that privilege was reserved only for the Emperor. Thus, however unwieldy they might have been, togas were considered a mark of honour for many Romans, because non-citizens were forbidden from wearing them.

Female stola

Women quickly developed their own shapely, and less heavy, version of the toga called the stola, which did not need to be wrapped around the body. The stola was a rectangular-shaped, long-sleeved dress, which covered both shoulders and ran down to the ground. Women often wrapped a shawl called a palla over the top of the stola to complete their outfit. If a woman was from a particularly wealthy family her palla might have been made of silk, an exceptionally rare commodity, imported all the way from China.

Gold cameo ring with profile portrait of a man wearing a diadem.

Tunics

In the early Republic, togas were usually worn directly over undergarments, but this was incredibly uncomfortable, especially because togas were made from wool, which often irritated the skin. Roman men and women began to wear a tunic under their togas or stolas.

Ordinary Roman men, who only wore a toga occasionally, wore a tunic most of the time. During the summer when it was hot, just one tunic would suffice, but several tunics were layered on to keep warm in winter.

Men's tunics comprised two rectangles of wool sewn together; they were usually short-sleeved and tied with a belt so as to make the garment stop at the knees. Women's tunics were longer in both the sleeve and the length. The tunics worn by slaves had stripes running down the sides to indicate their social status.

To clean the woollen material used in their clothing, the Romans would visit a fuller. First the clothes were stiffened using urine and then rubbed with special clay called 'fuller's earth' to remove any impurities before being washed in water. It was also the fuller's job to prepare the cloth used to make clothes, by stretching and dyeing it. A Roman woman would then use the cloth to make clothes for her family.

Footwear

Roman footwear was relatively uniform for men and women. In their own home or at the houses of friends or family, Romans wore informal, open-toe sandals. Soldiers wore a form of booted sandal called *caligae*. Outside of the home, Romans wore *calcei*, leather shoes, which covered the feet entirely; it was rare for Romans to leave the house with their sandals on and only *calcei* would ever be worn with a toga.

Although Romans did not wear socks with their shoes, many took to using some kind of material to prevent rubbing because fashion demanded that shoes be worn tightly.

The Emperor Gaius Julius Caesar Germanicus became known as Caligula, meaning 'little boot', because his mother used to dress him up in a miniature soldier's outfit, including a small pair of these boots.

A female figure from the fresoes in the Villa of the Mysteries in Pompeii shows typical Roman dress of the first century AD.

Statue of Helena which shows the drapes of the stola *and the* palla.

Hairstyles

During the Republic, Roman haircuts were relatively unremarkable because most men wore short hair while most women simply tied their hair into a bun. During the Empire, women's tastes became more ostentatious and dyes, products and wigs became popular.

Although the majority of Roman women had dark hair, many sought to be blonde or red-headed, either by using dyes or by cutting the hair from north European slaves to turn into wigs or extensions.

During the Flavian Dynasty, it became popular for women to have an elaborate hairstyle, involving several layers of mounted ringlets at the front of the head. Such a fashion could only be followed by the wealthy because it required women to visit a hairdresser, or to own a slave who could perform the extensive and time-consuming curling and pinning involved.

Men's haircuts remained largely unchanged until the second century AD, when Hadrian popularized a trend for curled hair when he had his own hair carefully styled into ringlets using heated tongs.

Beards

Few Roman men shaved during the early Republic because it was not fashionable, and the Romans did not have the necessary equipment. That changed in the third century BC, when Romans came under the influence of the Greeks in the south of the Italian peninsula, where shaving was more commonplace. Roman men would not shave themselves because shaving equipment was still relatively primitive; instead they would visit a barber, particularly one with a reputation for smoothness.

The shaved-look remained popular for several centuries, although men often decided to sport a short, tidy beard. When Emperor Hadrian came to the throne, he reintroduced the beard, allegedly because he wanted to hide a slight disfigurement to his face. The beard remained popular until the time of Constantine the Great, when shaving became fashionable again.

Hadrian initiated the popular trend of sporting a beard. It was rumoured that the Emperor first grew his beard to cover up a facial defect.

During the Flavian Dynasty, it became popular for women to have an elaborate hairstyle involving several layers of mounted ringlets at the front of the head. Such a hairstyle was a statement of wealth and status as only the rich could afford invest the time and money required to achieve such a confection.

Jewellery and Make-up

Signet rings

Roman men usually limited themselves to one piece of jewellery, a signet ring with a personalized engraving, which allowed the owner to make a seal by dipping the ring in melted wax. Signet rings were initially made of iron, but later gold rings became standard. Over time, richer Roman men took to wearing more than just one ring, probably because the fact that the majority of Roman men wore one ring meant that wearing more would be an outward sign of the owner's wealth.

Unlike their menfolk, Roman women wore a good deal of jewellery – especially rings, necklaces, earrings, bracelets, brooches, and hairpins. Most wedding rings were made from iron, which was the main metal used in jewellery in the early Republic. As Rome expanded and gained access to more materials, gold and silver jewellery became extremely popular, and remained so for the duration of the Empire. However, this did not preclude some women from seeking other types of jewellery, fashioned from materials such as mother-of-pearl or bone.

As with the men, Rome's wealthiest women liked to show off their riches; in order to stand out in a society in which most woman owned at least some jewellery, the wealthiest women liked to have their jewellery encrusted with rare gems such as sapphires, rubies and emeralds.

Crushed snails and ants

Roman women desired to appear paler than they actually were. Many achieved this look simply by staying out of the sun, but make-up was always on hand to help them look even paler. Powdered chalk, or even poisonous white lead, was applied to give the necessary pale complexion to the face and arms, and crushed snails were applied as a face cream. The fair-skinned appearance could be accentuated by darkening the eyebrows with crushed ants or ash. Reddish clay or dye was applied as a blusher and a lipstick, in order to complete the desired facial appearance.

Gold necklace with gemstones found at Pompeii.

Complex and intricate gold earring with five pendants.

Constantine and the Christian State

Constantine

Diocletian's tetrarchical rule quickly broke down and Constantine emerged as the sole ruler of the Roman world. He attributed his victories over his rivals to the divine intervention of the Christian God. Christianity was favoured over Roman paganism and eventually became the state religion.

Breakdown of the Tetrarchy

Diocletian's abdication in favour of his second-in-command, Galerius, was the beginning of the end for the Tetrarchy. In the West, Maximianus had also stepped down to allow Constantius to become Augustus in his stead. It was supposed to be a managed transfer of power.

In 305 AD the two junior Emperors, Constantius and Galerius were proclaimed Augusti in place of Diocletian and Maximianus. However, the following year, Constantius died at Eburacum (York) in Britannia and the Tetrarchy faced a serious crisis.

Diocletian had, in part, established the Tetrarchy to ease the succession process, with the junior Emperors taking power upon the death of the senior. But things did not go according to Diocletian's plan when the troops declared Constantius' son, Flavius Valerius Constantinus (Constantine) as Augustus, despite the fact that he had not been named as the vice-Emperor.

The serving vice-Emperor, Flavius Valerius Severus, declared power for himself in Rome, but he was defeated by another would-be ruler, Maxentius, the son of Maximianus. The East faced a similar breakdown when Galerius died in 311 and the territory was carved up between two prominent individuals, Licinius and Daia.

Battle for the Western Empire

In October 312, the battle between Constantine and Maxentius for the western portion of the Empire took place at the Milvian Bridge on the River Tiber.

En route to the battlefield, Constantine believed he had a divine vision that encouraged him to go into battle under the banner of Christianity. He obliged the vision and entered the battle under the sign of the Christian cross.

Although considerably outnumbered, Constantine managed to defeat Maxentius, who drowned when the bridge across the river collapsed while he was still on it.

Constantine's surprise victory, and the circumstances of Maxentius' death, convinced some people of a divine intervention by the Christian God.

The Gate of Diocletian on the temple island of Philae in the River Nile.

The Edict of Milan

Following his victory, Constantine marched on Rome, where the people and the Senate readily accepted him as Emperor. Although he was not yet a Christian, he legislated to protect them from persecution.

In 313 AD he passed the 'Edict of Milan', which stipulated that the Roman government would tolerate all religions. The agreement was co-signed by Licinius, who had allied with Constantine against Daia, his rival in the East. Licinius was firm in his pagan beliefs, but signed the edict to gain Constantine's support for his war against Daia, who had been persecuting the Christians. With Constantine's backing, Licinius was soon victorious over Daia and Christians were freed from tyranny across the entire Empire.

Constantine favours Christianity

The alliance between Licinius and Constantine gradually broke down as Constantine turned ever more to Christianity. At the dedication of the Arch of Constantine – a memorial to his triumph against Maxentius – he refused to make the traditional sacrifice to the pagan gods. In addition, state funds were channelled into the Christian Church at the expense of pagan temples.

Constantine's favouritism of Christianity over the traditional Roman gods frustrated the Senate, which looked to Licinius to help rid them of the heretical Constantine.

A Holy War

In 316, war broke out. Although it was essentially a power struggle between the two men, Constantine and Licinius, it was also a holy war between Christianity and Roman paganism. Neither man was able to score a decisive victory, so they reverted to an uneasy peace for seven years.

When Licinius began persecuting Christians another war became inevitable. This war ended in Constantine's favour after the Battle of Chrysopolis in 324, leaving him as the sole ruler of the Roman world.

Constantine's Arch, erected next to the Colosseum in Rome, stands as a memorial to his triumph over Maxentius, a victory which paved the way for him to assume sole command of the Roman Empire.

Constantinople: A New Capital

For much of Roman history, Rome was the most important city in the world. During the late Republic and early Empire period, the city had been made rich by the plunder from wars and occupied lands. Incredibly, the population had exceeded one million people and the city had become a hub for trade and transport across the Empire.

Rome declines

During the political crisis of the third century, the city had slipped into decline, as its economy stagnated because new sources of revenue became scarce. Trade through the city also began to dry up, as Rome was fast eclipsed by the East, where the economy flourished.

Rome's saving grace was the fact that it remained the political centre of the Empire, but even this was eroded when Diocletian introduced his reforms; the Western Ruler governed from Mediolanum (Milan), which was closer to the troublesome borders in the north, and the Eastern Ruler held his court at Nicomedia, in what is now the north-east region of Turkey.

Gold solidus depicting Emperor Constantine.

A decisive break with Rome

Constantine made the decisive break with Rome when he moved the capital of the Empire to Byzantium, modern-day Istanbul, which he renamed Nova Roma (New Rome).

Rome was considered too far from the new economic and cultural centre in the east of the Empire. Although Byzantium was favoured because Constantine had studied there, it was certainly a better location for the capital.

It brought the government closer to the geographical centre of the Empire, within easier reach of the trouble spots in both the East and the West. Furthermore, the city was situated in a perfect position to control much of the overland trade that passed between the East and West.

CONSTANTINOPLE

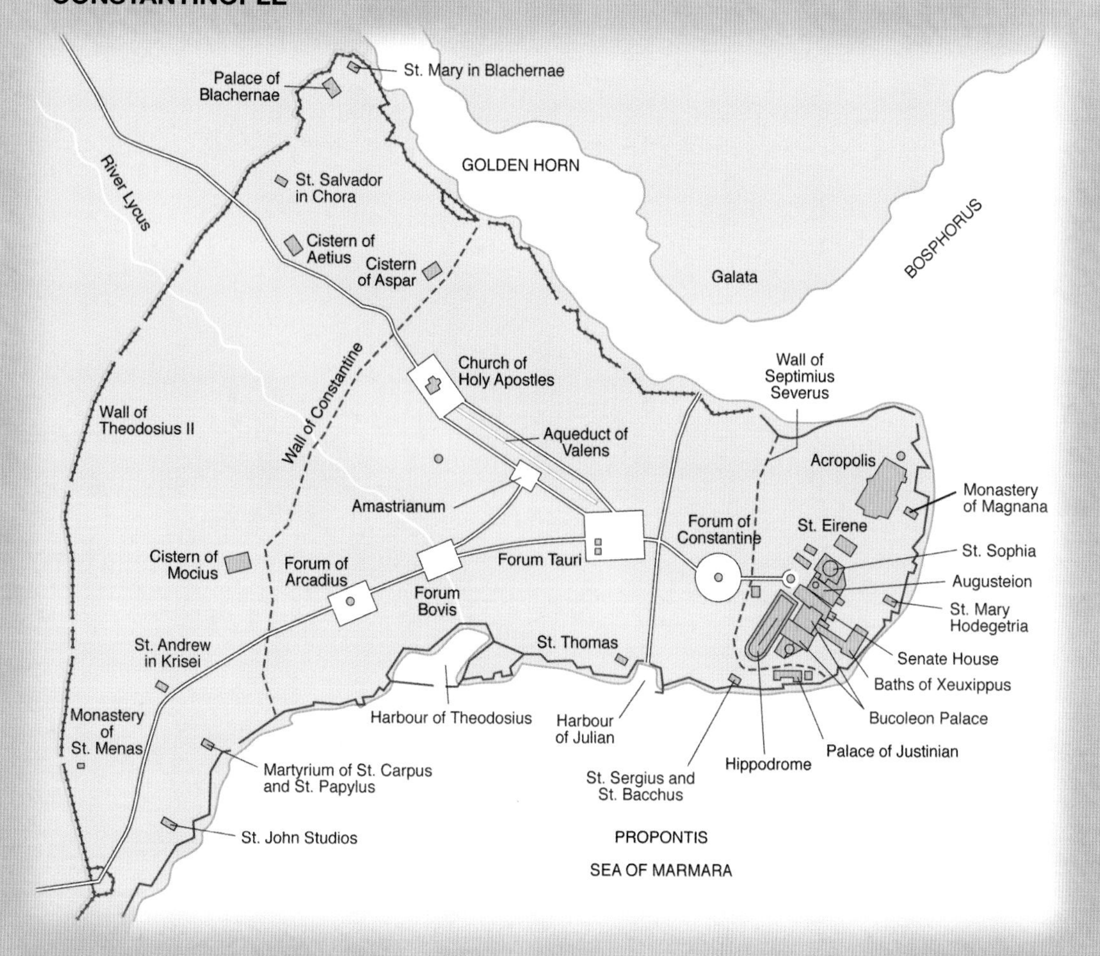

Lavish imperial capital

Cities across the Empire were forced to hand over treasures to make Nova Roma a lavish imperial capital. Although Rome maintained some prestige, there is little doubt that it became eclipsed as aristocrats, entertainers and merchants moved to the new capital.

After Constantine's death, Nova Roma was renamed 'Constantinople' in his honour.

Venus

The daughter of Dione and Jupiter, Venus was one of the most important Roman goddesses, mainly associated with love and beauty, and seen as the mother of all Roman people.

Unfaithful lover

Married to Vulcan, the god of fire and blacksmiths, she was sometimes unfaithful; lovers included Adonis and Mars.

Venus' particular cult began in 293 BC when the oldest-known temple dedicated to her was built and inaugurated on 18 August – the festival of *Vinalia Rustica* was then observed on this anniversary each year.

Temple of Venus and Rome

Venus is so closely identified with Rome that the largest temple in Ancient Rome was the 'Temple of Venus and Rome'. This structure, located at the eastern edge of the Forum, close to the Colosseum, was commissioned by Emperor Hadrian. Work began on construction in 121 AD and it was dedicated in 135, with the work being completed in the reign of Antoninus Pius.

Venus was very closely linked to the Greek goddess Aphrodite, taking over many of her myths.

Torso and head from a statue of Venus.

Statue of Mars from the Canopus at Hadrian's Villa. Mars was one of Venus' lovers.

Julian

Establishing Christianity

In 325 AD, Constantine convened the council of Nicaea to discuss matters of doctrine and practice in the Christian Church. It had far-reaching effects and the agreed statement of belief still underlies Christianity today. Constantine took to building churches, most significantly, the Church of the Nativity in Bethlehem and the Church of the Holy Sepulchre in Jerusalem, on the spots where Jesus is believed to have been born and to have died. Constantine went even further in the application of Christianity, crucifixion was abolished as a means of punishment and markets and offices were closed on a Sunday, the Christian holy day.

In spite of the changes he brought to Roman society, there is considerable debate as to whether Constantine was a true Christian, or whether the religion proved politically expedient. Although he continued to exhibit some impious behaviour, notably having Licinius, his wife and one of his sons disposed of rather than forgiven, he was sufficiently convinced by the religion to have himself baptised shortly before his death in 337.

The forces of paganism

While Constantine had made Christianity widely acceptable, it was not yet secure in its position as the orthodox religion of Ancient Rome; just over twenty years after Constantine's death, the forces of paganism were once again on the march.

Constantine had left the Empire to his three sons, who divided it up amongst them. However, infighting between the three rulers, as well as challenges from other family members and usurpers plunged the Empire back into division and chaos. The power struggle was eventually won by Constantine's nephew, Flavius Claudius Julianus (Julian), who became the sole ruler of Rome in 361.

He is known as Julian the Apostate because he brought back the traditional pagan gods of Rome and began to move against the Christians. A fully-fledged restoration was halted in 363, when Julian was killed in battle against the Persians. He was to be the last pagan Emperor of Ancient Rome – in 380, the devoutly Christian Emperor, Theodosius, acceded to the throne and made Christianity the official state religion.

Detail from the base on which the Egyptian obelisk is mounted shows Emperor Theodosius at the races.

The Missorium of Theodosius is a votive platter that was made to commemorate the tenth anniversary of his reign. These platters were made on significant occasions and given away as gifts. Since the platter was found in Spain and it has been suggested that the soldiers may be German, the cosmopolitan nature of the Empire is indicated.

Theodosius

Unlike Julian, the next Emperor, Flavius Jovianus (Jovian), was a Christian. The war against the Persians that had cost Julian his life was quickly ended when Jovian agreed to withdraw from several provinces in the East.

On his return to Constantinople, Jovian died in his sleep after less than eight months as Emperor. Officially he is thought to have suffocated on the fumes from a charcoal brazier nearby, but many people suspected foul play.

A return to diarchic rule

Flavius Valentinianus (Valentinian I) succeeded him and quickly resorted to a diarchic system of rule because he believed that the Empire was to be too large to govern alone. He appointed his brother, Valens, to rule the East while he took charge of the West. Valentinian proved a capable ruler and strengthened Rome's frontiers along the Danube and the Rhine, as well as in North Africa.

However, Valens proved to be less capable than his brother in the West. He ineffectively managed the challenges posed by the Persians and the Visigoths against him, and at one stage he even contemplated handing over control to a usurper, named Precopius, rather than stand and fight him.

Years of instability

In 375 AD, Valentinian died and his young sons, Gratian and Valentinian II took his place as rulers in the West. Three years later, Valens was killed in battle against the Visigoths at Adrianople. Gratian appointed Theodosius, the son of one of his father's greatest generals, as Emperor in the East.

Eight years after his appointment of Theodosius, Gratian was murdered at the hands of Magnus Maximus, a usurper who had been proclaimed Emperor by the troops serving under him in Britannia. Maximus had crossed into Gaul where he trapped and killed Gratian at Lugdunum (Lyon).

Theodosius refused to recognize Maximus' claim and continued to acknowledge Valentinian II as the rightful Western Emperor. Angered by this affront, Maximus invaded Italy to unseat Valentinian. Theodosius came to his rescue and swiftly defeated and killed Maximus.

Theodosius emerges as sole Emperor

To safeguard against future threats, Theodosius placed Valentinian under the protection of a Frankish soldier named Arbogast. When Valentinian was found hanged in 392, Arbogast claimed that the Emperor had committed suicide. However, Theodosius believed that Arbogast had murdered him; a suspicion that appeared to be confirmed when Arbogast appointed one of his allies, Eugenius, as Emperor in the West.

Theodosius promptly invaded from the East and defeated Arbogast at the Battle of the Frigidus River. He took up control of the West and became the sole ruler of the Roman world for three years until his death in 395.

Theodosius was a Christian and had curtailed the practice of traditional Roman religion during his tenure as Emperor in the East. In 391 AD, he took a further step by confirming Christianity as the official state religion across the Empire. His death marked the permanent division of the Empire, when his sons Arcadius and Honorius took control of the East and West respectively.

This Egyptian obelisk from Karnak was raised, on the instructions of Theodosius, in the Hippodrome (or racetrack) in Constantinople.

Religion

Genius and *juno*

The earliest form of Roman religion was animistic in character. Romans strove to please spirits they believed inhabited everything around them. Every place and object had its own spirit or *numen*, as did every person. People believed they were watched over by the spirits of their ancestors, called *genius* and *juno* for men and women, respectively.

Three prominent gods

Early in Rome's history three gods, Mars, Quirinus and Jupiter, came to prominence. It is thought that their importance was a result of the Sabine influence over Rome during the earliest years of the city.

Mars, the god of war, played a vital role in the story of the origins of Rome – he was thought to have been the father of Romulus and Remus. Quirinus, who watched over the people and government of Rome was the deified Romulus, and Jupiter was the leader of all the gods.

All three gods were worshipped at a temple on the Capitoline Hill, and were known as the Capitoline Triad. These new gods did not replace the traditional spirits, but both sets were worshipped alongside one another.

Etruscan influence

During the Roman Monarchy period, Rome came under the influence of the Etruscan civilization and the Capitoline Triad underwent a transformation. Jupiter remained at the pinnacle of Roman religion, but Mars and Quirinus were replaced with Juno and Minerva. Juno was the wife of Jupiter, and Minerva, their daughter, was the goddess of wisdom.

The religious ideas of the Greeks, who had settled in the south of the Italian peninsula, also infiltrated Roman beliefs. Roman gods traditionally had very limited or abstract characteristics, and it was under the influence of the Greeks that the Romans created a mythology surrounding their gods.

The characters of many Roman gods were borrowed from Greek gods, thus Jupiter began to share characteristics with the Greek god Zeus, Mars with Ares, and Minerva with Athena. This process, called syncretism, was applied to most Roman gods. However, reflecting Roman values, their gods displayed a distinctly frugal nature, not shared by their Greek counterparts.

Ara dei Gemelli ***from Ostia. This altar is dedicated to Silvanus, the ancient Italian god of nature and forests.***

Pontifex Maximus

The worship of these gods was part of an organized state religion. The faith was guided by a college of pontiffs, an assembly of the highest-ranking priests in Ancient Rome, who were charged with the control of all of the gods combined. It was the college's duty to ensure that each god was happy.

The college was presided over by the chief priest or *pontifex maximus*; originally this position was open exclusively to patricians, but after the third century BC a plebeian Roman could also hold the office.

Although the chief priest initially had a wholly spiritual function, during the late Republic, the position was increasingly politicized – for example, Julius Caesar was the *pontifex maximus* during the first Triumvirate. During the Empire, the role of chief priest was taken over by the Emperors.

Fresco painting from Pompeii showing the Punishment of Eros. The gods of Ancient Greece and their associated myths were important in the development of Roman religious beliefs, and while Roman gods might share some characteristics with their Greek counterparts, their mythological lifestyle were considerably more frugal.

Representing the gods

Each god had its own temple and each temple had its own priests, or *flamines*, who were exclusively dedicated to one god. While the college was tasked with managing the affairs of all the gods, the *flamines* would be present to represent their particular deity. The most important priests represented one of the three gods of the Capitoline Triad. With the exception of the priestesses to Vesta, the goddess of the hearth, all priests were men.

Detail of the altar to Matronae Aufaniae from the monument of Vettius Severus.

Vestal Virgins

The priestesses to Vesta were called the Vestal Virgins because they were ordered to remain celibate for the entire thirty years they were in service. The virgins were tasked with keeping the sacred fire of Vesta burning in the temple.

The vestals were extremely privileged because they were no longer under the control of their fathers, which meant they could vote and own property. Vestals were highly regarded in Roman society, so many patrician families wished to see their daughter become one of six vestals. Vestal Virgins were appointed by the *pontifex maximus*, who chose them by drawing lots.

Although Vestal Virgins had considerable advantages in society, there were also downsides – if a Vestal Virgin failed to remain celibate, the punishment was to be buried alive.

The Imperial Cult

Several Emperors were deified after their death. The trend began with Julius Caesar and was continued by his successor Augustus.

Initially, the government was quite discerning about which Emperor could become a god. Claudius, Vespasian and Titus were believed to have earned their divinity, while the less deserving, Caligula and Nero, were overlooked. After the accession of Nerva to the throne, deification became commonplace, unless the Emperor had been particularly unpopular or brief.

Worship of the Imperial Cult became commonplace during the Empire and a number of Emperors even believed themselves to be living gods. This was evident in Commodus, who thought he was the embodiment of Hercules, and the Emperor Diocletian found affinity with Jupiter. However, no Emperor promoted the idea of imperial divinity more than Caligula – he even ordered that his statue be placed in the temples of the monotheistic Jewish worshippers.

Christianity comes to Rome

Christianity started out as a marginal, often persecuted, sect but ended up as the official state religion.

As Christians grew in number, they became more prominent in society and managed to gain influence over the Emperor Constantine. Vaguely convinced by its teachings, Constantine decided to march into a battle under the banner of Christ. The odds were heavily stacked against Constantine, but he won a surprise victory and assumed it to be the result of divine intervention.

Constantine immediately released the Edict of Milan, which professed tolerance towards Christianity, and during his reign he increasingly favoured the religion. At the end of his life, Constantine was baptized and most of his successors were Christians. One exception was the Emperor Julian, who tried to re-instate the traditional Roman gods, to little avail. In 380 AD, Christianity was made the state religion and the Imperial Cult and the traditional, polytheistic Roman religion came to an end.

The pyramid of Caius Cestius is a funerary monument which contains a burial chamber.

Pantheon

The Pantheon

The Pantheon is undoubtedly the best-preserved Roman building in the world today, largely because it was saved from ruin by the Christian Church. The Pantheon was commissioned soon after the defeat of Antony and Cleopatra in 28 BC, by Marcus Vipsanius Agrippa, the famous general, and friend of the Emperor Augustus. The name Pantheon means 'temple to all Gods', which explains the function of the structure.

Agrippa's Pantheon is not the one that still stands. It was destroyed in a fire in 80AD during the reign of Titus. However, Hadrian began the rebuilding process after he came to the throne in 118 and the building that can be seen today dates from 126AD. Hadrian had a habit of not putting his name to his buildings, so the inscription on the portico still dedicates the building to Agrippa. It translates as, 'Marcus Agrippa, son of Lucius, built this during his third consulship'.

Right: Interior of the Pantheon.

Below: Aerial view of the Pantheon in Rome.

The Pantheon is a marvellous feat of ancient engineering. It is a huge domed structure, 45 metres at both the maximum height and diameter. It was the largest domed building for over a millennium. Thick walls and innovative concrete has allowed the building to remain standing. In the centre of the dome, there is a large eye, or *oculus*, designed to let light from the sun enter the building.

Most impressively, the Pantheon is still functioning in a somewhat similar capacity to that originally intended for it; it continues to be used as a place of worship by the Christian Church.

Collapse of Empire

Barbarian attack

After the death of Theodosius in 395 AD, the division of the Roman Empire became permanent. While the East flourished, the West fell into decline. Sensing weakness, various 'Barbarian' tribes picked away at the decaying West, and carved up the spoils between them.

The Visigoths

The endgame of the Roman Empire had begun with the migration of the Germanic Visigoths into Roman territory in 376. They were refugees who had fled attacks from the Huns, tough warriors from Central Asia.

Distracted by a war against the Sassanid (or Persian) Empire, the Roman Emperor, Valens, predecessor of Theodosius, had allowed the Visigoths to settle in Roman territory. It was hoped these peoples could replenish the Army legions and act as a bulwark against further invasions by the Huns.

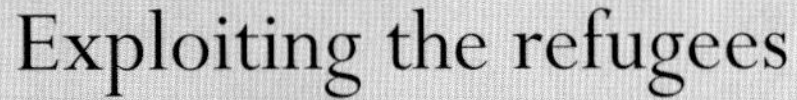

Exploiting the refugees

The men tasked with the resettlement exploited the refugees, by taking whatever possessions they had and leaving them worse-off than before they had entered Roman territory. Outraged, the Visigoths took up arms against the Romans, running amok over the Balkans. Valens had to take troops from the Eastern theatre to pacify the refugee army, but they defeated the his men at the Battle of Adrianople; Valens was killed the process.

The war had gone so badly for the Romans, that the new Emperor, Theodosius, had to agree to let the Visigoths settle in Thrace, as an ally of Rome. Allowing the Visigoths to establish an autonomous state within the Empire offered a clear display of quite how weak Roman power had become. This lesson was not wasted on the Visigoths, who pushed for more.

Visigoths lay siege to Rome

In the early fourth century, under the leadership of Alaric, the Visigoths menaced Greece and Illyricum, and also carried out raids into Italy. He tried to march on Constantinople, but the attack was averted when the Eastern Emperor offered him control of Illyricum instead. In 408, Alaric pushed into Italy once again and laid siege to Rome.

Again, the Visigoths were offered compensation, and the city managed to pay him off, but he returned the following year, and again in 410. On this last occasion the Visigoths actually entered the city – the first foreign army to do so in eight hundred years. The Visigoth Army plundered the city for three days, but owing to their Christian beliefs, they practised relative restraint.

Above: Although the Visigoths have a reputation as a 'barbarian' race, they were a Christian and civilized people. These gold crowns are an example of their metalworking skills.

Right: Alaric's entrance into Rome. The Visigoths became the first foreign army to capture Rome in eight hundred years when they plundered the city in 410 under the leadership of Alaric.

Peace treaty

Alaric moved his troops out of Rome into the south of Italy, where he prepared an invasion of North Africa. He died before the invasion could be carried out and his successor, Athaulf, moved the Army into the south of Gaul, where he hoped to settle.

However, the Visigoths had taken the Emperor Theodosius II's sister, Galla Placidia, hostage and were pursued by the Roman Army. Athaulf and his Visigoths were pushed into Spain. They later traded the return of Galla Placidia in exchange for peace. The treaty allowed the Visigoths to settle in northern Spain and southern Gaul.

Breaching the Rhine

While Rome had to deal with the Visigoths in the Balkan region, the Huns continued to menace the Germanic tribes of northern and eastern Europe. This forced many of these tribes to push westwards. In the winter of 407 AD, these Germanic tribes – the Vandals, the Suebi and the Alans – made use of the cold weather to cross the frozen River Rhine into Roman territory.

The 'barbarians' crossed near Moguntiacum (Mainz), where the Roman defences were weaker. They pushed into Gaul and crossed into the Pyrenees.

Weighed down by the difficulties posed by the Visigoths in Italy, attacks against Roman authority in Britannia and a parlously weakened Western Empire, there was little the Romans could do to stop the Huns' advance.

Control of North Africa

Moving south, the 'barbarian' tribes gained access to the Mediterranean. Here they resorted to piracy to fund their migrations. In 429, under the leadership of Gaiseric, the Vandals crossed the Mediterranean into Africa, the home of Rome's grain supply. Within just ten years, the Vandals had captured Carthage and the whole of North Africa had been conquered. Emperor Valentian III was forced to concede that the land was no longer subject to Roman rule.

Ruins from the port of Ostia which by the fifth century AD had declined in importance, although it was here that the Vandals landed in 455 AD to begin their march on Rome.

Control of the 'granary of the Empire'

Although the Vandals' control of North Africa threatened the grain supply which was vital for the Eastern Empire, there was little to be done to confront the challenge this posed. Constantinople was distracted by the invasion of the Huns.

In the early fifth century, the Huns had settled near to Roman territory on the east side of the River Danube. The Eastern Roman Emperors were happy to pay them tribute to keep them at bay.

Attila the Hun

However, in 434 AD, a ruthless new leader named Attila emerged. He demanded double the amount of money from the Romans, but was refused by the Emperor, Theodosius II, in Constantinople. The Huns crossed the Danube and exacted a brutal reign of terror in the Balkans, razing several Roman cities and butchering the populations.

By 443, the Huns had marched on Constantinople itself. They were unable to take the city, because it was too well defended by its great walls, but they had a sufficient psychological effect on Theodosius II to force him to negotiate terms. In the end, the Eastern Empire agreed to triple the tribute paid to the Huns and secede territory in the Balkans.

High price of deterrence

The Eastern Empire paid a high price to deter the Huns, but the poorer relation in the West did not have the same luxury and paid an even higher price. After agreeing terms with the Eastern Empire, the Huns set their sights on the Western Empire. Attila's army, together with an assortment of barbarian allies, crossed the Rhine in 451 and laid waste to several Gallic cities.

The Hun advance was only halted when it encountered the Roman Army at the Battle of Chalons. This battle is generally perceived as a Roman victory, albeit a pyrrhic one; thousands were killed on both sides. It was to be the last battle the Western Roman Empire would win.

When the Huns retreated across the Rhine, the Romans were too weak to go in pursuit. Consequently, the Huns undertook further attacks in Italy, and planned another march on Constantinople, but Attila died in 453 before he could carry it out.

The end of the Western Empire

After Attila's death, the threat from the Huns dissipated, but Italy was by no means safe, because the Vandals picked up where the Huns had left off. In 455, still under the leadership of Gaiseric, the Vandals landed at Ostia and marched into Rome. The city was completely sacked, leaving the Western Roman Empire in tatters.

In 476, Italy fell under the control of a barbarian named Odoacer, as the Visigoths moved in to occupy the peninsula, and the Empire in the West had reached a conclusion.

Farmers harvest their crop near the ruined city walls of Constantinople (Istanbul, Turkey) constructed by Emperor Theodosius II. During the fifth century the wall was constructed to keep out the raiding army of Attila the Hun. Theodosius also employed mercenary Viking warriors to help defend the city. In 447 most of the wall was destroyed by an earthquake. Wall construction began immediately to repair the damage before raiders could attack the city. The task of maintaining the wall was continued with successive Emperors.

GERMANIC KINGDOM
c. 500
movements of peoples
Huns
Slavs
Germanics
Celtics
N
COLLAPSE OF EMPIRE
Arctic Circle
Norwegian Sea
FINNO-UGRIANS
Faeroe Islands
North Sea
SCANDINAVIANS
Baltic Sea
CELT
ANGLO-SAXONS
JUTES
ANGLES
SAXONS
FRISIANS
SLAVS
FRANKS
BURGUNDIANS
ALEMANNI
KINGDOM OF THE THURINGIANS
FRANKISH KINGDOM
Lutetia
VANDALS
HUNS
ATLANTIC OCEAN
Namnetes
KINGDOM OF BURGUNDY
KINGDOM OF THE OSTROGOTHS
SUEVES
VISIGOTHS
Black Sea
Pavia
Ravenna
Spalatum
Naissus
Marcianopolis
KINGDOM OF THE SUEVES
BASQUES
Arelate
Massilia
Adriatic Sea
EAST ROMAN EMPIRE
Adrianople
Constantinople
Corsica
Rome
Salonica
KINGDOM OF THE VISIGOTHS
Toletum
Lisbon
Balearic Is.
Sardinia
Aegean Sea
Smyrna
Valentia
Hispalis
KINGDOM OF THE VANDALS
Athens
Carthago Nova
Panormus
Sicily
Mediterranean Sea
Hippo Regius
Carthage
VANDALS
Crete
BERBERS

ΙΟΥCΤΙΝΙΑΝΟC

Byzantium

Eastern Roman Empire

After the collapse of the Western Roman Empire, the Eastern Roman Empire continued to function. The Emperor, government and people still considered themselves part of the Roman Empire, but in reality the East had evolved into something new: the Byzantine Empire. The classical world had ended and the Middle Ages were beginning.

Gold cup from sixth century Byzantium.

Dawning of the Byzantine Empire

The 'Byzantine Empire' is a construction of historians. In reality the Empire was the Eastern Roman Empire. However, any claim to being 'Roman' had been weakened by the loss of the city of Rome, and the later replacement of Latin with Greek as the principal language. Over time, historians adopted the term 'Byzantine Empire' as a label for the East, coining the term from the name of its capital city, Byzantium, known also as Constantinople.

The precise date at which the Byzantine Empire began is debatable. The earliest proposed date is the division of the Empire by Diocletian at the end of the third century, but at this time the East was still integrated politically with Rome and court was held at Nicomedia, not Byzantium.

Another proposed start-date is in 330 AD, during the reign of Constantine, when Nova Roma (New Rome) was established on the site of Byzantium and was lavished with all the attentions of the Emperor. However, the most widely accepted date is 476 AD when the 'barbarian' king, Odoacer, took control of Rome and Italy, effectively severing the link between East and West.

A 'barbarian' Emperor

Odoacer had continued the pretence of being the Roman Emperor by resuming the Senate and holding public games, but there was little chance of a rapprochement between East and West because Odoacer was not a Roman citizen. Although Zeno, the Emperor in the East, initially acknowledged him, the relationship was not strong.

Unwilling to engage in open warfare to reclaim the West from the pretender to the imperial role, Zeno instead encouraged Theodoric, the king of the Ostrogoths, to go to war against Odoacer in exchange for control over the Italian peninsula.

Theodoric defeated and killed Odoacer, and ruled Italy in his place; Rome had simply replaced one 'barbarian' with another, more amenable, one. In theory, Theodoric was under the influence of the Emperors in the East, but in reality, by paying lip-service to Constantinople, he maintained a strong degree of independence.

Mosaic from San Vitale Cathedral in Ravenna, Italy, depicting the Byzantine Emperor Justinian.

Justinian

Despite the uneasy relationship with Byzantium, Theodoric ruled over a relatively peaceful and stable Italy, but order began to break down when he died in 526 AD.

Justinian moves to take control

The new Byzantine Emperor, Justinian, decided to take advantage of the unrest in the West, to make one last bid to control the former Western Empire.

His first move was to dispatch a small force to retake North Africa in 533, where the Vandal king had been persecuting Christians who held different doctrinal beliefs to those held by the Vandals. The mission was led by Belisarius, a general who had made his name suppressing an extremely violent riot in Constantinople which erupted as a result of a chariot race.

North Africa regained

Belisarius and his men faced only limited resistance in North Africa because the Vandal forces were preoccupied in Sardinia. What troops the Vandals had to hand were sent from Carthage to engage the Byzantine Army ten miles south of the city itself. The battle is referred to as 'The Battle of *Ad Decimum*', meaning 'the battle at the ten-mile post'.

Although the Vandals, lead by King Gelimer, were in a strong position, the result was an easy victory for the Byzantines. Belisarius and his men were able to re-occupy Carthage, defeat the remainder of the Vandal forces in the Battle of Tricamerum, and take back the province of North Africa in the process.

Minarets in present-day Istanbul, formerly known as Byzantium or Constantinople. By the end of the fifteenth century, the city had fallen to the Islamic Ottoman Empire, after more than one thousand turbulent years, during which it had been subject to attack, siege and decline.

Rome recaptured

Justinian then ordered Belisarius to push on into Sicily and Italy to take advantage of Theodoric's death to annex the peninsula. Belisarius marched through southern Italy and, by the end of 536, even captured Rome. The Byzantine troops had faced little resistance because the ruling Ostrogoths were distracted by the Franks, whom Justinian had encouraged to invade from the north.

In January 537, after paying a large indemnity to the Franks, the Ostrogoths were free to march south to try to reclaim Rome. They laid siege to the city for more than a year, but failed to break the will of Belisarius' smaller force. The siege was only broken when Constantinople sent more men to relieve Belisarius' beleaguered troops in early 538. The tables were quickly turned and the Byzantine force laid siege to the Ostrogoth capital at Ravenna in 540.

By 554, Justinian's army, supported by thousands of mercenaries, had succeeded in redeeming a sizeable amount of territory in the West; as well as Italy, Sicily and North Africa, the Byzantines occupied Sardinia, Corsica and southern Spain.

Despite the immense gains, it quickly became apparent that Constantinople could not hope to hold on to the West for long because its army had become dangerously overstretched, and opposition was galvanizing.

Over the following two centuries the Empire was attacked by a host of enemies, including Magyars, Slavs, Bulgars, Persians, Avars, Lombards, Goths and Arabs, forcing it into retreat.

Legacy

In the centuries following Justinian's death in 565 AD, the Byzantine Empire ebbed and flowed, intermittently gaining control of territory in Italy. For the most part, the Empire was restricted to the Balkans and modern Turkey. Rome became something of a backwater, as its population plummeted to just tens of thousands, a far cry from the height of the Empire when more than a million people crammed into the city.

Charlemagne: Holy Roman Emperor

Justinian's war against the Ostrogoths had ravaged the Italian peninsula. After the Byzantines and the Ostrogoths were pushed out, the Lombards, a Germanic people from northern Europe, moved in. The Lombards did very little to regenerate Italy, and were eventually ousted by the Franks, another Germanic tribe, at the end of the eight-century. The Frankish king, Charlemagne, was rewarded with the title 'Emperor of the Romans' by the Pope, and became the first of the Holy Roman Emperors.

After Charlemagne's death, his territories were split in half, with the Franks continuing to control the area of Roman Gaul, and the Holy Roman Empire being carved out of northern Italy and Germany.

A Holy Roman Empire

The creation of a Holy Roman Empire was partly an attempt to rekindle the Western Roman Empire. The Emperors were appointed by the Pope, and ruled over vast swathes of central Europe for almost a millennium, until Napoleon reorganized the region in 1806. However, the Holy Roman Empire was really quite different to the Roman Empire; it was a confederation of small states and principalities, and it was centred on Germany, neither of which had been true of Ancient Rome.

The Byzantine Empire continued the Roman Empire in the East for many centuries. Over time it grew gradually weaker as new, powerful tribes moved into the region under the banner of Islam. At times only Constantinople's near-impenetrable walls kept the city safe. The city was sacked in 1204 during the fourth crusade, which set in motion a steady decline as the population plummeted. Two and a half centuries later, in 1453, Constantinople finally fell to the Ottomans and the Byzantine Empire passed into history.

Ruins of a great hall at Emperor Hadrian's Villa, just outside Tivoli, Italy, one of the many wonderfully preserved structures which give us an insight into the way in which the peoples of the Ancient Roman civilization lived.

Ruins of a carved column sitting on the Palatine Hill, where Rome's first settlement was established.

Italy divided

In the West, Italy remained divided for centuries, ownership of the land being carved up between foreign invaders, wealthy families and the Catholic Church. After a series of wars and a conscious nationalist effort, Italy was reunified during the nineteenth century.

Much of the reunification task was completed by 1861, but Rome still remained elusive because it was under papal control, backed by French support. Paris finally removed its backing in 1870 and Italian troops took the city.

Italy was unified as a nation; Rome was established as the capital, and once again placed at the heart of a short-lived Empire, ruling over parts of Africa, the Balkans and Greece.

Relics of Rome

The array of fascinating Roman relics that litter Europe, North Africa and the Middle East strike awe into the millions that visit them each year. But the Romans have bequeathed so much more to us than just ruined buildings; we continue to be influenced by Roman politics, law, time, literature, town planning, sanitation and road building. Even Roman education and medicine, which are now largely discredited, were upheld until very recently.

The political systems of the Roman Republic have influenced the American and French systems among many others, and the word 'Caesar' was still evident in the German 'Kaiser' and Russia 'Tsar' until these positions were purged during the First World War.

The Romans were also largely responsible for the removal of the Jews from Judea, an act that was to have fateful consequences in the twentieth century, and which still impacts international relations to this day.

Legacy of language

One of Rome's greatest legacies is its language; Latin forms the root of a number of European languages, including Italian, French, Portuguese, Spanish and Romanian. Even the Germanic English language, that has replaced Latin as the *lingua franca* of our time, owes much of its vocabulary to Latin words.

Rome's other greatest legacy is religion; since Jesus' disciple, Saint Peter, was crucified in the city, Rome became an important religious centre of the Christian Church. The Bishop of Rome, later called the Pope, could claim to be the successor of Saint Peter, which meant that through the centuries he retained an important role, despite the relegation of Rome to the sidelines.

Over time, theological and political differences led to a split between the Christian Churches of the East and West and the Pope became the highest authority of the western, Catholic Church. Today the Catholic Church has the most followers of all the world's religions; one in every six people in the world is thought to be Catholic. At the heart of such a massive religion, the city of Rome has been able to retain its position at the centre of the world, long after the Roman Empire disappeared.

Rome remains an important international city, where the ruins ofAncient Roman lie alongside modern building.

Ancient Rome Timeline

ROMAN MONARCHY 753-509 BC

753 BC Traditional Date for the foundation of Rome.

According to Roman mythology founded by Romulus and Remus. In a dispute over who should rule, Romulus killed Remus, gave the city his own name and went on to reign for the next 38 years.

715 Numa Pompilius elected as king.

From the Sabine tribe, he created the Roman Senate.

673 Reign of Tullus Hostilius.

During his reign, the Curia Hostilia (the Senate House) was built.

642 Reign of Ancus Marcius.

617 Reign of Lucius Tarquinius Priscus.

Also known as Tarquin the Elder, he was responsible for the building of the Circus Maximus and the construction of the city's first sewer system.

578 Reign of Servius Tullius.

534 Reign of Lucius Tarquinius Superbus.

The last Roman king whose reign was characterized by bloodshed and violence.

509 Violation of Lucretia, by king's son, Sextus Tarquinius.

Uprising by Lucius Junius Brutus against Tarquin dynasty and their expulsion.

ROMAN REPUBLIC 509 – 27 BC

509 BC Establishment of the Roman Republic.

War with the Etruscans begins and lasts 13 years.

495 Temple of Mercury built.

494 1st Tribune of the Plebs (the People) established.

449 The Twelve Tables codified – the ancient laws comprising the foundation of Roman law.

They were said to have been written on 12 ivory tablets and placed in the Forum for all Romans to read.

445 Marriage permitted between patricians and plebeians.

433 Temple of Apollo built.

396 Roman soldiers are paid for the first time.

390 Roman Army defeated at the Battle of Allia. Sacking of Rome by Gauls.

388 Temple of Mars built.

387 The city walls built.

344-41 First Samnite War.

Between the Republic and the tribes of Samnium. The three Samnite Wars, extending over 50 years, involved almost all of the Italian states and concluded with the domination of the Samnites by Rome.

329 Circus Maximus completed in Rome.

326-04 Second Samnite War.

With victory, Rome increased its colonisation and control of most of central and southern Italy.

312 Building of the Appian Way.

The Via Appia was the most important of all Roman roads, running from the Forum Romanum out of the city walls, south and east to Brindisi (Brundisium). Construction of first aqueduct, Aqua Appia.

298-90 Third Samnite War.

After Rome's great victory at Sentinum in 295 BC it emerged as the dominant force throughout the Italian peninsula, except for the extreme south and the Po Valley.

280-75 The Pyrrhic War.

The Empire fought the Greek ruler, Pyrrhus of Epirus. With the surrender of Tarentum to the Romans at the end of the war, Pyrrhus returned to Epirus and Rome won control over the whole of Italy.

C270 Minting of the first Roman coinage.

First gladiatorial games in Rome.

264-41 First Punic War against Carthage (now Tunisia).

Rome emerged victorious in the battle for supremacy in the western Mediterranean Sea and won Sicily.

218-02 Second Punic War (the 'War against Hannibal').

216 Hannibal invades Italy and inflicts defeat on the Romans at Cannae.

215-05 First Macedonian War.

212 New denarius coin introduced.

206 Carthaginians defeated in Spain.

Spain becomes two Roman provinces.

204 Scipio invades Africa.

202 Scipio defeats Hannibal at Zama.

204-169 Career of Plautus, a comedic playwright, attaining huge popularity in the Republic.

200-196 Second Macedonian War.

The Roman victory meant Macedonian control of Greece was ended.

171-67 Third Macedonian War.

The Kingdom of Macedon was destroyed at the Battle of Pydna in 168 BC.

149-46 Third Punic War against Carthage.

Resulted in complete destruction of Carthage, the Carthaginian population being sold into slavery and the annexing by Rome of the province of Africa.

149-48 Fourth Macedonian War.

Macedon was defeated and became a Roman province.

133 Murder of the tribune Tiberius Gracchus after proposing land reform.

126 Gaius Gracchus (Tiberius' brother) becomes tribune.

121 Gaius Gracchus murdered after proposing to extend Roman citizenship.

112-01 War against Germanic tribes – the Cimbri and the Teutons.

111-05 War against Jugurtha, King of Numidia.

107-86 Gaius Marcus elected consul seven times.

91-98 Social War between the Republic and its Italian allies over citizenship reforms.

The end of the war saw citizenship extended in some form to much of Italy.

88-85 First Mithridatic War.

88-86 Civil War between Sulla and Marius.

83-72 Sertorius' rebellion in Spain.

82 Sulla appointed dictator of Rome, with total control of the city and Empire of Rome.

He instituted a reign of terror, proscribing his political opponents and ordering the execution of 1500 nobles.

79 Sulla resigns dictatorship.

73-71 Slave rebellion led by Spartacus, brutally put down by Crassus.

63 Consulship of Cicero.

Catiline conspiracy – an attempt by Lucius Sergius Catiline to overthrow the Republic and the power of the Senate. Julius Caesar appointed chief priest/pontifex maximus.

60 First triumvirate of Pompey, Julius Caesar and Crassus.

58-50 Caesar fights Gallic wars and conquers Gaul.

55-54 Caesar's first expeditions to Britain.

53 Crassus defeated and killed in a campaign against the Parthian empire.

Triumvirate collapses.

49 Caesar crosses the Rubicon in a deliberate act of war against Pompey and the Republicans.

49-45 Civil war.

48 Pompey killed in Egypt.

46 Reform of the Roman calendar.

45 Caesar defeats the Republicans and declared dictator of the Roman Republic for life.

44 Caesar assassinated on the Ides of March (15th).

44-42 Third Roman civil war between the assassins of Caesar (Cassius and Brutus) and Caesar's heirs – Octavian and Mark Antony.

43 Second triumvirate between Octavian, Mark Antony and Lepidus.

42 Caesar's death avenged at the Battle of Philippi by the defeat of Cassius and Brutus.

Murder of Cicero.

41 Triumvirs divide up Empire – Octavian in West, Antony in East, Lepidus in North Africa.

Mark Antony joins Cleopatra in Egypt.

32 End of peaceful relations between Octavian and Mark Antony.

Octavian declares war on Cleopatra.

31 Octavian defeats Antony and Cleopatra at the Battle of Actium.

30 Mark Antony commits suicide.

Cleopatra commits suicide.

27 The end of the Roman Republic.

THE ROMAN EMPIRE
27 BC – 476 AD

27 BC Octavian becomes sole ruler of Rome and named Princeps or "First Citizen" Augustus.

Agrippa's Pantheon built.

25 Baths of Agrippa built.

19 Virgil's Aeneid completed.

Livy's history of Rome Ab Urbe Condita written. Death of Virgil.

16-6 AD Campaigns against the Germanic tribes and conquest of the Danube provinces.

2 Forum of Augustus completed.

Ovid's Metamorphoses published.

2 AD Augustus adopts Tiberius.

Tiberius was the son of Augustus' wife (Livia Drusilla) from her first marriage. When Augustus' adoptive heirs Gaius Caesar and Lucius Caesar died, Tiberius was recalled to Rome and became Augustus' heir apparent.

6 Judea becomes a Roman province.

8 Exile of Ovid.

9 Battle of Teutoburg.

Three Roman legions lost. The outcome of the battle defined the Rhine as the boundary of the Roman Empire.

14 Death of Augustus.

Tiberius becomes Emperor.

17 Death of Livy.

Death of Ovid.

19 Death of Germanicus.

Tiberius had been compelled by Augustus to name Germanicus as his heir.

23 Tiberius' natural son, Drusus, dies.

26 Tiberius governs Rome by proxy from self-imposed exile in Capri.

Pontius Pilate appointed prefect in Judea.

31 Death of Sejanus.

A confidant of Tiberius, Sejanus' influence increased further on his betrothal to the Emperor's niece, Livilla. He plotted to seize power but was discovered, arrested and condemned to death.

37 Death of Tiberius.

Caligula becomes Emperor.

41 Assassination of Caligula by Praetorian Guard.

Claudius becomes Emperor.

43 Conquest of Britain.

54 Nero becomes Emperor.

60-61 Boudica's uprising.

Queen of the Iceni tribe in Norfolk, she led a revolt against the Roman forces. Boudica was ultimately defeated at the Battle of Watling Street, but not before she had destroyed the cities of Camulodunum (Colchester), Londinium (London) and Verulamium (St Albans), killing tens of thousands in the process.

64 Fire in Rome.

Large proportion of the city was destroyed. In the aftermath, Nero found a scapegoat in the form of the small Christian sect in the city. On his orders, Christians were thrown to the lions and many others were crucified.

65 Suicides of Seneca and Lucan.

A statesman who influenced the early years of Nero's rule, Seneca was accused of being involved in a plot to kill the emperor. Nero ordered him to commit suicide, and it is reported that he died a slow and painful death. The poet Lucan was also implicated in the conspiracy and committed suicide at the age of 25.

66-73 First Jewish-Roman War.

Also known as the Great Revolt. Sparked by persecution of their race, it ended in defeat for the Jews: Jerusalem was looted and destroyed and Jews were killed on a massive scale or enslaved.

68 Nero commits suicide.

End of the Julio-Claudian dynasty. Succeeded by Galba.

68-69 Civil war and the Year of the Four Emperors.

Galba succeeded by Otho, Vitellius and finally Vespasian. Vespasian becomes the first ruler of the Flavian Dynasty.

79 Titus becomes Emperor.

Pompeii and Herculaneum destroyed by the eruption of Vesuvius. Death of Pliny the Elder at nearby Stabiae.

80 The Colosseum in Rome completed.

Capable of holding more than 50,000 spectators it was used for gladiatorial contests. Fire engulfs Rome, destroying Agrippa's Pantheon.

81 Domitian becomes emperor.

96 Domitian killed. End of Flavian Dynasty.

Nerva becomes Emperor – first of the 'Five Good Emperors', known for their moderate rule.

97-109 Letters of Pliny the Younger published.

These included an account of the eruption of Vesuvius and the death of his uncle Pliny the Elder. The nine published books gave an insight into everyday life in first-century Rome.

98 Trajan succeeds Nerva as Emperor.

Born in Spain, Trajan was the first non-Italian to become Emperor. During his reign the Empire grew to its maximum boundary.

101-102 First Dacian War.

105-106 Second Dacian War.

Dacia was conquered and annexed as a province of Rome.

112 Trajan's forum and column completed and dedicated.

Death of Pliny the Younger.

113-16 Trajan's war against the Parthian Empire.

Parthian capital Ctesiphon captured. Mesopotamia becomes Roman province. Empire reaches Persian Gulf.

117 Hadrian becomes Emperor.

118-134 Hadrian's Villa built at Tibur.

c119 Biographies of Suetonius on The Twelve Caesars published.

Under Hadrian, Suetonius became his secretary, but was dismissed in 122.

122 Building of Hadrian's Wall begun in Britain.

On a visit to Britain in 122, Hadrian decided the wall was needed to protect the province from possible invasion from the tribes in Caledonia (now Scotland).

132-35 Second Jewish Revolt

The building of a pagan temple in Jerusalem sparked the second Jewish-Roman War. The revolt was eventually crushed after three years, and it is thought that hundreds of thousands of Jews were slaughtered. Hadrian took draconian measures to outlaw Judaism – prohibiting Jews from entering the holy city, romanizing Judaea and renaming the region Syria Palaestria.

138 Antoninus Pius becomes Emperor.

142 Construction of the Antonine Wall begins.

Made from turf and stone and stretching 37 miles, it was built to replace Hadrian's Wall to the south. Despite the 19 forts built along its course, it came under many attacks, and was abandoned soon after Antoninus' death.

161 Marcus Aurelius becomes Emperor.

162-66 Campaigns against the Parthian Empire (now Iran).

168-80 Campaigns against Germanic tribes on the Republic's border with the Danube.

180 Commodus becomes Emperor.

192 Commodus murdered.

Pertinax briefly Emperor. Replaced with Didius Julianus.

193 Septimius Severus becomes Emperor.

His reign begins with immediate opposition: Pescennius Niger was proclaimed Emperor by the Syrian legions, and Clodius Albinus was hailed as Emperor by his own troops.

194 Niger defeated by Severus at the Battle of Issus.

197 Clodius Albinus defeated and killed at the Battle of Lugdunum.

211 Caracalla and Geta proclaimed joint emperors after the death of their father, Septimius Severus.

Within months of accession, Caracalla had Geta assassinated.

212 Roman citizenship granted to freemen throughout the Empire.

217 Caracalla murdered by Praetorian Guard on the order of Macrinus.

Macrinus declared Emperor.

218 Macrinus defeated and killed outside Antioch.

Elagabalus becomes Emperor.

222 Elagabalus murdered.

Alexander Severus becomes Emperor.

235 Maximinus Thrax becomes the first of the 'Soldier Emperors'.

238 Gordian I and II proclaimed joint Emperors but reigned for less than 40 days.

Succeeded by Pupienus and Balbinus as joint emperors but were themselves killed by the Praetorian Guard. Maximinus assassinated by the Praetorian Guard. Gordian III declared Emperor.

244 Marcus Iulius Philippus becomes Emperor.

249 Philippus killed in battle with Decius.

Decius becomes Emperor.

250 Persecution of Christians.

251 Decius killed in battle with the Goths.

Gallus becomes Emperor with his son Volusianus.

252 Romans defeated at Barbalissos by Shapur I of Persia.

253 Gallus and Volusianus killed.

Aemilianus becomes Emperor for 3 months. Valerian and Gallienus become joint emperors.

257 Valerian captured by Shapur I of Persia.

Gallienus continues to rule.

258 Goths invade Asia Minor.

260 Postumus declares break away 'Gallic Empire' in the West.

267 Zenobia forms break away 'Palmyrene Empire' in East.

268 Gallienus murdered.

Claudius II becomes Emperor.

269 Postumus killed.

Victorinus proclaimed Emperor in Gaul and Britain.

270 Claudius dies of plague.

Aurelian becomes Emperor. His reign was known for reunification of the Empire. Victorinus murdered. Tetricus I proclaimed Gallic Emperor.

271 Campaigns against Vandals, Juthung and Sarmatians.

272 Palmyra retaken.

Dacia abandoned.

273 Gallic Empire reincorporated by Aurelian.

274 Tetricus defeated by Aurelian.

275 Aurelian murdered by Praetorian Guard.

Tacitus becomes Emperor.

276 Tacitus dies.

Probus becomes Emperor and re-establishes security of the Empire's frontiers.

282 Probus killed by own troops when they changed sides in support of Carus.

Carus becomes Emperor.

283 Carus dies whilst invading Persia.

Numerian, his son, becomes Emperor.

284 Diocletian becomes Emperor, bringing the period of anarchy for the previous 50 years to an end.

287 Diocletian appoints Maximian as Emperor in the Western Regions.

Diocletian takes Western Regions. Carausius revolts and declares himself Emperor in Britain and Northern Gaul.

293 Establishment of Tetrarchy: Two Caesars appointed to each Augustus: Galerius to Diocletian, Constantius Chlorus to Maximian.

Carausius murdered by Allectus. Allectus declares himself Emperor in Britannia.

296 Constantius Chlorus defeats Allectus and returns Britannia to the Empire.

301 The Edict on Maximum Prices issued.

303 Diocletian's Edict Against the Christians.

Persecution of Christians increases.

305 Diocletian and Maximian abdicate.

Constantius and Galerius become Augusti (Emperors) of West and East respectively. Severus and Maximinus appointed Caesars.

306 Constantius dies.

Constantine, Severus and Maxentius all declared Emperor of West.

307 Severus defeated and killed by Maxentius.

Maximian comes out of retirement to rule with Maxentius.

308 Diocletian persuades Maximian to step down.

Licinius appointed Emperor in the East.

310 Maximian captured by Constantine and commits suicide.

311 Galerius dies.

Licinius and Maximinus Daia rule in the Eastern Region.

312 Battle of Milvian Bridge – Constantine defeats Maxentius and becomes sole Emperor in West.

313 Edict of Milan – legalised Christianity in the Empire.

Maximinus Daia dies.

314 Licinus defeated at Cibalae by Constantine.

316 Diocletian dies.

324 Licinius defeated by Constantine for third time and abdicates.

326 Crispus executed on the order of his father, Constantine.

330 Constantinople becomes capital of the Roman Empire.

337 Constantine I dies.

His sons succeed him: Constantine II and Constans (West) and Constantius (East).

340 Constantine II killed by his brother at Aquileia.

350 Magnentius proclaims himself Emperor in the West.

Constans is captured and killed.

353 Magnentius defeated by Constantius II and commits suicide.

Constantius II now sole Emperor with Julian and Gallus appointed as Caesars in West and East respectively.

361 Constantius dies.

Julian named as his successor. Attempts to reintroduce pagan religion.

363 Julian invades Persia and is killed in battle.

Jovian declared Emperor.

364 The Empire again divided into East and West.

Valens Emperor in the East. Valentinian Emperor in the West.

380 Theodosius I becomes Emperor.

He reunited the two parts of the Empire, but after his death they split again, this time permanently. Makes Christianity official state religion.

410 Sacking of Rome by Alaric.

455 Sacking of Rome by Vandals.

475 Romulus Augustulus becomes Emperor of Western Empire.

476 Romulus Augustulus abdicates.

Traditional date for the fall of the Western Roman Empire.

The Romar

27 BC – 14 AD	Augustus
14 -37	Tiberius
37-41	Gaius (Caligula)
41-54	Claudius
54-68	Nero
68-69	Galba
69	Otho
69	Vitellius
69-79	Vespasian
79-81	Titus
81-96	Domitian
96-98	Nerva
98-117	Trajan
117-38	Hadrian
138-61	Antoninus Pius
161-80	Marcus Aurelius
161-69	Lucius Verus
180-93	Commodus
193	Pertinax
193	Didius Julianus
193-211	Septimius Severus
211-12	Geta
211-17	Caracalla
217-18	Macrinus
218-22	Elagabalus
222-35	Alexander Severus
235-38	Maximinus
238	Gordian I
238	Gordian II
238	Balbinus
238	Pupienus
238-44	Gordian III
244-49	Philip the Arab
249-51	Decius
251-53	Trebonianus Gallus
251-53	Volusianus
253	Aemilianus
253-60	Valerian
253-68	Gallienus
268- 70	Claudius II, Gothicus
270	Quintillus
270-75	Aurelian
275-76	Tacitus
276	Florianus

Emperors

276-82	Probus
282-83	Carus
283-84	Carinus
283-84	Numerianus
284-86	Diocletian

West		East	
286-305	Maximian	286-305	Diocletian
305-06	Constantius Chlorus	305-11	Galerius
306-07	Severus		
306-12	Maxentius	309-13	Maximinus
307-24	Constantine		
324-37	Constantine I		

West		East	
337-40	Constantine II	337-53	Constantius II
337-50	Constans		
350-353	Magnentius (usurper)		
353-61	Constantius II		
361-63	Julian		
363-64	Jovian		

West		East	
364-75	Valentinian I	364-78	Valens
375-83	Gratian	379-92	Theodosius I
375-92	Valentinian II		
383-88	Magnus Maximus (usurper)		
392-94	Eugenius (usurper)		
392-95	Theodosius		

West		East	
395-423	Honorius	395-408	Arcadius
423-25	Iohannes (usurper)	408-50	Theodosius II
425-55	Valentinian III	450-57	Marcian
455	Petronius Maximus		
455-56	Avitus		
457-61	Majorian	457-74	Leo
461-65	Librius Severus		
467-72	Anthemius		
472	Olybrius		
473	Glycerius		
473-75	Nepos	474-91	Zeno
475-76	Romulus Augustulus	475-76	Basiliscus

Places to Visit

Roman ruins are littered throughout Europe, the Middle East and North Africa. Here is just a limited selection of the most impressive Roman sites to visit.

Algeria
Djémila • Timgad

Britain
Bath • Hadrian's Wall • London
St Albans • York

Croatia
Split

France
Nîmes • Arles • Orange

Germany
Saalburg • Trier

Israel
Caesarea • Masada

Italy
Herculaneum • Ostia • Pompeii • Ravenna
Rome • Tivoli

Jordan
Jerash

Lebanon
Baalbeck

Libya
Leptis Magna • Sabratha

Spain
Italica • Merida • Segovia • Tarragona

Syria
Bosra • Palmyra

Tunisia
Carthage • Dougga • El Djem

Turkey
Aphrodisias • Ephesus • Istanbul

Opposite above: The best-preserved Roman Baths can be found at Bath, England, a day trip from London.

Opposite centre: The ruins of Ostia, the ancient city-port of Rome, are among the finest and most extensive in the world. Despite suffering a natural decline, the ruins are almost as impressive as the better known Pompeii and Herculaneum, which were frozen in time by the eruption of Vesuvius in 79 AD.

Opposite below: This remarkable amphitheatre, the largest in Africa, can be found at El Djem, Tunisia.

Above: This spectacular temple, the Maison Carrée, in Nîmes, France, explains why the city is often called the 'Rome of France'. However, Arles, with its magnificent amphitheatre, is also a strong contender for this title.

Centre: The view from within the Colosseum in Rome is equally as breathtaking as the view from without.

Below: The Canopus *is among the many spectacular sights at Hadrian's Villa at Tivoli near Rome.*

Index

Acknowledgements

All photographs copyright Corbis© except the following:

G.N.Photography:

1, 3, 9, 14, 15t, 16t, 17l, 19b, 22t, 23b, 26t, 26b, 29b, 31t, 31b, 37b, 41b, 45b, 64, 67r, 75b, 96b, 97b, 101t, 102t, 102b, 103t, 103b, 114, 116l, 116r, 117t, 118, 119, 125t, 126, 134l, 134r, 135t, 135b, 142, 149t, 151, 154, 155b, 156t, 156b, 157b, 158t, 158b, 159tr, 160, 162r, 163, 165t, 165b 166t, 167b, 168l, 169t, 169b, 170b, 171t, 171b, 172b, 173b, 180b, 182b, 190r, 196, 197t, 197b, 199, 202, 206b, 208b, 209t, 214, 217, 219l, 222, 226, 229, 236l, 236r, 238b, 240l, 240c, 241t, 242b, 243b, 244b, 245t, 245b, 246c, 246t, 247b, 249t, 249b, 250c, 251c, 251b.

Cartographica:

14, 33, 42, 60, 74, 83, 86b, 101, 121, 189, 195, 205, 231

Thanks also to John Dunne and Mark Brown for the design;
Simon Taylor and Gordon Mills for the diagrams;
Sarah Rickayzen and Alison Gauntlett for their supplements;
Sunny Dhillon, Ryan Near, Guy Nettleton, Jo Newson, Cliff Salter,
Richard Betts and Jill Dorman.